TOURO COLLEGE LIBRARY
Kings Hwy

WITHDRAWN

BEHAVIORAL DISORDERS: IDENTIFICATION, ASSESSMENT, AND INSTRUCTION OF STUDENTS WITH EBD

ADVANCES IN SPECIAL EDUCATION

Series Editor: Anthony F. Rotatori

Recent Volumes:

ADVANCES IN SPECIAL EDUCATION   VOLUME 22

BEHAVIORAL DISORDERS: IDENTIFICATION, ASSESSMENT, AND INSTRUCTION OF STUDENTS WITH EBD

EDITED BY

JEFFREY P. BAKKEN
Illinois State University, Normal, IL, USA

FESTUS E. OBIAKOR
University of Wisconsin-Milwaukee, Milwaukee, WI, USA

ANTHONY F. ROTATORI
Saint Xavier University, Chicago, IL, USA

TOURO COLLEGE LIBRARY
Kings Hwy
WITHDRAWN

United Kingdom – North America – Japan
India – Malaysia – China

KH

Emerald Group Publishing Limited
Howard House, Wagon Lane, Bingley BD16 1WA, UK

First edition 2012

Copyright © 2012 Emerald Group Publishing Limited

Reprints and permission service
Contact: booksandseries@emeraldinsight.com

No part of this book may be reproduced, stored in a retrieval system, transmitted in any
form or by any means electronic, mechanical, photocopying, recording or otherwise
without either the prior written permission of the publisher or a licence permitting
restricted copying issued in the UK by The Copyright Licensing Agency and in the USA
by The Copyright Clearance Center. No responsibility is accepted for the accuracy of
information contained in the text, illustrations or advertisements. The opinions
expressed in these chapters are not necessarily those of the Editor or the publisher.

British Library Cataloguing in Publication Data
A catalogue record for this book is available from the British Library

ISBN: 978-1-78052-504-4
ISSN: 0270-4013 (Series)

Emerald Group Publishing
Limited, Howard House,
Environmental Management
System has been certified by
ISOQAR to ISO 14001:2004
standards

Awarded in recognition of
Emerald's production
department's adherence to
quality systems and processes
when preparing scholarly
journals for print

INVESTOR IN PEOPLE

11/26/12

CONTENTS

LIST OF CONTRIBUTORS

Alfredo J. Artiles	Department of Culture, Society, & Education, Arizona State University, Tempe, AZ, USA
Aydin Bal	Department of Rehabilitation Psychology & Special Education, University of Wisconsin-Madison, Madison, WI, USA
Stacey Jones Bock	Department of Special Education, Illinois State University, Normal, IL, USA
Christy Borders	Department of Special Education, Illinois State University, Normal, IL, USA
Yojanna Cuenca-Sanchez	Department of Special Education, Illinois State University, Normal, IL, USA
R. Kenton Denny	Special Education Programs, Louisiana State University, Baton Rouge, LA, USA
Shelley L. Neilsen Gatti	Department of Special Education, University of St. Thomas, Minneapolis, MN, USA
Philip L. Gunter	Provost's Office, Valdosta State University, Valdosta, GA, USA
Kristine Jolivette	Department of Educational Psychology & Special Education, Georgia State University, Atlanta, GA, USA

Timothy J. Lewis	Department of Special Education, University of Missouri, Columbia, MO, USA
Sarup R. Mathur	Division of Educational Leadership & Innovation, Arizona State University, Tempe, AZ, USA
Nichelle Michalak	Department of Special Education, Illinois State University, Normal, IL, USA
Barbara S. Mitchell	Department of Special Education, University of Missouri, Columbia, MO, USA
Paul Mooney	Special Education Programs, Louisiana State University, Baton Rouge, LA, USA
April L. Mustian	Department of Special Education, Illinois State University, Normal, IL, USA
Festus E. Obiakor	Department of Exceptional Education, University of Wisconsin-Milwaukee, Milwaukee, WI, USA
Theresa A. Ochoa	Department of Curriculum and Instruction, Indiana University, Bloomington, IN, USA
Cynthia A. Plotts	Department of Counseling, Leadership, Adult Education & School Psychology, Texas State University-San Marcos, San Marcos, TX, USA
Diana L. Rogers-Adkinson	Department of Special Education, University of Wisconsin-Whitewater, Whitewater, WI, USA
Joseph B. Ryan	The Eugene T. Moore School of Education, Clemson University, Clemson, SC, USA

Stanley C. Trent	Department of Curriculum, Instruction, and Special Education, University of Virginia, Charlottesville, VA, USA
Kathleen King Thorius	Department of Special Education, Indiana University at Indianapolis, Indianapolis, IN, USA
Stacy L. Weiss	Department of Curriculum and Instruction, Indiana University, Bloomington, IN, USA
Mitchell L. Yell	Department of Educational Studies, University of South Carolina, Columbia, SC, USA

PREFACE

Behavioral Disorders are divided into two volumes; Volume 22, *Identification, Assessment and Instruction of Students with EBD*, and Volume 23, *Practice Concerns and Students with EBD*. Since the beginning of the field of emotional and behavioral disorders (EBD), professionals have argued and debated about what society accepts as normal emotional and behavioral developmental patterns of children and youth in school environments. This situation has led to many approaches concerned with the identification, assessment, instruction, and clinical practices applied to students with EBD. Unfortunately, some of these approaches were unwarranted, inappropriate, misguided, misinterpreted, over generalized, unneeded, and lacking in fidelity of treatment. In addition, some of the approaches did not take into consideration how treatment and instruction needs to be modified as society changes in regard to opinions, beliefs, and knowledge base information about children and youth with EBD. Positively, special education EBD professionals have gravitated toward the utilization of scientific and research based analysis to evaluate past and current approaches. Such an approach produces greater fidelity of treatment as the EBD knowledge base evolves. This is the emphasis that is used by chapter authors as they analyze and discern current perspectives and issues in identification, assessment instruction, and practice of working with children and youth with EBD.

Volumes 22 and 23 address the current top perspectives and issues in the field of EBD by providing chapters written by active researchers and scholarly university professors who specialize in this area. Volume 22 first delineates legal issues, themes, and dimensions related to the historical development of the EBD field. Then this volume addresses best practices for the assessment and placement of students with EBD. These discussions are followed by innovative examinations of critical issues that have faced the field of EBD for many years such as the disproportionate placement of culturally and linguistically diverse learners with EBD, prevention strategies for at-risk students with EBD and the dilemma of instructing English language learners with EBD. The volume concludes with comprehensive discussions of instructional issues such as the effective use of behavioral modification techniques to develop appropriate behavior, the need to differentiate instruction to produce positive academic change and a rational for using multidimensional intervention choices for culturally linguistic learners with EBD. Volume 23 begins with a strong ideological rationale and convincing research arguments for the inclusion of students with EBD in general education classes. This chapter is supported by an examination of academic instruction parameters that are currently being practiced in the EBD field to support inclusion practices. Next, the volume reviews for general and special educators, knowledge base components that are associated with effective practices and interventions such as social skills training factors, positive behavior supports and response to intervention. Successful inclusion for students with EBD necessitates that educators understand the students' mental health issues and transitional adjustments factors. There are two informative chapters that deal with these aspects. The volume concludes with chapters that are devoted to secondary aspects of successful inclusion by students with EBD such as the utilization of technology in instruction, working with families of the students, and effectively preparing teachers of the students.

Volume 22 is composed of 10 chapters and Volume 23 is composed of 11 chapters that are written by well-known university professors who are actively involved in teaching undergraduate and graduate special education courses and engaged in research in the EBD field. *Behavioral Disorders: Identification, Assessment and Instruction of Students with EBD* is an excellent supplementary text for advanced undergraduate special education majors and graduate students who are looking for detailed, comprehensive, and current information for their research papers or theses.

Jeffrey P. Bakken
Festus E. Obiakor
Anthony F. Rotatori
Editors

CHAPTER 1

LEGAL ISSUES AND TEACHERS OF STUDENTS WITH EMOTIONAL AND BEHAVIORAL DISORDERS

Mitchell L. Yell and Shelley L. Neilsen Gatti

ABSTRACT

Federal and state laws exert an important influence on the education of students with emotional and behavioral disorders. The most important of these laws is the Individuals with Disabilities Education Act. States and school districts must adhere to the requirements of IDEA when educating students with disabilities in special education programs. In addition to IDEA, other federal and state laws also affect special education programs for students with EBD. Two other important areas are laws that address (a) supervisory responsibilities of teachers of students with emotional and behavioral disorders and (b) issues of bullying in schools. The purpose of this chapter is to provide an overview of Individuals with Disabilities Education Act, and to examine the ways that this and other important laws affect the education of students with EBD and their teachers.

Keywords: Legal issues; Individuals with Disabilities Education Act; individual education programs; legal issues regarding supervisory responsibilities of teachers; legal issues regarding bullying

Behavioral Disorders: Identification, Assessment, and Instruction of Students with EBD
Advances in Special Education, Volume 22, 1–29
Copyright © 2012 by Emerald Group Publishing Limited
All rights of reproduction in any form reserved
ISSN: 0270-4013/doi:10.1108/S0270-4013(2012)0000022004

Federal and state laws exert a significant influence on special education programs. Although special education administrators are most directly responsible for ensuring that special education programs in their school districts meet legal requirements, it is also very important that teachers understand their important roles with respect to these laws. Moreover, because teachers are charged with serving on their student's individual education program (IEP) planning teams as well as being accountable for the day-to-day operations of their classrooms, the ability to implement programs in a manner that is consistent with these laws is very important. In this chapter, we briefly review the primary federal law that is of special importance to special education teachers: The Individuals with Disabilities Education Act (IDEA). In particular we emphasize how teachers can ensure that they develop IEPs for their students that are educationally appropriate and legally sound. We also examine teachers' responsibilities when supervising students, and addressing bullying and harassment. We first discuss the IDEA and how to develop educationally meaningful and legally sound IEPs.

THE INDIVIDUALS WITH DISABILITIES EDUCATION ACT AND TEACHERS OF STUDENTS WITH EBD

The most important law in special education is the IDEA. Table 1 lists and briefly describes the major principles of the IDEA. The purpose of the law is

Table 1. Major Principles of the IDEA.

Principle	Description
Zero reject	School districts must locate, identify, and provide special education services to all eligible students with disabilities
Protection in evaluation	School districts must conduct full and individualized assessments of students with disabilities before initially providing special education services
Free appropriate public education	School districts must provide special education and related services at public expense, that meet the standards of the SEA, and are provided in conformity with students' IEPs
Least restrictive environment	School districts must ensure that to the maximum extent appropriate students with disabilities are to be educated with students who do not have disabilities
Procedural safeguards	School districts must adopt or develop procedures developed to ensure that students and their parents are involved in the special education process
Parental participation	Parents must be meaningfully involved in IEP development (i.e., assessment, programming, and placement)

to ensure that all eligible students with disabilities in public schools are provided with a free appropriate public education (FAPE), which consists of special education and related services that are designed to meet students' unique educational needs.

FREE APPROPRIATE PUBLIC EDUCATION

Students who are eligible for special education under the IDEA must receive an education that confers an FAPE, which means that students have the right to receive special education and related services that (a) are provided at public expense, under public supervision and direction, and without charge; (b) meet the standards of the state educational agency (SEA); (c) include preschool, elementary school, or secondary school education in the child's state; and (d) are provided in conformity with an IEP (IDEA, 2004).

The key to provide an FAPE is for school personnel to develop and implement an IEP. A student's IEP must be based on a full and individualized assessment and must be designed to confer meaningful educational benefit to the student (Yell, 2012). Because the IEP is the primary evidence of the appropriateness of the student's education, the IEP is frequently at the center of IDEA disputes that wind up in due process hearings and in court (Bateman, 2011). This is because, as Bateman (2011) asserted, the IEP is accepted in legal proceedings as an accurate depiction of a student's special education program and unless there is evidence of implementation failures, the IEP is the primary basis for finding whether FAPE was delivered. Thus it is extremely important that teachers fully understand and be able to develop meaningful IEPs.

THE INDIVIDUALIZED EDUCATION PROGRAM DEVELOPMENT PROCESS

The most basic of the requirements of the IDEA is that a student's parents must be full and equal participants with school district personnel in the development of an IEP (Bateman, 2011). Developing a student's special education program is a collaborative process between a student's parents and a team of school-based personnel. This process begins with an assessment of a student, which forms the basis of his or her IEP, which is then developed through this collaborative process. A student's placement is also determined during this process. The student's IEP team often determines the placement,

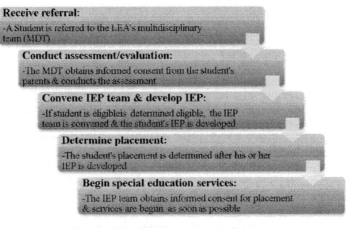

Receive referral:
-A Student is referred to the LEA's multidisciplinary team (MDT)

Conduct assessment/evaluation:
-The MDT obtains informed consent from the student's parents & conducts the assessment

Convene IEP team & develop IEP:
-If student is eligibleis determined eligible, the IEP team is convened & the student's IEP is developed

Determine placement:
-The student's placement is determined after his or her IEP is developed

Begin special education services:
-The IEP team obtains informed consent for placement & services are begun as soon as possible

Fig. 1. The IEP Development Process.

during which the parents must be involved. Fig. 1 depicts this process. We next describe the development of the IEP.

Conducting the Assessment

The IEP process begins with a full and individualized assessment or evaluation of a student's educational needs. The assessment must reveal all of a student's academic and functional needs upon which the IEP will be developed. If the assessment is incomplete or inaccurate the rest of the IEP will likely be inaccurate. In *Kirby v. Cabell County Board of Education* (2006), a U.S. District Court judge accurately described the critical importance of conducting an accurate, relevant, and meaningful assessment:

> If the IEP fails to assess the 'child's present levels of academic achievement and functional performance' the IEP does not comply with [IDEA]. This deficiency goes to the heart of the IEP; the child's level of academic achievement and functional performance is the foundation on which the IEP must be built. Without a clear identification of [the child's] present levels, the IEP cannot set measurable goals, evaluate the child's progress and determine which educational and related services are needed. (p. 694)

The IEP must stand solidly on a foundation of current, accurate assessment of a student's level of performance in academic and functional areas (Bateman, 2011).

Because the initial assessment/evaluation is the keystone of students' IEPs, conducting the assessment is a very important part of providing FAPE. Table 2 includes the IDEA's rules for conducting assessments.

Table 2. IDEA's Evaluation Requirements.

Evaluation Requirements	Description
The team must use a variety of assessment tools and strategies to gather relevant functional, developmental, and academic information, including information provided by the parent, that may assist in determining (a) whether the student has a disability and (b) the content of the student's IEP	Assessments should not only involve formal tests, but curriculum-based measurements, functional-based assessments, interviews, observations, and other procedures that will assist the team to determine eligibility and instructional needs
The team cannot use a single measure or assessment as the sole criterion for determining whether a student has a disability or determining an appropriate educational program for a student	No single measure (e.g., an IQ test) can be the basis for determining eligibility of instructional programming
The team must use technically sound instruments to assess the contribution of cognitive, behavioral, physical, and developmental factors	Assessment procedures that are used should have good technical characteristics and be appropriate to assess different factors that may be involved with a student's disability
Assessment and other evaluation materials (a) must not be discriminatory on a racial or cultural basis; (b) must be provided and administered so as to yield accurate information on what a students knows and can do academically, developmentally, and functionally; (c) must be used for purposes for which the assessments are reliable and valid; (d) must be administered by trained and knowledgeable personnel; and (e) are administered in accordance with the instructions provided by the producer of the assessments	The persons who conduct the assessments must have been trained in administering tests and other assessment procedures. Moreover, all assessments must be reliable, valid, and accurate assessments of academic and functional factors
A student must be assesses in all areas of suspected disability	When a student is assessed, the team must ensure that all areas of concern are addressed
Assessment tools and strategies must provide information and directly assist the team in determining the educational needs of a student	It is important that assessments not only be used for determining eligibility but that they are useful for instructional planning

The following key areas are important when conducting the assessment:

- Include a student's parents in the assessment process. The IDEA requires that a student's parents be included in their child's assessment. Because plays play an important role in the assessment, the team must give full consideration to their opinions and views regarding their child's academic and functional needs.
- Assess all suspected areas of academic or functional needs thoroughly so that a student's instructional program can be planned. Too often the assessment process just involves giving a student norm-referenced tests that are used to determine eligibility, an action that Reschly (2000) noted was inappropriate because it would not result in the type of information necessary to plan a student's IEP. Although norm-referenced tests can give the team clues to help identify a students' needs to accurately plan instruction more fine-grained assessments using procedures such as curriculum-based assessment, curriculum-based measurement, direct observation, and functional behavioral assessment are needed (Yell, Thomas, & Katsiyannis, in press). Such tests and procedures will be much more useful to the team in determining the students' present levels of performance and skill deficits in areas in which they need individualized instruction or programming.
- Include professionals on the team with specialized expertise in assessment if needed. The IDEA requires that the IEP team include a person who can interpret the instructional implications of the assessment. Often a school psychologist who specializes in assessment will be included on the team, although the IDEA does not specify who the team member must who can interpret the instructional implications of the assessment person must be. Depending on students' suspected needs, a person with specialized assessment expertise may also be needed on the team. For example, in the case of students who may require assistive technology devices or services include a person with expertise in conducting and interpreting assistive technology assessments on the team.
- Include a team member with behavioral expertise on the team when a student has been referred for behavior problems.
- Consider the assessment information as the baseline upon which students' IEP goals will be measured. The assessment is the path to good goals and subsequent monitoring of student progress. Thus, if a student has serious behavioral problems, the team should conduct a functional behavioral assessment. The result of this assessment will lead directly to the measurable annual goals and special education services, and the team's system for monitoring the student's progress.

Developing the IEP

Developing students' IEPs refers to the process of creating a students individualized program of special education and related services. Thus, the IEP is the blueprint of a student's FAPE. The IDEA mandates the process and procedures for developing the IEP. We next briefly review these procedures. The IDEA mandates the persons who must be on IEP team, although other school-based personnel are permitted, but not required, to attend the IEP meeting. Table 3 lists and describes the required members of students' IEP teams.

Having the appropriate IEP team members at IEP meetings is so important that Lake (2007) observed that very few procedural errors will foil a school district's ability to provide an FAPE as will having an inappropriate IEP team. In fact, courts and due process hearing officers have invalidated IEPs when the required participants were not involved in the process and their absence affected the development of the IEP (Lake, 2007; Yell, 2012).

Table 3. IEP Team Members.

IEP Team Members	Description
The parents of the student	Either one or both of a student's parents
*General education teacher of the student	At least one general education teacher who has had or does have the student
*Special education teacher of the student	At least one special education teacher who has had or does have the student
*LEA representative	A representative of the school district. This person is often a principal or assistant principal of the student's school
*Individual who can interpret the instructional implications of the assessment/evaluation	A person who understands and can interpret the instructional implications of the assessment. This person is often a school psychologist although it may be another person already on the IEP team (e.g., special education teacher)
Other persons who have knowledge of special expertise regarding the student, including related services personnel	The student's parents or the school personnel may appoint other members who have knowledge of the student or the student's disability
The student, when appropriate	The student must be invited to the IEP team if transition services are considered

*Required members.

As is the case with the assessment, the IDEA requires that a student's parents must be full and equal participants in developing the IEP. In fact, Bateman (2011) asserted that courts more vigorously protect parental participation than any of the IDEA's procedural rights. Having a student's parents participate fully in the special education process is so important that failing to do so is one of the two procedural grounds by which a due process hearing officer may rule that a school district has denied a student an FAPE, this violating the IDEA (Individuals with Disabilities Education Act Regulations, 2006).

The Supreme Court ruling in *Winkleman v. Parma City School District* (2007) emphasized the critical importance of parental participation throughout the special education process. In this decision, the unanimous high court held that "We conclude IDEA grants independent, enforceable rights. These rights, which are not limited to certain procedural and reimbursement-related matters, encompass the entitlement to a free appropriate public education for the parents' child' (p. 2005). The high court thus ruled that the IDEA mandates that (a) parents must be meaningfully involved in the development of their child's IEP; (b) parents have enforceable rights under the law; and (c) parental participation in the special education process is crucial to ensuring that children with disabilities receive an FAPE (Yell & Crockett, 2011).

The IEP, therefore, is a process in which a student's parents and school district personnel develop the student's IEP and determine the placement where his or her special education services will be delivered. An illegal practice, called predetermination, occurs when school personnel develop a student's IEP and determine his or her placement outside of the IEP process. In other words, the school personnel develop a student's IEP before an IEP meeting, thereby not involving the student's parents. This is a serious violation of the IDEA, and could result in a ruling that a school district had denied a student an FAPE (Lake, 2007; Slater, 2010). It is a red flag that predetermination has occurred when IEP team members make definitive statements about what the school will and will not consider putting in the IEP (e.g., "We always ..." or "We never ...").

On the contrary, it is permissible for IEP team members to hold informal preparatory meetings and even to come to an IEP meeting with a draft IEP. It is important that a student's parents understand that the IEP is only a draft and is subject to changes during the IEP meeting. It is advisable that when IEP teams bring a draft IEP have the words "DRAFT" printed on the IEP. It is useful to remember the opinion in *Doyle v. Arlington* (1992) in which the judge wrote that, "School Officials must come to the IEP table with an open mind. But this does not mean they should come ... with a blank mind" (p. 156).

The following key areas are important when developing the content of students' IEPs:

- Ensure that the parents attend the initial IEP meeting. Keep good documentation of all attempts to get the parents to come to the meeting (e.g., emails, phone calls, and home visits) in case they cannot be contacted or choose not to come.
- Come to the IEP meeting with an open mind and seriously consider suggestions made by a student's parents. You may come with a draft IEP but write "draft" at the top of the IEP and ensure that parents understand that it is not a final IEP.
- Ensure that all the required team members are at the initial IEP meeting. Remember, a student's general education teacher must be involved in the IEP process.
- Include members on the IEP team who have specialized expertise in areas that may be needed to meet the unique educational needs of a student (e.g., functional behavioral assessment, positive behavior support, and progress monitoring). Of course this will depend on the needs of the particular student.

Determining Placement

To determine a student's placement a team of persons, which includes a student's parents, reviews the student's IEP and determines the least restrictive environment in which his or her special education can be implemented and an FAPE can be provided. The IDEA requires that a placement team, consisting of a student's parents, persons knowledgeable about the child, the meaning of the evaluation data and the placement options, determine a student's placement. Although the IDEA does not require that the placement decision be part of the IEP process Bateman (2011) asserted that it is acceptable for the IEP team to determine a student's placement because parents are participating members of both the placement and the IEP team.

The following three requirements are extremely important in determining a student's placement. First the placement decision can only be made after the IEP is written. This is because the team needs to have a basis for determining where a student's unique educational needs can best be met, and this basis is his or her IEP (Individuals with Disabilities Education Act Regulations, 2006). According to Bateman (2011) the case law has been very clear on this point: A school district cannot assign placement before the education program is developed. Lake (2007) also noted that IEP teams need to avoid a practice called "shoehorning." Shoehorning occurs when an IEP team places a student in a particular program (e.g., a special call for students with EBD) and then develops his or her IEP (i.e., goals and services) to fit the program. This is a clearly illegal practice and must be avoided (Lake, 2007; Slater, 2010).

Second, a student's placement must be individually determined and based on his or her needs rather than factors such as the students' category of disability, severity of disability, the availability of special education or related services, availability of space, or administrative convenience (Federal Register, 2006). Although these factors may be considered in determining a student's placement, they cannot be the sole determining factor (Lake, 2007).

Third, the IDEA's least restrictive environment (LRE) principle must be kept in mind when determining a student's placement (see Table 1). The LRE principle requires that teams must ensure that to the maximum extent appropriate students with disabilities are educated with students who are not disabled. The team may decide to remove a student to a more restrictive placement but only when education in the general education classroom with supplementary aides and services cannot be achieved satisfactorily. Thus, IEP team members must make good-faith efforts to educate a student in the LRE before proposing a more restrictive placement. Additionally, such deliberations should be documented.

Placement issues have engendered a considerable amount of litigation because IEP teams often make procedural and substantive errors when determining a student's placement (Slater, 2010). The following suggestions offered by Yell et al. (in press) are provided to assist IEP teams to ensure that they correctly determine appropriate placements for students with disabilities.

- Ensure that IEPs team members develop students' IEPs before determining placement.
- Ensure that a student's parents are on the team that determines their son or daughter's educational placement.
- Ensure that a student's IEP or placement team determines his or her placement based on the student's individual needs and not on the

student's category of disability or severity of disability. Similarly, do not substitute a policy of full inclusion for the consideration of a student's individual needs.

• Ensure that IEP teams make diligent, good faith efforts to educate students with disabilities in general education settings with supplementary aids and services. Monitor a student's progress and if a student is not succeeding in a placement, the IEP or placement team should meet to consider placement in a more appropriate, and sometimes more restrictive, setting.

• Ensure that when a decision is made to place a student in a more restrictive setting that the team thoroughly documents the decision-making process, including that they followed the continuum of alternative placements in a step-by-step manner. Additionally, in such situations the team should make all efforts to include opportunities for students with disabilities to be included in integrated settings.

• Ensure that placement and IEP teams avoid predetermining a student's placement.

DEVELOPING THE CONTENT OF THE IEP

The IDEA requires that, at a minimum, eight components be present in the IEP. States and local agencies, however, may require additional elements. The required components of IEPs are listed and described in Table 4. It is crucial that these elements be discussed at the IEP meeting and included in the IEP document. Courts have often determined that IEPs are invalid when any of these components are missing from a student's IEP and the student's special education is adversely affected (Bateman, 2011; Yell, 2012).

These components reveal the following four questions that are at the heart of the IEP process: (1) What are the student's unique educational needs that must be considered in developing the individualized program? (2) What measurable goals will enable the student to achieve meaningful educational benefit? (3) What services will the school provide to the student to address each of his or her educational needs? (4) How will the team monitor the student's progress to determine if the instructional program is effective? These questions are answered in the IEP process in developing the present levels of academic and functional performance, developing the measurable annual goals and special education services, and determining how the student's progress will be measured.

Table 4.   Required Components of IEPs.

IEP Components Required for All Students	IEP Components Required for Some Students
Present levels of academic achievement and functional performance	Transition goals and services for students aged 16 or younger if required by a state or determined by an IEP team
Measurable annual goals (and in some states short-term objectives)	For students who take alternate state assessments, a description of benchmarks or short-term objectives
Description of how progress will be measured and when a student's progress reported to his or her parents	If students take a state alternate assessment, a statement of why they cannot participate in the regular assessment and what assessment they will take
Statement of special education and other services provided to a student. These services must be based on peer-reviewed research	For students whose behavior impedes their learning the team must consider positive behavioral interventions and supports
An explanation of the extent, if any, that a student will not participate with nondisabled students in the general education classroom	IEP teams must consider whether a student needs assistive technology devices and services and they must be included in the IEP
A statement of accommodations that a student needs on state or district wide assessments	Additional special factors if required – Limited English proficiency, blind/ visually impaired, deaf/hard of hearing
Projected dates of services and frequency, location, and duration of these services	

Present Levels of Academic Achievement and Functional Performance

The present levels of academic achievement and functional performance (PLAAFP) statements reflect the information that was gathered from the full and individualized assessment of a student's unique educational needs. The PLAAFPs serve as the foundation of the IEP. The information is the baseline data from which the IEP team can determine the annual goals and measure a student's progress.

The U.S. Department of Education's question and answer document on IEPs described the relationship between the present levels and other aspects of the IEP as follows:

> There should be a direct relationship between the present levels of performance and the other components of the IEP. Thus, if the statement describes a problem with the child's

reading level and points to a deficiency in reading skills, the problem should be addressed under both goals and specific special education and related services provided to the child. (Question and Answer, p. 36)

Measurable Annual Goals

Since the enactment of the EAHCA in 1975, annual goals have been required in all students' IEPs. In the reauthorization of the IDEA in 1997 (hereafter IDEA '97), the requirement was changed from "annual goals" to "measurable annual goals." Annual goals are projections the team makes regarding the progress of the student in one school year; the IDEA '97 requirement meant that this progress must be measured. Now when IEP teams fail to include measurable goals for each area of need and then actually measure student progress toward those goals an IEP can be rendered inappropriate, and thus violate the FAPE provisions of the IDEA (Bateman, 2007; Bateman & Linden, 2006; Yell & Crockett, 2011).

According to Bateman (2011) only a fraction of IEPs contain goals that are actually measurable. When the goals are not measurable, an IEP will likely not provide an FAPE, which may violate the IDEA and when goals are not measured, an IEP will not provide an FAPE, which may violate the IDEA (Bateman & Linden, 2006). Thus it is critical that IEP teams develop measurable annual goals, measure them, and then make instructional changes if the measures indicate that they are necessary.

The importance of including measurable annual goals in the IEP was shown in the opinion of the following due process hearing. A hearing officer in New Mexico found that a school district's IEP did not provide FAPE when the:

Student's annual goals and objectives in each IEP simply do not contain objective criteria which permit measurement of Student's progress ... A goal of 'increasing' reading comprehension skills or 'improving decoding skills' is not a measurable goal ... Even if [present levels of performance] were clearly stated, an open-ended statement that Student will 'improve' does not meet the requirement ... for a 'measurable' goal. The addition of a percentage of accuracy is not helpful where the IEP fails to define a starting point, an ending point, the curriculum in which Student will achieve 80 to 85% accuracy, or a procedure for pre and post-testing. (*Rio Rancho Public Schools*, 2003, p. 563)

According to Bateman (2011) too few special education teachers know how to write measurable goals and too few goal writers intend that anyone will actually measure the progress the student has made, which makes IEP goals meaningless and useless. It is important that IEP team members, especially special education teachers and school psychologists, understand how to write measurable goals. Fig. 2 contains four guides to writing measurable goals.

In 1962 Robert Mager wrote a small book titled *Preparing instructional objectives: A critical tool in the development of effective instruction.* Mager (1962) suggested that goals and objective could be made measurable by including three components in the goal: The target behavior, the stimulus material, and the criteria for acceptable performance. Table 5 is an example of goals written in accordance with Mager's format.

In the IDEA reauthorization of 2004, Congress eliminated the requirement that IEPs must include short-term objectives (STOs), except for special education students who are assessed on state/district tests using

---

- Bateman, B.D. (2007). *From Gobbledygook to clearly written annual IEP goals.* Verona WI: Attainment Company

- Johnston, T.C. (2010) *without tears: How to write measurable educational goals and collect meaningful data.* Champaign, IL: Research Press

- Mager, R. F. (1997). *Preparing instructional objectives: A critical tool in the development of effective instruction.* Atlanta, GA: Center for Effective Performance

- Yell, M.L., Meadows, N.D., Drasgow, E., & Shriner, J.G. (2009) *Evidence-based practices in educating students with emotional and behavioral disorders.* Upper Saddle River, NJ: Pearson/Merrill Education.

Fig. 2.   Guides to Writing Measurable Goals.

Table 5.   Writing Measurable Goals Using Mager's Criteria.

Component	Academic Goal	Behavior Goal
Goal	In 36 weeks when given a reading passage from the 4th grade reading textbook, Jeremy will read aloud 48 words per minute	In 36 weeks when observed for half an hour on three separate occasions in his reading class, Jeremy will be on task 75% of the time observed as measured by direct observation
Target behavior	Read aloud	On task
Stimulus condition	In 36 weeks when given a reading passage from the 4th grade reading textbook	In 36 weeks when observed for half an hour on three separate occasions in his reading class
Criteria for acceptable performance	48 Words per minute	75% of the time observed

alternate assessments and alternate standards. However, states have the option of continuing to require that IEPs of all special education students include STOs. The requirements regarding annual goals and objectives are identical except for the length of time anticipated for accomplishment. For example, STOs can be similar to the goals, but written in shorter time frames. For example, use the same basic goal but write it for nine weeks rather than one year. Short-term objectives can also be written in the form of a task analysis. Therefore, the STOs represent progressive and sequential steps that a student must accomplish in order that he or she reaches the goal.

When developing annual goals, IEP teams should ensure that they are ambitious, but reasonable. This is because if goals are written that call for only small amounts of student growth it is likely that even if the goals are achieved the progress a student achieves will not be meaningful. In fact, if a hearing officer or court determines that if a student achieves the goals in his or her IEP but the goals were trivial in the first place, it becomes much more likely that the IEP will be found to be deficient and a violation of an FAPE (Bateman, 2011). IEP team members do not need to be concerned that a student's goals are too ambitious as long as the LEA has made good faith efforts in providing special education services and have the data to prove that a student made educational progress.

Special Education Services

All students' IEPs must include a statement of the specific educational services, related services, and supplementary aids and services that will be provided by the school. The purpose of the statements is to clarify the services that the school will provide to help a student (a) progress toward his or her annual goals and (b) be involved in and progress in the general education curriculum. The IDEA's definition of special education is "specially designed instruction to meet the unique needs of a student with a disability" (Individuals with Disabilities Education Act Regulations, 2006).

In IDEA 2004, Congress added the requirement that IEPs must include "a statement of the special education and related services and supplementary aids and services, based on peer-reviewed research (PRR) to the extent practicable (IDEA, 20U.S.C. § 1414(d)(1)(A)(i)(IV)). This requirement applies to the (a) selection and provision of special education methodology;

(b) selection and provision of related services, which are services that are required to assist a student to benefit from special education; and (c) selection and provision of aids, services and supports provided in regular education settings. PRR is research that has been accepted by a peer-reviewed journal or approved by a panel of independent experts through a comparably rigorous, objective, and scientific review (*Elementary and Secondary Education Act*). In the final regulations to the IDEA issued on August 14, 2006, the U.S. Department of Education defined PRR in the commentary as generally referring "to research that is reviewed by qualified and independent reviewers to ensure that the quality of the information meets the standards of the field before the research is published" (Federal Register, 2006). According to Etscheidt and Curran (2010) the intent of this section of the IDEA was to ensure that IEP teams' selection of educational approaches reflect sound practices which have been validated empirically whenever possible. Table 6 includes a number of websites that include information on PRR.

Measuring Student Progress

Progress monitoring is a generic term that refers to a simple procedure for repeated measurement of student growth toward long-range instructional goals (Deno, 1985). When teachers monitor students' progress they frequently and systematically collect data to determine how their students are progressing in a specific academic or functional areas (Yell, Meadows, Drasgow, & Shriner, 2009). According to the National Center on Progress Monitoring (2010), "Progress monitoring is a scientifically based practice that is used to assess students' academic and functional performance and evaluate the effectiveness of instruction." Monitoring a student's progress toward meeting IEP goals and objectives is essential because without conducting such monitoring it will be impossible to determine if the student's program is working and if he or she is making progress in achieving the goals in his or her IEP. If the goals and objectives of the IEP cannot be measured or evaluated, the IEP will not appropriately address the student's needs, which may result in the denial of FAPE. On the contrary, if students' progress is monitored and students do make growth toward their goals hearing officers and courts would likely rule that an IEP delivered FAPE.

To ensure that progress is monitored, The IEP must include a statement of how a student's progress toward the annual goals will be measured. The statement must also describe how a student's parents will be regularly

Table 6. Websites with Peer-Reviewed Research.

Center and URL	Description
Center on Positive Behavioral Interventions and Supports (PBIS) http://www.pbis.org/	The Technical Assistance Center on PBIS is devoted to giving schools information and technical assistance for identifying, adapting, and sustaining effective school-wide disciplinary practices
Council for Children with Behavioral Disorders (CCBD)	A professional organization dedicated to supporting the professional development and enhancing the expertise of those who work on behalf of children with challenging behavior and their families. It is a division of the Council for Exceptional Children (CEC)
Doing What Works: Research-Based Education Practices Online (http://www.ed.gov/)	U.S. Department of Education website that provides information to help educators to practical tools to improve classroom instruction
National Center on Response to Intervention (NCRTI) http://www.rti4success.org/	The NCRTI mission is to provide technical assistance to states and districts and build the capacity of states to assist districts in implementing proven models for RTI
National Dissemination Center for Children with Disabilities (NICHCY) www.nichcy.org	A central source of information on infants, toddlers, children, and youth with disabilities. Includes information on law and PRR
National Early Childhood Technical Assistance Center (NECTAC) http://www.nectac.org/	The NECTAC is dedicated to improving service systems and outcomes for children with disabilities and their families in all 50 states and 10 jurisdictions
National Secondary Transition Technical Assistance Center (NSTTAC) http://www.nsttac.org/	The NSTTAC is dedicated to ensuring full implementation of the IDEA and helping youth with disabilities achieve desired post-school outcomes
Promising Practices Network www.promsingpractices.net	This center offers research-based information on what works to improve the lives of children and families
What Works Clearinghouse http://ies.ed.gov/ncee/wwc/	The What Works Clearinghouse is an initiative of the U.S. Department of Education's Institute of Education Sciences. It is a central source of scientific evidence for what works in education

informed about their child's progress toward the annual goals. Parents of students with disabilities must be informed about their child's progress as regularly as are parents of children without disabilities (e.g., through regular report cards).

In a decision in *Escambia County Public School System* (2004) the importance of progress monitoring was described as follows: "Periodic review of progress on the goals and objectives provides the disabled student's teacher with supportive data needed to make a determination of the success of the intervention ..." (p. 248). How much progress a student makes has also been a factor in court's determination of whether FAPE was provided (Bateman, 2011). For example, in *Cranston School District v. Q.D.* (2008), *Taylor v. Sandusky* (2005), and *Draper v. Atlanta Independent School System* (2007) the courts ruled that school districts had failed to provide FAPE because students had failed to make academic gains. However, in *M.P. v. South Brunswick Board of Education* (2008), the court found that a school district had provided FAPE despite having a flawed IEP because the data collected by a special education teacher showed that the student had made meaningful academic progress. The decisions in these cases show that when a student does not make meaningful progress, or an IEP team fails to collect data regarding student progress, it is possible that a school district could be found in violation of the FAPE mandate of the IDEA. However, when an IEP collects legitimate data, and the data shows that a student has made progress, the school district has clearly provided FAPE.

Special education teachers should also skills in collecting and analyzing data. Although teachers of use anecdotal data to determine progress, using anecdotal data and other subjective procedures are not appropriate for monitoring progress, and should not be the basis of a progress monitoring system (Yell et al., 2009). The most appropriate progress monitoring systems are those in which objective numerical data are collected, graphed, analyzed, and used to make instructional decisions (Yell, 2012). Two examples of such systems are curriculum-based measurement (Deno, 1985) and applied behavior analysis (Alberto & Troutman, 2009).

A Federal District Court in Virginia commented on the nature of the data collected in *County School Board of Henrico County, Virginia v. R.T.* (2006). The case involved the parents of a young child with autism, R.T. The parents had placed R.T. in a private school because he had failed to make progress in the school district's program. R.T.'s teacher and other school district personnel asserted that R.T. had made progress in the school's program. The court, however, did not find the testimony credible because the evidence of R.T.'s progress was based only on anecdotal information and no data had been collected. The Court wrote, "(the teacher's) assessment of R.T. is entitled to little weight because it is based on anecdotal, rather than systematic, data collection" (p. 685). In *Board of Education of the Rhinebeck Central School District* a school district's IEP was invalid because no legitimate data were collected to show student progress. In fact, the student's goals were measured by teacher observation. According to the decision "although subjective teacher observation provides valuable information, teacher observation is not an adequate method of monitoring student progress" and "Without supporting data, teacher observation is opinion which cannot be verified" (p. 156).

The following key areas are important when developing the content of students' IEPs:

- Base the IEP on a student's needs not on the availability of services.
- Ensure that all student needs that are identified in the PLAAFP are addressed in the annual goals, service statements, or both.
- Ensure that IEP goals are measurable and are actually measured.
- Be a good consumer of PRR. Know how to access the latest research and be able to implement research-based procedures in the classroom.
- Conduct frequent and systematic monitoring of student progress. Collect legitimate date and make instructional decisions based on the data.
- Ensure that all required components are included in all students' IEPs (see Table 4).
- Include positive behavioral supports and interventions when behavior is an issue.

SUMMARY OF THE IDEA AND TEACHERS OF STUDENTS WITH EBD

To develop, implement, and evaluate special education programs requires a thorough knowledge of the IDEA and the development of IEPs. Because mistakes made during the IEP process can result in school district liability it is extremely important that teachers understand their responsibilities and duties under the IDEA. Additionally, because the law is always evolving, special education teachers should be especially aware of developments in the law. For example, the IDEA is re-authorized, and often amended, every 4 or 5 years, so teachers should keep current in these developments in special education law. Special education teachers should be supported and encouraged to attend professional conferences in their fields, where such responsibilities are discussed.

Because the IEP is the heart and soul of the IDEA, teachers should have expertise in (a) conducting assessments that provide relevant information for educationally planning, (b) writing measurable annual goals that are ambitious, (c) planning programming using empirically validate procedures,

(d) monitoring student progress, and (e) analyzing progress monitoring data. When IEP teams develop ambitious goals and special education teachers use research-proven practices in their instruction, monitor student progress, and react in accordance with the information from the data, it is increases the likelihood that students will make meaningful educational progress, thus meeting the FAPE requirement of the IDEA.

SUPERVISORY RESPONSIBILITIES OF TEACHERS OF STUDENTS WITH EBD

In recent years there has been an increase in the number of personal injury lawsuits filed on behalf of students seeking compensation from school districts (Lewis & Brunner, 2004). Moreover, school districts, and even teachers, may have legal liability when student's injuries are caused by negligence on part of school personnel (Rinato, 1998). In fact, lawsuits by students seeking compensation for injuries caused by negligence of school personnel are a major source of school litigation (Lewis & Brunner, 2004).

Although a school district's liability is more a function of the location and conditions under which an injury occurred, rather than whether or not a student has a disability, students with disabilities may be more susceptible to injury (Rinato, 1998). This may be especially true for students with EBD who may be more impulsive and more likely to put themselves in dangerous situations that may lead to injury.

When an injured student brings a negligence claim it is often brought under a state's tort law. Tort laws offer remedies to persons who have been injured by the intentional or negligent actions of others. According to Schimmel, Stellman, and Fischer (2011) state tort laws are based on the legal premise that individuals are liable for the consequences of their conduct if it results in injury to others. In negligence lawsuit four things have to be proven: (a) the school had a duty to take reasonable care to prevent the injury, (b) the school breached its duty failing to exercise a reasonable standard of care, (c) the student was injured, and (d) the school's breach of duty was the proximate cause of the student's injury.

The second element is a factor that teachers should pay particular attention to because if a teacher fails to exercise a reasonable standard of case to protect students from injury, then the teacher, and school, could be found negligent. Courts in negligence cases will gauge a teacher's conduct on how a "reasonable" teacher in a similar situation would have behaved (Yell,

2012). Moreover, thee degree of care exercised by a "reasonable" teacher is determined by a number of factors including (a) the training and experience of the teacher in charge, (b) the student's age, (c) the environment in which the injury occurred, (d) the type of instructional activity, (e) the presence or absence of the supervising teacher, and (f) a student's disability, if one exists (Schimmel et al., 2011). A number of cases have held that the student's IEP, disability, and unique needs are all relevant factors in determining the level of supervision that is reasonable (Yell, 2012).

Because of issues like student impulsivity, distractibility, and aggression students with EBD clearly require a high standard of care, especially younger students. The implications are clear that teachers of students with EBD must be mindful of their supervisory duties, especially in situations that could result in student accidents or injury. If there are any student problems that may involve safety issues, either to a particular student or his/her peers this may be a matter to be address in an IEP meeting. Moreover, teachers should keep documentation, signed by witnesses, if potential problems do arise.

Teachers of students with EBD should not worry needlessly about liability. In fact there are less liability lawsuits involving education than there are among the general public and the odds of being involved in litigation are quite small. Nevertheless, teachers should exercise a heightened sensitivity to the standard of care they assume when working in their important professions.

ADDRESSING BULLYING IN SCHOOLS

Bullying is a major concern among students and staff in the nation's school (Rodkin, 2011). Bullying in schools is a common experience for children and adolescent with over 50% of students reporting having being bullied mentally, verbally or physically some time during their school career (American Academy of Child Adolescent Psychiatry, 2011). Students with disabilities experience bullying even more than their nondisabled peers (Carter & Spencer, 2006). Students with significant social skills challenges may be at particular risk for bullying and victimization. For example, a study of U.S. mothers found that 94% of children with Asperger's syndrome faced bullying (Little, 2002) and 34% of students taking medication for ADHD reported being bullied at least 2–3 times a month (Unnever & Cornell, 2003). Students with EBD may also be at-risk for being the bully AND the victim. Clearly bullying in schools is a common occurrence.

Bullying is characterized by repeated harmful actions and an imbalance of power (Sampson, 2009). These harmful actions include physical behaviors (e.g., hitting, kicking, pushing, and choking), verbal behaviors (e.g., by calling names, threatening, taunting, malicious teasing, and spreading nasty rumors), or psychological attacks or intimidation. The Olweus Bullying Prevention Program characterizes bullying by the following criteria (a) it is aggressive behavior or intentional "harmdoing;" (b) it repeated and carried out over time; and (c) it occurs within a relationship characterized by an imbalance of power (Olweus, Limber, & Mihalic, 1999).

Although bullying is not a new phenomenon, new technologies, such as smart phones, facebook, and twitter allow students to expand their reach and the extent of their bullying. This is referred to as Cyberbullying and is defined as using computers, cell phones, and other electronic devices to harass, threaten, or humiliate peers (Hinduja & Patchin, 2011). According to Hinduja and Patchin (2011), the differences between cyber- and traditional bullying is that cyberbullying is (a) typically anonymous, (b) can involve a large number of people with just a few key strokes or click of the mouse, (c) more cruel than face-to-face interaction because the bully does not see the immediate impact on the victim, and (d) less noticeable by adults due to lack of adult supervision and technological know-how to keep up with teens' online activities.

Regardless of the type of bullying, it has a significant impact on all involved and unfortunately may be a prevailing part of the school day for some students. Without effective intervention the consequences of bullying and victimization are serious for individuals, schools, families, and communities. For the student being bullied it can have an impact on the student's physical (Vaillancourt, McDougall, Hymel, & Sunderani, 2010) and mental health (Cook, Williams, Guerra, Kim, & Sadek, 2010; Espelage & Swearer, 2011) as well as their academic performance (Glew, Fan, Katon, Rivara, & Kernic, 2005). For the student engaged in bully behavior it also has an impact; children who bully are significantly more likely than others to lead lives marked by school failure, depression, violence, crime, and other problems (Cook et al., 2010) and students may be victims themselves.

Legal Protections Under the Law for Students with Disabilities

Even though this is a pervasive issue in the schools, there is no federal policy in place governing bullying in the schools. To date, there are only state laws on bullying, however there is a call for bullying prevention and antibullying language in Elementary, Secondary Education Act (Young, Ne'eman, & Gesler, 2011). At the end of 2010, 45 states had bullying laws (states without antibullying laws: DC, Hawaii, Michigan, Montana, North Dakota, and South Dakota). For examples of various state and district law, see Arne Duncan's "Dear Colleague" letter (U.S. Department of Education, 2010b).

Regardless of state and federal law, existing federal legal and policy tools focused on disability nondiscrimination and educational access are available to address bullying against students with disabilities. As Duncan (U.S. Department of Education, 2010b) and Ali (U.S. Department of Education, 2010a) pointed out "under certain circumstances, bullying may trigger legal responsibilities for schools under the civil rights laws enforced by OCR and the Department of Justice that prohibit discrimination and harassment based on race, color, national origin, sex, disability, and religion" (p. 1). At minimum schools must protect students with disabilities from bullying and harassment, in addition to any actions governed by state and local law. The description of the laws and how they protect students with disabilities is described below.

Section 504 of the rehabilitation act and title II of the americans with disabilities act (ADA)

In 2000, the Department of Education's Office of Special Education and Rehabilitative Services (OSERS) and Office on Civil Rights (OCR) issued a joint letter highlighting the issue of disability harassment (U.S. Department of Education, 2000). In this letter, they highlighted laws protecting students with disabilities from harassment (Section 504 of the Rehabilitation Act; Title II of the Americans with Disabilities Act). When harassment is severe, persistent, or pervasive and it creates a hostile environment for the student, it can violate a student's rights under Section 504 or Title II of ADA (Young et al., 2011). Recently, the Office for Civil Rights issued a "Dear Colleague" letter including disability in a list of protected classes and added that schools MUST respond to bullying and harassment perpetrated on the basis of membership in these protected classes (U.S. Department of Education, 2010a). This most recent letter from OCR spells out the legal obligations schools must follow under Section 504 of the Rehabilitation Act and Title II of ADA. These actions include:

1. A school is responsible for addressing harassment incidents about which it knows or reasonably should have known.
2. A school must take immediate and appropriate action to investigate or otherwise determine what occurred.
3. If the investigation revealed that discriminatory harassment occurred, the school must take prompt and effective steps to end the harassment,

eliminate any hostile environment and prevent the harassment from recurring.

4. The school may need to provide training or other interventions for the larger school community to ensure that all students, their families, and school staff can recognize harassment and know how to respond.

5. The school should take steps to stop future harassment and prevent retaliation against the victim, the family, or any witnesses who provided information.

Individuals with Disabilities Education Act

Failure to address disability harassment may constitute a violation of the Individuals with Disabilities Education Act's (IDEA) guarantee of an FAPE and LRE for all eligible students. When harassment prevents or diminishes the ability of a student to benefit from his or her education, this violates FAPE. Additionally, if the bullying is left unaddressed, and it forces a student with a disability to a more restrictive educational placement, in order to benefit from their educational experience, this violates LRE. These provisions in IDEA may require districts a legal responsibility to act to protect students with disabilities.

Additionally, a student's IEP can also provide an important mechanism to address bullying through proactive, preventative, and reactive ways. The IEP can be used to include goals targeting pro-social behaviors or replacement behaviors to replace the bully behavior as well as self-advocacy skills to teach the student how to avoid or effectively respond to bullying and harassment. In addition, positive behavioral support plans can outline how educators can intervene to help teach these skills in their natural context as well as help protect students from bullying behaviors. Some states are using the IEP to help address bullying for students with disabilities. For example, Massachusetts passed a law that requires that IEPs address skills and behaviors required to avoid and respond to bullying (Young et al., 2011).

The IDEA also protects students with disabilities through the discipline provisions. These provisions are somewhat complex and confusing (Yell et al., 2009). In regards to bullying, the school needs to be sure that the state or local antibullying measures do not come in conflict with or serve to restrict the rights of students with disabilities under IDEA. For students with disabilities laws and policy tools, such as the IEP, FAPE, and LRE exist to protect students. These tools need to be used and districts may need ongoing training and support to help them interpret and apply these laws appropriately for students with disabilities.

IMPLICATIONS FOR EDUCATORS

One of the most important obligations for schools and educators is to deal with bullying issues in a proactive manner by addressing these issues early and providing documented action to ameliorate issues of bullying and harassment. There is not a quick fix to these issues and in fact the quick fix solutions may do more harm than good. For example brief assemblies or one-day awareness activities are insufficient to address bullying. Furthermore, tolerance policies, such as suspension are also ineffective and may result in under-reporting of bullying due to the perceptions that these consequences are too harsh or punitive (Bradshaw & Waasdorp, 2011). Importantly, there is little evidence that suspension is effective in curbing aggressive or bullying behavior (American Psychological Association (APA) Zero Tolerance Task Force, 2008).

Instead, bully prevention and response requires school-wide, multi-tiered systems that involve families and community and are sustainable. These efforts need to focus on school climate, supervision, and a consistent, proactive discipline system (Bradshaw & Waasdorp, 2009; Sugai & Horner, 2009).

One example of a school-wide, multi-tiered model is school-wide Positive Behavior Interventions and Supports (PBIS). School-wide PBIS promotes a learning environment that is positive, safe, and productive (Scott, Park, Sawain-Bradway, & Landers, 2007). Through this three-tiered prevention system educators proactively teach and acknowledge pro-social behaviors and prevent or reduce challenging behaviors. This tiered system provides universal intervention for the entire school as well as more explicit, small group instruction for students (both the victim and the student engaging in the bullying behavior) who need a more targeted level of support to be successful. In addition, PBIS includes intensive support for students who need individualized intervention. At this individualized levels, teams conduct functional behavioral assessments and design individualized positive behavior support plans. The team examines bullying using a functional approach and asks questions such as, why is bullying working from the perspective of the bully and what goals are being served by the bullying behavior. Through this tiered model, schools can create positive environments so that all children feel safe and can learn.

There are a variety of bully prevention programs available. The most extensively researched program is the Olweus Bullying Prevention Program (Olweus et al., 2007). This program is also implemented school-wide and includes classroom activities and meetings, targeted interventions for students identified as victims and students displaying bullying behavior, and activities for community involvement.

Regardless of the type of program used, the essential elements of a bully prevention program include parent training activities, high levels of playground supervision, consistent disciplinary methods, classroom management strategies, classroom and school-wide rules related to bullying and training of teachers (Farrington & Ttofi, 2009). Additionally, students who bully and are isolated or part of a deviant peer group (e.g., students with EBD), may need additional support, such as social skills training and opportunities for prosocial interactions with peers, such as peer tutoring and leadership roles (Charpie & Wehby, in press). Bullying is a complex phenomenon that requires prevention, early intervention, and the application of the legal protections due to students with disabilities.

CONCLUSION

It is important that teachers of students with EBD understand their responsibilities under IDEA and other laws affecting the education of students with EBD. The most important law that special education teachers need to follow is the IDEA. Teachers especially need to understand how to develop and implement a student's IEP. An educationally appropriate and legally correct IEP is developed according to the rules and regulations of IDEA, and is intended to serve as a blueprint for a student's special education program. The IEP is both a process and a document that determines and defines a student's free appropriate public education. Teachers of students with EBD should understand their heightened supervisory activities under state liability laws.

REFERENCES

Alberto, P. A., & Troutman, A. C. (2009). *Applied behavior analysis for teachers* (8th ed). Upper Saddle River, NJ: Pearson/Merrill Education.

American Academy of Child & Adolescent Psychiatry. (2011). Bullying: Facts for families. Washington DC: American Academy of Child & Adolescent Psychiatry. Available from www.aacp.org

American Psychological Association (APA) Zero Tolerance Task Force. (APA). Are zero tolerance policies effective in the schools? An evidentiary review and recommendations. *American Psychologist, 63*, 852–862.

Americans with Disabilities Act, 42 U.S.C. 12101 *et seq.*

Bateman, B. D. (2007). *From Gobbledygook to clearly written IEP goals.* Verona, WI: Attainment.

Bateman, B. D. (2011). Individual education programs for children with disabilities. In J. M. Kauffman & D. P. Hallahan (Eds.), *Handbook of special education* (pp. 91–106). New York: Routledge.

Bateman, B. D., & Linden, M. A. (2006). *Better IEPs.* Verona, WI: Attainment Co.

Board of Education of the Rhinebeck Central School District, 39 IDELR 148 (SEA, NY, 2003).

Bradshaw, C. P., & Waasdorp, T. E. (2009). Measuring and changing a "culture of bullying". *School Psychology Review, 38,* 356–361.

Bradshaw, C. P., & Waasdorp, T. E. (2011). Effective strategies in combating bullying. In Whitehouse Conference on Bullying Prevention. Retrieved from http://www.stopbullying.gov/references/white_house_conference/white_house_conference_materials.pdf#effective_strategies

Carter, B. B., & Spencer, V. G. (2006). The fear factor: Bullying and students with disabilities. *International Journal of Special Education, 21:* 11–23. Retrieved from http://www.internationaljournalofspecialeducation.com/articles.cfm?y=2006&v=21&n=1

Charpie, E., & Wehby, J. H. (in press). The effects of a leadership role on the engagement of students at-risk for emotional and behavioral disorders. *Journal of Behavioral Education.*

Cook, C. R., Williams, K. R., Guerra, N. G., Kim, T. E., & Sadek, S. (2010). Predictors of bullying and victimization in childhood and adolescence: A meta-analytic investigation. *School Psychology Quarterly, 25,* 65–83.

County School Board of Henrico County, Virginia v. R.T., 433 F.Supp.2d 657 (E.D. VA 2006).

Cranston School District v. Q. D., 51 IDELR 41 (D. R.I. 2008).

Deno, S. L. (1985). Curriculum-based measurement: The emerging alternative. *Exceptional Children, 52,* 219–232.

Doyle v. Arlington, 806 F. Supp. 1253 (E.D. VA 1992).

Draper v. Atlanta Independent School System, 47 IDELR 260 (N.D. Ga. 2007).

Elementary and Secondary Education Act, 20 U.S.C. § 1208(6)(B)]

Escambia County Public School System, 42 IDELR 248 (SEA NY 2004).

Espelage, D. L., & Swearer, S. M. (Eds.). (2011). *Bullying in North American schools* (2nd ed.). New York: Routledge.

Etscheidt, S., & Curran, C. M. (2010). Reauthorization of IDEA 2004: The peer-reviewed research requirement. *Journal of Disability Policy Studies, 21,* 29–39.

Farrington, D. P., & Ttofi, M. M. (2009). *School-based programs to reduce bullying and victimization. (Campbell Systematic Reviews No. 6).* Oslo, Norway: Campbell Corporation.

Federal Register, 71, 46,588-46,674 (2006).

Glew, G. M., Fan, M., Katon, W., Rivara, F. P., & Kernic, M. A. (2005). Bullying psychosocial adjustment and academic performance in elementary school. *Archives of Pediatric Adolescent Medicine, 159,* 1026–1031.

Hinduja, S., & Patchin, J. (2011). Overview of cyberbullying. In *Whitehouse Conference on Bullying Prevention.* Retrieved from http://www.stopbullying.gov/references/white_house_conference/white_house_conference_materials.pdf#overview_of_cyberbullying.

Individuals with Disabilities Education Act (IDEA) of 2004, 20 U.S.C. § 1401 et seq.

Individuals with Disabilities Education Act Regulations of 2006, 34 C.F.R. § 300.1 et seq.

Johnston, T. C. (2010). *Data without tears: How to write measurable educational goals and collect meaningful data.* Champaign, IL: Research Press.

Kirby v. Cabell County Board of Education, 46 IDELR § 156 (S.D. W. VA 2006).

Lake, S. E. (2007). *Slippery slope! The IEP missteps every IEP team must know – and how to avoid them.* Horsham, PA: LRP Publications.

Lewis, D. K., & Brunner, J. M. (2004). *Providing teachers tools for safe classrooms (video).* Horsham, PA: LRP Publications.

Little, L. (2002). Middle-class mothers' perceptions of peer and sibling victimization among children with Asperger's syndrome and nonverbal learning disorders. *Issues in Comprehensive Pediatric Nursing, 25,* 43–57.

Mager, R. F. (1997). *Preparing instructional objectives: A critical tool in the development of effective instruction.* Atlanta, GA: Center for Effective Performance.

Mager, R. (1962). *Preparing instructional objectives.* Palo Alto, CA: Fearon.

M.P. v. South Brunswick Board of Education, 51 IDELR 219 (D. N.J. 2008)

National Center on Progress Monitoring. Retrieved from June 24, 2010 from www.student progress.org.

Olweus, D., Limber, S. P., Flerx, V. C., Mullin, N., Riese, J., & Snyder, M. (2007). *Olweus bullying prevention program: Schoolwide guide.* Center City, MN: Hazelden.

Olweus, D., Limber, S., & Mihalic, S. F. (1999). *Blueprints for violence prevention, book nine: Bullying prevention program.* Boulder, CO: Center for the Study and Prevention of Violence.

Reschly, D. (2000). Assessment and eligibility determination in the Individuals with Disabilities Education Act of 1997. In C. Telzrow & M. Tankersley (Eds.), *IDEA Amendments of 1997: Practice guidelines for school-based teams* (pp. 65–104). Bethesda, MD: National Association of School Psychologists.

Rinato, P. (Ed.) (1998). *Limiting your school's exposure to negligence supervision and safety claims.* Horsham, PA: LRP Publications.

Rio Rancho Public School, 40 IDELR 140 (SEA N.M. 2003).

Rodkin, P. C. (2011). Bullying and children's peer relationships. *Proceedings from Whitehouse Conference on Bullying Prevention.* Retrieved from http://www.stopbullying.gov/references/white_house_conference/white_house_conference_materials.pdf#bullying_and_peer_relationships.

Sampson, R. (2009). *"Bullying in Schools." Problem-oriented guides for police.* Washington, DC: U.S. Department of Justice.

Schimmel, D., Stellman, L., & Fischer, L. (2011). *Teachers and the law* (8th ed). Boston: Allyn & Bacon.

Scott, T., Park, K., Sawain-Bradway, J., & Landers, E. (2007). Positive behavior support in the classroom: Facilitating behaviorally inclusive learning environments. *International Journal of Behavioral Consultation and Therapy, 3*(2), 223–235.

Section 504 of the Rehabilitation Act of 1973, 29 U.S.C. § 794 *et seq.*

Slater, A. E. (2010). *Placement under the IDEA: Avoiding predetermination and other legal pitfalls.* Horsham, PA: LRP Publication.

Sugai, G., & Horner, R. H. (2009). Responsiveness to intervention and school-wide positive behavior supports: Integration of multi-tiered approaches. *Exceptionality, 17,* 223–237.

Taylor v. Sandusky, 43 IDELR 4 (D. Md. 2005).

Unnever, J. D., & Cornell, D. G. (2003). Bullying, self-control, and ADHD. *Journal of Interpersonal Violence, 81*(2), 129–147.

U.S. Department of Education. Dear Colleague Letter: Prohibited Disability Harassment (July 25, 2000). Retrieved from http://www2.ed.gov/about/offices/list/ocr/publications.html#Section504-Docs

U.S. Department of Education. Dear Colleague Letter: Harassment and bullying, background, summary, and fast facts (October 26, 2010a). Retrieved from http://www.stopbullying. gov/references/white_house_conference/white_house_conference_materials.pdf#dear_ colleague.

U.S. Department of Education. Dear Colleague Letter: Secretary of Education bullying law and policy memo (December 16, 2010b). Retrieved from http://www.stopbullying.gov/ references/white_house_conference/white_house_conference_materials.pdf#secretary_ memo.

Vaillancourt, T., McDougall, P., Hymel, S., & Sunderani, S. (2010). Respect or fear? The relationship between power and bullying behavior. In S. R. Jimerson, S. M. Swearer & D. L. Espelage (Eds.), *Handbook of bullying in schools. An international perspective* (pp. 221–222). New York: Routledge.

Winkleman v. Parma City School District, 550 U.S. 516 (2007).

Yell, M. L. (2012). *The law and special education* (3rd ed). Upper Saddle River, NJ: Pearson/ Merrill Education.

Yell, M. L., & Crockett, J. B. (2011). Free appropriate public education. In J. M. Kauffman & D. P. Hallahan (Eds.), *Handbook of special education* (pp. 91–106). New York: Routledge.

Yell, M. L., Meadows, N. B., Drasgow, E., & Shriner, J. G. (2009). *Evidence-based practices for educating students with emotional and behavioral disorders*. Upper Saddle River, NJ: Pearson/Merrill Education.

Yell, M. L, Thomas, S. S., & Katsiyannis, A. (in press). Special education law for leaders and administrators of special education. In J. B. Crockett, B. S. Billingsley, & M. L. Boscardin (Eds.), *Handbook of leadership and administration for special education*. New York: Taylor & Francis.

Young, J., Ne'eman, A., & Gesler, S. (2011). Bullying and students with disabilities. *Proceeding from Whitehouse Conference on Bullying Prevention*. Retrieved from http://www.stop bullying.gov/references/white_house_conference/white_house_conference_materials.pdf# bullying_and_disabilities

CHAPTER 2

THEMES AND DIMENSIONS OF EMOTIONAL AND BEHAVIORAL DISORDERS

April L. Mustian and Yojanna Cuenca-Sanchez

ABSTRACT

Students with emotional and behavioral disorders (EBD) are one of the most underserved populations in today's schools (Kauffman, Mock, & Simpson, 2011). Many of these students also have additional disabilities in conjunction with an EBD identification, such as Learning Disabilities (LD), Attention Deficit Disorder (ADD), Attention Deficit Hyperactivity Disorder (ADHD), Oppositional Defiant Disorder (ODD), or Obsessive Compulsive Disorder (OCD), among other psychiatric disorders (Henley, Ramsey, & Algozzine, 2009; Kauffman, 2005).

Because the identification of EBD examines behaviors that tend to be more subjective in nature than other disabilities and because these pervasive behaviors are manifested in a variety of forms, EBD is one of the most misidentified disability categories (Skiba, Poloni-Staudinger, Gallini, Simmons, & Feggins-Azziz, 2006). For students with EBD, the behavior(s) they exhibit contribute to learning difficulties in multiple academic and functional areas. This chapter provides in-depth information on the common characteristics and behavioral dimensions of this

Behavioral Disorders: Identification, Assessment, and Instruction of Students with EBD
Advances in Special Education, Volume 22, 31–49
Copyright © 2012 by Emerald Group Publishing Limited
All rights of reproduction in any form reserved
ISSN: 0270-4013/doi:10.1108/S0270-4013(2012)0000022005

population. Additionally, the in-school performance and long-term outcomes of students with EBD are discussed.

Keywords: EBD; characteristics; dimensions; outcomes; behaviors

Students with emotional and behavioral disorders (EBD) are one of the most underserved populations in today's schools (Kauffman, Mock, & Simpson, 2011). Many of these students also have additional disabilities in conjunction with an EBD identification, such as Learning Disabilities (LD), Attention Deficit Disorder (ADD), Attention Deficit Hyperactivity Disorder (ADHD), Oppositional Defiant Disorder (ODD), or Obsessive Compulsive Disorder (OCD), among other psychiatric disorders (Henley, Ramsey, & Algozzine, 2009; Kauffman, 2005).

Because the identification of EBD examines behaviors that tend to be more subjective in nature than other disabilities, it is also one of the most misidentified disability categories (Skiba, Poloni-Staudinger, Gallini, Simmons, & Feggins-Azziz, 2006). The pervasive behaviors exhibited by these students take on a vast array of forms, such as: (a) aggression, (b) self-injury, (c) social withdrawal, (d) excessive fear or anxiety, (e) impulsivity (f) immaturity, (g) social skill deficits, and (h) poor peer and adult relationships. For students with EBD, the behavior(s) they exhibit contribute to learning difficulties in multiple academic areas. This chapter will provide in-depth information on the common characteristics and behavioral dimensions of this population. Additionally, the in-school performance and long-term outcomes of students with EBD will be discussed.

WHAT CONSTITUTES IDENTIFICATION OF EBD UNDER IDEA?

In order to fully understand the characteristics of students who become identified with EBD, it is important to examine the actual definition under law by which students may be eligible. The Individuals with Disabilities Education Improvement Act (IDEA) amendments of 2004 defines the disability category of *emotional disturbance* as:

> a condition exhibiting one or more of the following characteristics over a long period of time and to a marked degree that adversely affects a child's educational performance: (a) an inability to learn which cannot be explained by intellectual, sensory, or health factors, (b) an inability to build or maintain satisfactory interpersonal relationships with peers

and teachers, (c) inappropriate types of behavior or feelings under normal circumstances, (d) a general pervasive mood of unhappiness or depression, (e) a tendency to develop physical symptoms or fears associated with personal or school problems ... includes schizophrenia ... does not apply to children who are socially maladjusted, unless it is determined that they have an emotional disturbance. (§ 300.8 [a][4][i])

This 2004 revision to IDEA uses the term *emotional disturbance* to describe students with emotional and/or behavioral disorders (EBD). Previous versions of IDEA used the term *serious emotional disturbance*, but *serious* was dropped in 1999 when the regulations for the 1997 version of IDEA were created (U.S. Department of Education, 1999). With this change to the disability term, the government made it clear that the definition was not changed; specifically, the U.S. Department of Education (1999, p. 12,542) stated, "[It] is intended to have no substantive or legal significance. It is intended strictly to eliminate the pejorative connotation of the term 'serious'."

Though the terms used to refer to students with EBD have changed over the years, the definition in itself has remained consistent. Although many students have probably experienced social maladjustment, withdrawal, or anxiety at moments in their educational lives, the law states that to be identified with a true disability in this category, a student must exhibit one or more behaviors to the extent that it significantly impacts his or her academic performance. Additionally, the behavior or behaviors for which the student is being referred must either be intense in nature and/or have evidence of occurrence over a long period of time. More in-depth information on the actual identification process of students suspected of having EBD can be found in Chapter 3 of this book.

RISK FACTORS FOR DEVELOPING EBD

One of the most common terms used in the field of education to describe students who do not achieve academically or socially when compared to their same-age peers is "at risk." Even though states are given the opportunity to define for themselves what it means to be at risk, some salient characteristics are evident across the nation. Lane and Menzies (2003) described students at risk, as those who "deviate from normative performance" (p. 431) in an academic, behavior, and/or social domain, which results in problems with learning and behavior. At-risk students are also characterized as children living in poverty, English Language Learners (ELL), migratory students, neglected and delinquent children, homeless children, immigrant students, teen parents, refugee children, or ethnically identified students (U.S. Department of Education, 1994).

Researchers have further defined the meaning of "at risk" with specific regard to behavioral concerns. For example, Severson, Walker, Hope-Doolittle, Kratochwill, and Gresham (2007) define behaviorally at-risk students as those "(a) who are on a trajectory to later destructive outcomes due to risk factor exposure in the first five years of life and (b) who present moderate to severe behavioral challenges to their teachers, peers, and sometimes primary caregivers" (p. 194). These behavioral risk factors have been defined as "events that occur at the child, family, and environmental levels that increase the probability of diagnosis or the severity of a serious emotional disturbance (e.g., physical abuse, sexual abuse, family violence, and drug-alcohol abuse; family history of mental illness, violence, or drug-alcohol abuse)" (U.S. Department of Health and Human Services, Substance Abuse and Mental Health Services Administration, 1998).

Much research has been conducted on such potential risk factors in children for developing EBD. Some of the most salient environmental risk factors associated with the development of chronic behavior problems identified in the literature include (a) poverty, (b) subjection to domestic violence, and (c) child maltreatment (Conroy & Brown, 2004). Nelson, Stage, Duppong-Hurley, Synhorst, and Epstein (2007) found five factors that were most predictive of problem behavior including (a) externalizing behaviors, (b) internalizing behaviors, (c) child maladjustment, (d) family functioning, and (e) maternal depression. Without effective early interventions, these at-risk students are likely to experience increased difficulty with social adjustment and in meeting academic and behavior expectations; many eventually become eligible for EBD as a result (Farmer et al., 2008).

CHARACTERISTICS OF STUDENTS WITH EBD

Externalizing/Internalizing Behaviors

Externalizing and/or internalizing behavior problems are typically the two broad categories used to describe the type of behaviors students with EBD might exhibit (Furlong, Morrison, & Jimerson, 2004; Gresham & Kern, 2004). Externalizing types of behaviors are more visible and disruptive. Within this broad category, conduct disorder (CD), ADHD, and ODD are discussed due to the interrelatedness among them and because they are characterized by behavioral difficulties linked to aggressive, noncompliant, and violent behavior that severely affect students' performance in school and at home (Furlong et al., 2004; Kauffman, 2005).

CD typically encompasses an array of antisocial behaviors that impede students' abilities to follow major social rules and behave according to social expectations. According to the American Psychiatric Association (APA, 2000, pp. 98–99) a student diagnosed with CDs should exhibit a pattern of behaviors that violate social rules and the rights of others. Students might manifest at least three of the following behaviors within a year (with at least one behavior present in the past six months): (a) aggression to people or animals in the form of bullying, threatening, fighting, using a weapon, or cruelty; (b) destruction of property in the form of fire setting, vandalism; (c) deceitfulness, lying, or stealing; and (d) serious violations of rules, such as running away from home, school truancy, or staying out of home despite parental objections. CD is classified by age of onset and those students who manifest the "childhood-onset type" (i.e., CD types of behaviors before age 10 years), will most likely continue to develop a severe impairment and have worse prognosis in comparison to students who manifest CD types of behaviors after age 10 years, that is the "adolescent-onset type" (Eddy, Reid, & Curry, 2002; Walker, Ramsey, & Gresham, 2004).

ODD and ADHD are other types of disorders that are commonly associated with CD. In fact, the coexistence of CD with ADHD and ODD is very high (Kauffman, 2005). Studies have shown that many children and youngsters with a CD diagnosis manifested ODD types of behaviors early on (Eddy et al., 2002). Moreover, according to the *Diagnostic and Statistical Manual of Mental Disorders, Text Revisions, Fourth Edition(DSM-IV-TR)* (APA, 2000) if a child does not meet the criteria for CD, but exhibits defiant, angry, hostile, irritable, or spiteful behaviors they might be diagnosed with ODD. However, if children or adolescents exhibit a persistent pattern in which social rules and the rights of others are violated, then they might be diagnosed with CD. Following are the criteria the DSM-IV-TR (APA, 2000, p. 102) established for the diagnosis of ODD with four or more of the following behaviors frequently present during at least six months: (a) loses temper easily; (b) argues with adults; (c) is noncompliant; (d) annoys people deliberately; (e) blames others for his/her misbehavior; (f) is irritable and easily annoyed by others; (g) shows anger and resentfulness; (h) is spiteful or vindictive.

ADHD is thought to affect 3–5% of school-age children in the United States (American Psychiatric Association, 2000). The DSM-IV-TR (APA, 2000, p. 87) establishes three types of ADHD: (a) inattentive type, where the main difficulty is an inability to stay focused on a task or activity; (b) hyperactive-impulsive type, where the person acts impulsively and is very active (e.g., fidget, run around constantly, and cannot play quietly); and (c) combined type, where the person is inattentive, impulsive, and excessively active. Boys are more likely to be diagnosed with ADHD than girls and tend to display more externalizing types of behaviors as well (Abikoff et al., 2002).

Under IDEA, ADHD is classified under the other health impairments (OHI) category. However, according to Special Education Elementary Longitudinal (SEELS) data, the prevalence of ADHD in other special education categories is high, especially for LD and ED. Fifty percent of students with ADHD qualified for the LD category and 60% for the ED category. Due to the coexistence of this disorder with ODD, CD, and other psychiatric disorders students with ADHD are more likely to receive special education services under the ED category (Schnoes, Reid, Wagner, & Marder, 2006).

Internalizing behavior problems are manifest when a student turns inward in social or emotional conflict (Henley et al., 2009). Contrary to externalizing type of behaviors, students who suffer from internalizing types of behaviors will frequently go unnoticed. There are several types of internalizing disorders: (a) anxiety-related disorders; (b) mood disorders; and (c) suicidal ideation or planning (Gresham & Kern, 2004).

Anxiety-related disorders are typically co-morbid with CD and depression (Kauffman, 2005). Within anxiety disorders some of the major disorders are: (a) separation anxiety; (b) obsessive-compulsive disorder; (c) selective mutism; and (d) posttraumatic stress disorders.

Separation anxiety is a disorder in which children become excessively fearful and nervous when separated from home or loved ones. For this disorder to be diagnosed, children have to exhibit severe and persistent separation anxiety that impedes their ability to function in social and academic contexts. To be diagnosed, three or more of the following characteristics must be present for at least four weeks: (a) excessive distress when separated from home or important figures; (b) worry about losing major subjects of attachment or an event that might cause them to be detached from loved ones; (c) fear about being left alone; (d) refusal to go to sleep or sleep away from home if significant figures are not present; (e) nightmares about separations; and (f) physical symptoms (e.g., crying, headaches, nausea, and vomiting) when they know they will be separated from loved ones (APA, 2000, p. 125).

Obsessive-compulsive disorder is another type of anxiety disorder in which individuals engage in a cycle of repetitive thoughts, fears, or an obsession in regard to nonrelated real-life problems. For instance, obsessions might be related to fear of contamination by germs, repeated doubts, urge to have things in order, or aggressive impulses and images. These obsessions are difficult to control and cause individuals to engage in patterns of routines (compulsions) in an attempt to make the obsessive thought to go away. They might wash hands constantly, arrange things in a certain order, count or repeat words in silence, or frequently check things (e.g., oven turned off, and door locked) that they associate with harm or danger (Gresham & Kern, 2004).

Selective mutism is a disorder in which children exhibit a persistent failure to speak in social settings. This disorder is rare as it occurs in less than 1% of the school-age population. These children know how to have normal conversations, but they choose to communicate only with certain individuals. They are to some degree socially withdrawn, exhibit compulsive traits, negativism, and temper tantrums that severely affect social and school functioning (APA, 2000, p. 125; Kauffman, 2005).

Post-Traumatic Stress Disorder (PTSD) is an anxiety disorder that can develop after a person has been exposed to life-change events or ordeals (e.g., accidents, natural disasters, and violent personal assaults) in which grave physical harm or near-dead experience occurred or had the potential for occurring. People who suffer from PTSD will develop intense fear, helplessness, and horror. Symptoms might manifest in irritability or anger, difficulties with sleep, inability to concentrate, and obsessive worry (APA, 2000).

Mood disorders are mental health problems that have many characteristics and dimensions. For instance, they may involve and array of extreme emotions from the feeling of unhappiness or anguish to a state of euphoria. Often times these emotions are not in proportion to actual circumstances. Depression is one major mood disorder that affects children and adolescents. According to the APA (2000) a major depressive disorder is characterized by one or more depressive episodes that would cause the person to lose interest in all activities. Depression usually manifest by the following characteristics: feeling down, unworthy, guilty, helpless, restless, irritable, lethargic, increased or decrease in sleep, inability to concentrate or remember, increase or decrease in appetite, and thoughts of death or suicide. In children, a major depressive disorder is typically characterized by irritability rather than sadness. The co-occurrence of depression with anxiety disorders and CDs is high (Gresham & Kern, 2004; Kauffman, 2005). Dysthymic disorder is another depressive disorder. In children and adolescents it manifests by irritability and, during a year period, they experience two or more of the following characteristics without the symptoms for more than two months at a time: (a) poor appetite or overeating, (b) sleeping problems; (c) fatigue or low energy; (d) hopelessness and low self-esteem; and (e) lack of concentration and difficulty making decisions (APA, 2000).

Suicidal behavior is a major health concern as it is the third leading cause of death for 10- to 24-year-olds. Males commit suicide five times more than female youth (American Association of Suicidology, 2010). Children and adolescents who are depressed are at a greater risk to commit suicide (Kauffman, 2005). Some warning signs include: (a) talks about suicide or no reason to live; (b) withdrawn from friends and social activities; (c) experience a recent severe loss; (d) drastic changes in behavior (e.g., loss of interest in hobbies and activities and in personal appearance, increase use of alcohol and drugs); (e) give away possessions and make final arrangements; and (f) depression (e.g., feelings of helplessness and hopelessness).

Without doubt, the types of externalizing and internalizing behaviors children and youth might exhibit is vast. Both present unique challenges in the education and treatment of children with EBD in school settings as they also influence and impact language, processing ability, and overall academic performance.

Language Skills and Processing Ability

The types of externalizing and internalizing behaviors that students with EBD experience can not only co-occur among each other, but they can also influence students' language skills and processing speed. Research has shown that language deficits and EBD frequently coexist (Benner, Nelson, & Epstein, 2002; Nelson, Benner, & Rogers-Adkinson, 2003), that the presence of externalizing type of behaviors tend to accentuate students' expressive language deficits (Nelson, Benner, & Cheney, 2005) as well as their academic fluency deficits (Benner, Allor, & Mooney, 2008).

In a literature review of 26 quantitative studies, spanning from 1993 to 1996 (Benner et al., 2002) examined the (a) prevalence and types of language deficits (e.g., receptive, expressive, and pragmatic) in children with EBD and (b) the prevalence of EBD in children diagnosed with language deficits. The sample included 2,358 children with EBD and 438 without EBD between the ages of 4 and 19 years. Researchers reported that an average of 71% of children with EBD experienced significant language deficits. When looking at language deficits by type, the majority of students experienced pragmatic deficits, followed by expressive deficits, and lastly receptive deficits. Finally, approximately 57% of children with language deficits also experienced EBD.

In a similar study, Nelson et al. (2003)Nelson, Benner, and Rogers-Adkinson (2003) conducted a cross-sectional study that included a sample of 152 students, in grades K-12, in an urban school district in the Midwest. The purpose was to further investigate the characteristics of students with co-morbid EBD and language deficits. Findings revealed that 45% of the sample selected had some type of language deficit. Specifically, 32% of children and 54% of adolescents experienced difficulties with receptive and expressive language. Additionally, across age groups, students who exhibited EBD and language deficits were more likely to have severe expressive language deficits. Further, these students exhibited mild to moderate achievement deficits in reading, mathematics, and written language.

Nelson et al. (2005) examined deficits in language skills across age and gender for a random sample of 166 students with EBD, in public school settings, across grades K-12. They also examined the specific types of problem behaviors that were related to deficits in language skills. Findings revealed that gender did not influence language deficits across grade levels (boys and girls experienced similar expressive and receptive language deficits); however, they were more likely to experience more expressive, rather than receptive, language deficits. Moreover, type of behavior did influence the type of language deficit. Those students who exhibited externalizing behaviors were more likely than students who exhibited internalizing behaviors to experience expressive language deficits (Nelson et al., 2005).

The relationship between processing ability (i.e., the rate with which a student is able to process information automatically and rapidly), has also been examined in regard to the contribution to the externalizing, internalizing, and attention problems of students with EBD. Benner et al. (2008) conducted a cross-sectional study of 133 students with EBD, in grades K-12, to assess the frequency of fluency deficits in reading, mathematics, writing, academic skills, and language in students with EBD. Results showed that more than half of the sample (57%) evidenced an academic processing deficit. Students with fluency deficits in reading, math, and writing evidenced more externalizing and attention problems than did students who evidenced academic skills or language deficits. This study found that academic fluency deficits have a greater impact on social adjustment than language or academic skills of students with EBD.

Social Skills Deficits

Social competence is considered a necessity in order for students to lead successful and healthy lives both in school and beyond. The ability of a child to apply appropriate verbal and nonverbal social responses, such as eye-contact, posture, social distance, voice, volume, handling conflict, expressing feelings, and cooperating with peers and adults allows him or her to gain the social competence necessary to create and maintain positive interpersonal relationships with peers, family, and adults (Gresham, Sugai, & Horner, 2001; Gresham, Van, & Cook, 2006; Spence, 2003). Gresham et al. (2001) define social skills from a conceptualized standpoint by stating, "social skills are the specific behaviors that an individual uses to perform competently or successfully on particular social tasks" (p. 333).

In alignment with this definition, today's education focuses on promoting social competence of all students. Although many students are fluent in the ability to interact with peers and adults and perform socially appropriate behaviors, other students may not naturally possess these capabilities. Students with disabilities are one population of students for which this statement is highly accurate. In fact, more than 70% of youth with disabilities have deficits in social interaction and communication skills (Wagner, Newman, Cameto, Levine, & Garza, 2006). Students with EBD are at the forefront of this disparaging statistic, especially when compared to their same-age, typically developing peers. By definition, students with EBD often experience social skills deficits that lead to inappropriate peer and adult interactions, as well as social withdrawal and poor academic achievement in the educational setting (Christensen, Young, & Marchant, 2007; Gresham, et al., 2001). For these students, simple exposure to social settings alone is an insufficient remedy. The acquisition of appropriate social skills for students with EBD often require more direct and systematic instructional approaches that often take the form of an integrated multimodel involving modeling, behavior rehearsal/role-play, immediate feedback, and reinforcement (Chen, 2006; Spence, 2003). Without such explicit social skill instruction, students with EBD continue on a trajectory of school failure and poor post-school outcomes in employment, education, independent living, and social and leisurely activities.

WHO AND WHERE ARE STUDENTS WITH EBD: NATIONAL PERSPECTIVE

Now that the most salient characteristics of students with EBD have been identified and explained, it is important to examine the current status and trends of these students within the national context.

Representation of Students with EBD

According to the U.S. Department of Education (2009), national data indicate that of the 6,608,446 students with disabilities, ages 6 through 21 years, receiving special education services, a total of 405,475 were classified under the EBD category. Many factors influence the social and academic progress for these students. Three longitudinal studies funded by the Office of Special Education Programs (OSEP), Special Education Elementary Longitudinal Study (SEELS); National Longitudinal Transition Study-2 (NLTS2); and the Study of State and Local Implementation and Impact of IDEA (SLIIDEA) provide a comprehensive perspective on students with EBD across grade levels (Bradley, Doolittle, & Bartolotta, 2008; Bradley, Henderson, & Monfore, 2004; Wagner et al., 2006). Findings from these longitudinal studies are discussed in more detail below.

Demographics of Students with EBD

Approximately 8% of special education students are identified with EBD as their primary disability. The majority of those are male. Specifically, an astounding 80% of elementary and middle school children and 76% of secondary school youth with EBD are male. Across racial and ethnic backgrounds of the EBD population, 57% of elementary and middle school children are White, 27% African American, and 12% Hispanic (Wagner, Kutash, Duchnowski, Epstein, & Sumi, 2005). These percentages indicate a disproportionate representation of African Americans identified as EBD. In fact, the National Research Council & Committee on Minority Representation in Special Education (NRC, 2002) reported that African American students are 1.92 times more likely than Caucasian students to be labeled with EBD. Further, African American students make up 17% of the total school population but disproportionately represent 27% of the students with EBD (NRC, 2002). Socioeconomic status is also a factor associated with students with EBD, as 33% of elementary and middle school children with EBD are living in poverty compared with 16% of students in the general education population (Wagner et al., 2005). Additionally, students with EBD are more likely to live with one parent, in foster care, or in another alternative living arrangement (Cullinan, Epstein, & Sabornie, 1992; Wagner, 1995).

Although many children with EBD exhibit problems at an early age (Knitzer, 1996), students are usually identified later than those with other disabilities, despite the availability of valid and reliable screening tools. In fact, according to NLTS-2 (2004) data, more than half of all secondary school students identified with EBD do not begin receiving services until age nine years. Research suggests that behavioral and emotional problems identified during adolescence can often be linked to early childhood behavioral patterns (Hinshaw, Lahey, & Hart, 1993; Walker, Colvin, & Ramsey, 1995).

EDUCATIONAL AND LONG-TERM OUTCOMES OF STUDENTS WITH EBD

Although many of the previously described behavioral dimensions are common across students with disabilities, much of the research examining the academic achievement for this group yields highly variable results (Reid, Gonzalez, Nordness, Trout, & Epstein, 2004; Wiley et al., 2008). Though statements can be made regarding the overall educational outcomes of this group, many studies have found that characteristics such as school income and educational placement are also significant indicators of academic performance deficits of students with EBD (e.g., Lane, Wehby, Little, & Cooley, 2005a, 2005b; Wiley et al., 2008). The academic performance and post-school outcomes for these students are discussed in more detail below.

Overall Intelligence

Much research has been dedicated to examining the intelligibility of students with EBD when compared to students with other disabilities and to their peers without disabilities. The majority of studies have concluded that students with EBD tend to fall in the low-average range (i.e., mean IQ of 96) when compared to their peers without disabilities (Kauffman, 2005). The results of a meta-analysis conducted by Sabornie, Cullinan, Osborne, and Brock (2005) also echo similar results when comparing IQ to two other disability categories, LD and Mild Intellectual Disabilities (MID). The authors found 58 studies that matched their inclusion criteria and included all necessary data to run analyses. The participants in the studies ranged from preschool to 12th grade, and school placements included general education classrooms, resource rooms, and self-contained settings. The results indicated that the IQ scores of students with EBD were similar to students with LD (i.e., average to low-average range). Further, there was a large statistically significant difference (i.e., $ES = -2.17$) between students with EBD and students with MID, indicating that students with EBD had higher IQ scores.

Academic Performance

Despite the large number of studies that indicate students with EBD have general cognitive abilities in the average and low-average ranges, this group consistently has the worst outcomes across all academic domains (Bradley

et al., 2004, 2008). In fact, the majority of students with EBD are functioning at least one or more grade levels below the one in which they are
assigned (Cullinan, 2007). Extant research on students with EBD has been
conducted in an effort to better understand the variables that significantly
affect the academic performance of this student population. For example, in
an extensive literature review of academic research trends and performance
of students with EBD that spanned almost 40 years (i.e., 1961–2000) Trout,
Nordess, Pierce, and Epstein (2003) found that students with EBD were
performing below grade level in all included studies. Specifically, these
students showed below-grade level performance in the areas of reading,
mathematics, and written expression.

Reid et al. (2004) found similar results in a meta-analysis conducted on
the academic status of students with EBD. Results of this study suggested
that 75% of students with EBD across the included 25 studies had overall
academic achievement below the mean when compared to students without
disabilities. Additionally, the authors found that students with EBD
performed lower in all academic areas compared to their peers without
disabilities, especially in spelling and mathematics.

Wagner et al. (2005) examined conducted bivariate and multivariate
analyses on existing SEELS data to examine how students with EBD differ
in academic performance, among other measures, when compared to other
disability categories. The authors found that, in reading, 61.2% of students
with EBD have percentile scores in the bottom quartile (i.e., lowest scoring
25% of children in the general population). Further, 24.5% score in the
second quartile, 9.2% in the third, and only 5.1% in the top quartile.
Though scores in mathematics calculation for students with EBD were
better than those in reading, they were still considerably below students in
the general population. Specifically, 43% of students with EBD scored in the
lowest quartile, 30% in the second, 18.8% in the third, and only 8.1% in the
top quartile. These scores are comparable to student with MID, autism, and
multiple disabilities.

In a recent study, investigating the academic performance of students with
EBD, Lane, Barton-Arwood, Nelson, and Wehby (2008) found that both
elementary and secondary students with EBD performed below the 25th
percentile in reading, mathematics, and written expression. Moreover, as
students became more fluent in reading, their reading comprehension skills
failed to improve.

Even more disconcerting, there is evidence to suggest that academic
performance deficits among students with EBD do not tend to improve over
time (Anderson, Kutash, & Duchnowski, 2001), and have actually been

shown to get worse as students grow older (Nelson, Benner, Lane, & Smith, 2004). More specifically, Nelson et al. (2004) conducted a cross-sectional study of school-aged students with EBD. The authors found significant differences between children with EBD and adolescents with EBD, with mathematics performance being poorer at adolescent age; reading and writing achievement of these students remained stable across the years.

The Effects of Setting on School Performance

Researchers have been especially interested in determining how academic performance of students with EBD compares across different educational placements. For example, when examining general education classes, resource classes, self-contained classes, and special school settings, Reid et al. (2004) found that students with EBD exhibited academic delays regardless of the instructional setting.

Other evidence, however, suggests the performance of students with EBD varies depending on the setting in which instruction is provided. For example, Lane et al. (2005a) compared the behavioral, social, and academic characteristics of students with EBD educated in self-contained schools versus the characteristics of students with EBD self-contained classrooms within general education schools. Their sample included 72 students with high-incidence disabilities (ED, LD, and ADHD). To assess progress, behavioral rating scales, standardized, and curriculum-based measures were used. Results showed that students who were educated in self-contained classrooms had higher academic skills in reading comprehension, reading fluency, oral language, written language, and mathematics when compared to students educated in self-contained schools. There were no differences, however, in the students' social skills in either setting. Additionally, students with EBD in self-contained classrooms exhibited significantly higher levels of internalizing behaviors than students in self-contained schools.

In another study, Lane et al. (2005b) examined how students with EBD progressed and benefited over time, either in a self-contained school or in a self-contained classroom, from the beginning to the end of the school year. Results showed that students in both settings made limited academic improvement. Across settings, no significant differences were found. Although students educated in the self-contained school experienced modest progress in reading comprehension and oral language skills, they showed significant decreases in writing scores as compared to students educated in self-contained classrooms. The latter group showed no changes on writing measures.

Long-term Outcomes

When investigating the overall educational and post-school outcomes of students with EBD, results are consistent and stable across time. A plethora of research exists that indicates students with EBD experience the most discouraging outcomes compared to any other group of students (Kauffman, 2005; Walker et al., 2004).

For students with EBD, success during school and beyond is often poor because the many deficits described previously in this chapter impact almost every aspect of daily life. In fact, 44% of students with EBD exit school without finishing; this represents the highest dropout rate among all disability categories (Wagner et al., 2006). Thirty-five percent of young adults with EBD no longer live with parents, and they are the only group among all disability categories to show a significant increase in the likelihood of living in criminal justice or mental health facilities, under legal guardianship, in foster care, or being homeless (Wagner et al., 2006). Additionally, one-third of this specific population lacks the social competence necessary to become actively engaged in their community after leaving high school (Wagner et al., 2006). Individuals with EBD were the largest group among all disability categories to indicate that they see friends often (i.e., at least weekly); however, they are among the least likely to take part in organized community groups, volunteer activities, or to be registered to vote. Finally, more than three-fourths of individuals with EBD have been stopped by police for an offense other than a traffic violation, 58% have been arrested a minimum of one time, and 43% have been on probation or parole (Wagner et al., 2006). These are harrowing post-school statistics for this population.

SUMMARY

The information provided in this chapter captures the multifaceted nature that often characterizes students with EBD. This population of students makes up the smallest percentage of students identified with high incidence disabilities, yet they are the most underserved (Kauffman et al., 2011). Many students who become identified with EBD often exhibit a number of risk factors, such as (a) poverty, (b) subjection to domestic violence, and (c) child maltreatment (Conroy & Brown, 2004). Although early identification of any disability is critical, students with EBD still tend to be identified years after the behavioral warning signs are exhibited (Knitzer, 1996). Additionally, students with EBD share many common characteristics, including (a) diagnoses of additional disabilities or psych disorders, (b) externalizing and/ or internalizing behaviors, (c) social skill deficits, (d) language and processing deficits, (e) low academic performance, and (e) poor long-term outcomes. To address the many complex characteristics and dimensions of students with EBD, it is critical to examine and implement the most effective identification, assessment, and instructional strategies to best meet their needs. These issues are explored more thoroughly in subsequent chapters.

REFERENCES

Abikoff, H. B., Jensen, P. S., Arnold, E. A., Hoza, B., Hechtman, L., & Pollack, S. (2002). Observed classroom behavior of children with ADHD: Relationship to gender and comorbidity. *Journal of Abnormal Child Psychology, 30*, 349–359.

American Association of Suicidology. (2010). Youth suicidal behavior-fact sheet. Retrieved form http://www.suicidology.org/c/document_library/get_file?folderId=232&name=DLFE-335.pdf

American Psychiatric Association. (2000). *Diagnostic and statistical manual of mental disorders, text revisions: DSM-IV-TR* (4th ed). Washington, DC.

Anderson, J. A., Kutash, K., & Duchnowski, A. J. (2001). A comparison of the academic progress of students with EBD and students with LD. *Journal of Emotional and Behavioral Disorders, 9*, 106–111.

Benner, G. J., Allor, J. H., & Mooney, P. (2008). An investigation of the academic processing speed of students with emotional and behavioral disorders served in public school settings. *Education and Treatment of Children, 31*, 307–332. doi:10.1353/etc.0.0006.

Benner, G. J., Nelson, R., & Epstein, M. H. (2002). Language skills of children with EBD: A literature review. *Journal of Emotional and Behavioral Disorders, 10*, 43–59. doi:10.1177/106342660201000105.

Bradley, R., Doolittle, J., & Bartolotta, R. (2008). Building on the data and adding to the discussion: The experiences and outcomes of students with emotional disturbance. *Journal of Behavioral Education, 17*, 4–23. doi:10.1007/s10864-007-9058-6.

Bradley, R., Henderson, K., & Monfore, D. A. (2004). A national perspective on children with emotional disorders. *Behavioral Disorders 29*: 211–223. Retrieved from http://www.ccbd.net

Chen, K. (2006). Social skills intervention for students with emotional/behavioral disorders: A literature review from the American perspective. *Educational Research and Reviews, 1*(3), 143–149.

Christensen, L., Young, K. R., & Marchant, M. (2007). Behavioral intervention planning: Increasing appropriate behavior of a socially withdrawn student. *Education and Treatment of Children, 30*, 81–103.

Conroy, M. A., & Brown, W. H. (2004). Early identification, prevention, and early intervention with young children at risk for emotional and behavioral disorders: Issues, trends, and a call for action. *Behavioral Disorders, 29,* 224–236.

Cullinan, D. (2007). *Students with emotional and behavioral disorders: An introduction for teachers and other helping professionals* (2nd ed). Upper Saddle River, NJ: Merrill Prentice Hall.

Cullinan, D., Epstein, M. H., & Sabornie, E. J. (1992). Selected characteristics of a national sample of seriously emotionally disturbed adolescents. *Behavioral Disorders, 17,* 273–280.

Eddy, J. M., Reid, J. B., & Curry, V. (2002). The etiology of youth antisocial behavior, delinquency, and violence and a public health approach to prevention. In M. R. Shinn, H. M. Walker & G. Stoner (Eds.), *Interventions for academic and behavior problems: Preventive and remedial approaches* (pp. 88–111). Bethesda, MD: National Association of School Psychologists.

Farmer, T. W., Estell, D. B., Hall, C. M., Pearl, R., Van Acker, R., & Rodkin, P. C. (2008). Interpersonal competence configurations, behavior problems, and social adjustment in preadolescence. *Journal of Emotional & Behavioral Disorders, 16,* 195–212.

Furlong, M. J., Morrison, G. M., & Jimerson, S. R. (2004). Externalizing behaviors of aggression and violence and the school context. In R. B. Rutherford, M. M. Quinn & S. R. Mathur (Eds.), *Handbook of research in emotional and behavioral disorders* (pp. 243–261). New York: Guilford Press.

Gresham, F. M., & Kern, L. (2004). Internalizing behavior problems in children and adolescents. In R. B. Rutherford, M. M. Quinn & S. R. Mathur (Eds.), *Handbook of research in emotional and behavioral disorders* (pp. 262–281). New York: Guilford Press.

Gresham, F. M., Sugai, G., & Horner, R. H. (2001). Interpreting outcomes of social skills training for students with high-incidence disabilities. *Exceptional Children, 67,* 331–344.

Gresham, F. M., Van, M. B., & Cook, C. R. (2006). Social skills training for teaching replacement behaviors: Remediating acquisition deficits in at-risk students. *Behavioral Disorders, 31,* 363–377.

Henley, M., Ramsey, R. S., & Algozzine, R. F. (2009). *Characteristics of and strategies for teaching students with mild disabilities* (6th ed). Upper Saddle River, NJ: Pearson Education.

Hinshaw, S. P., Lahey, B. B., & Hart, E. L. (1993). Issues of taxonomy and comorbidity in the development of conduct disorder. *Development and Psychopathology, 5,* 31–50.

Individuals with Disabilities Education Improvement Act of 2004, 31 U. S. C.

Kauffman, J. M. (2005). *Characteristics of emotional and behavioral disorders of children and youth* (8th ed). Upper Saddle River, NJ: Pearson Merrill Prentice Hall.

Kauffman, J. M., Mock, D. R., & Simpson, R. L. (2011). Problems related to underservice of students with emotional or behavioral disorders. *Behavioral Disorders, 33,* 43–57.

Knitzer, J. (1996). Meeting the mental health needs of young children and families: Service needs, challenges and opportunities. In B. Stroul (Ed.), *Systems of care for children and adolescents with serious emotional disturbances: From theory to reality* (pp. 236–253). Baltimore, MD: Brookes.

Lane, K. L., Barton-Arwood, S. M., Nelson, J. R., & Wehby, J. (2008). Academic performance of students with emotional and behavioral disorders served in a self-contained setting. *Journal of Behavioral Education, 17,* 43–62.

Lane, K. L., & Menzies, H. M. (2003). A school-wide intervention with primary and secondary levels of support for elementary students: Outcomes and considerations. *Education and Treatment of Children, 26*, 431–451.

Lane, K. L., Wehby, J. H., Little, M. A., & Cooley, C. (2005a). Academic, social, and behavioral profiles of students with emotional and behavioral disorders educated in self-contained classrooms and self-contained schools: Part I – are they more alike than different? *Behavioral Disorders, 30*: 349–361. Retrieved from http://www.ccbd.net

Lane, K. L., Wehby, J. H., Little, M. A., & Cooley, C. (2005b). Students educated in self-contained classrooms and self-contained schools: Part II – how do they progress over time? *Behavioral Disorders, 30*: 363–374. Retrieved from http://www.ccbd.net

National Research Council, Committee on Minority Representation in Special Education. (2002). *Minority students in special and gifted education*. Washington, DC: National Academy Press.

Nelson, J. R., Benner, G. J., & Cheney, D. (2005). An investigation of the language skills of students with emotional disturbance served in public school settings. *Journal of Special Education, 39*, 97–105. doi:10.1177/00224669050390020501.

Nelson, R. J., Benner, G. J., Lane, K., & Smith, B. W. (2004). Academic achievement of k-12 students with emotional and behavioral disorders. *Exceptional Children, 71*: 59–73. Retrieved from http://www.cec.sped.org

Nelson, J. R., Benner, G. J., & Rogers-Adkinson, D. L. (2003). An investigation of the characteristics of k-12 students with comorbid emotional disturbance and significant language deficits served in public school settings. *Behavioral Disorders, 29*: 25–33. Retrieved from http://www.ccbd.net

Nelson, J. R., Stage, S., Duppong-Hurley, K., Synhorst, L., & Epstein, M. H. (2007). Risk factors of the problem behavior of children at risk for emotional and behavioral disorders. *Exceptional Children, 73*, 367–379.

NLTS-2 Data Brief: The characteristics, experiences, and outcomes of youth with emotional disturbances. A Report from the National Longitudinal Transition Study-2 (2004, August). Retrieved from www.ncset.org/publications/viewdesc.asp?id=1687.

Reid, R., Gonzalez, J. E., Nordness, P. D., Trout, A., & Epstein, M. H. (2004). A meta-analysis of the academic status of students with emotional/behavioral disturbance. *Journal of Special Education, 38*, 130–143. doi:10.1177/00224669040380030101.

Sabornie, E. J., Cullinan, D., Osborne, S. S., & Brock, L. M. (2005). Intellectual, academic, and behavioral functioning of students with high incidence disabilities: A cross-categorical meta-analysis. *Exceptional Children, 72*, 47–63.

Schnoes, C., Reid, R., Wagner, M., & Marder, C. (2006). ADHD among students receiving special education services: A national survey. *Exceptional Children, 72*, 483–496.

Severson, H. H., Walker, H. M., Hope-Doolittle, J., Kratochwill, T. R., & Gresham, F. M. (2007). Proactive early screening to detect behaviorally at-risk students: Issues, approaches, emerging innovations, and professional practices. *Journal of School Psychology, 45*, 193–223.

Skiba, R. J., Poloni-Staudinger, L., Gallini, S., Simmons, A. B., & Feggins-Azziz, R. (2006). Disparate access: The disproportionality of African American students with disabilities across educational environments. *Exceptional Children, 72*, 411–424.

Spence, S. H. (2003). Social skills training with children and young people: Theory, evidence and practice. *Child & Adolescent Mental Health, 8*, 84–96.

Trout, A. L., Nordess, P. D., Pierce, C. D., & Epstein, M. H. (2003). Research on the academic status of children with emotional and behavioral disorders: A review of the literature from 1961 to 2000. *Journal of Emotional and Behavioral Disorders, 11*, 198–210.

U.S. Department of Education. (1994). *The improving America's schools act of 1994; summary sheets.* Washington, DC: U.S. Department of Education.

U.S. Department of Education. (1999). Assistance to states for the education of children with disabilities and the early intervention program for infants and toddlers with disabilities: Final regulations. *Federal Register, 64*(48), CFR Parts 300 and 303.

U.S. Department of Education. (2009). *Twenty-seventh annual report to Congress on the implementation of the Individuals with Disabilities Education Act.* Washington, DC: U.S. Department of Education.

U. S. Department of Health and Human Services, Substance Abuse and Mental Health Services Administration. (1998). *Annual report to Congress on the evaluation of the comprehensive community mental health services for children and their families program.* Retrieved from http://www.mentalhealth.org/publications/allpubs/CB-E199E/default.asp

Wagner, M. (1995). Outcomes for youth with serious emotional disturbance in secondary school and early adulthood. *Future of Children, 5*(2), 90–111.

Wagner, M., Kutash, K., Duchnowski, A. J., Epstein, M. H., & Sumi, W. C. (2005). The children and youth we serve: A national picture of the characteristics of students with emotional disturbances receiving special education. *Journal of Emotional and Behavioral Disorders, 13*, 79–96. doi:10.1177/10634266050130020201.

Wagner, M., Newman, L., Cameto, R., Levine, P., & Garza, N. (2006). *An overview of findings from wave 2 of the National Longitudinal Transition Study-2 (NLTS2).* Menlo Park, CA: SRI International. Retrieved from www.nlts2.org/reports/2006_08/nlts2_report_2006_08_complete.pdf. Accessed on June 26, 2008.

Walker, H. M., Colvin, G., & Ramsey, E. (1995). *Antisocial behavior in schools: Strategies and best practices.* Pacific Grove, CA: Brooks/Cole.

Walker, H. M., Ramsey, E., & Gresham, F. M. (2004). *Antisocial behavior in schools: Strategies and best practices* (2nd ed). Pacific Grove, CA: Brooks/Cole.

Wiley, A. L., Siperstein, G. N., Bountress, K. E., Forness, S. R., & Brigham, F. J. (2008). School context and the academic achievement of students with emotional disturbance. *Behavioral Disorders, 33*, 198–210.

CHAPTER 3

ASSESSMENT OF STUDENTS WITH EMOTIONAL AND BEHAVIORAL DISORDERS

Cynthia A. Plotts

ABSTRACT

Assessment and identification of children with emotional and behavioral disorders (EBD) is complex and involves multiple techniques, levels, and participants. While federal law sets the general parameters for identification in school settings, these criteria are vague and may lead to inconsistencies in selection and interpretation of assessment measures. Assessment practice across school settings is greatly influenced by clinical guidelines such as the DSM-IV, which more specifically defines emotional and behavioral disorders and highlights the issue of co-morbidity. Before a student is assessed for special education eligibility under the IDEIA category of emotional disturbance, screening techniques and pre-referral interventions are needed. Positive Behavioral Supports and Response to Intervention models provide empirically supported frameworks for establishing the need for formal psychological assessment. Collaboration among members of the multidisciplinary team, including parents, helps to ensure that identification and intervention efforts have ecological validity. Tests and techniques vary considerably, but developmental histories, interviews, observations across settings, and behavioral checklists and rating scales

Behavioral Disorders: Identification, Assessment, and Instruction of Students with EBD
Advances in Special Education, Volume 22, 51–85
Copyright © 2012 by Emerald Group Publishing Limited
All rights of reproduction in any form reserved
ISSN: 0270-4013/doi:10.1108/S0270-4013(2012)0000022006

are recommended, along with cognitive and achievement testing. While problems exist in the reliability and validity of projective techniques, they continue to be used in school-based assessment for EBD. Multitrait, multisetting, and multimethod approaches are essential for culturally fair assessment and reduction of bias in identification and placement.

Keywords: Assessment; definition; co-morbidity; identification; DSM-IV; projectives

ISSUES IN IDENTIFICATION OF EMOTIONAL AND BEHAVIORAL DISORDERS

Since emotional and behavioral problems can significantly interfere with academic, interpersonal, and vocational development, early identification of these problems is imperative. With early recognition, effective educational interventions may be developed to prevent the need for special education placement; if special education services are required, then the duration of such intensive services may be reduced in individualized assessment that is linked to effective intervention. In any case, professionals must reach consensus on which students should be served through special education under the classification of emotional disturbance under Individuals with Disabilities Education Improvement Act (IDEIA, 2004).

The term emotional and behavioral disorders (EBD) is used in this discussion to refer to emotional disturbance as defined by IDEIA. Although federal regulations have provided some direction for definition and assessment, the identification procedures for these students are complex. The wide array of tests and techniques for assessment, vague guidelines regarding severity and duration, and the process for determining educational need further complicate the identification process. In the following section, the definition of emotional disturbance (ED) included in the IDEIA and the specific procedures required to identify children with EBD are reviewed. Additional professional guidelines for identification and intervention are also explored.

Federal Law Definition

The federal definition of emotional disturbance was first specified in Public Law 94-142 and later in the 1997 individuals with disabilities education act

(IDEA) and the 2004 individuals with disabilities education improvement act (IDEIA). The definition, as stated below, has not changed substantially with these reauthorizations.

(i) The term means a condition exhibiting one or more of the following characteristics over a long period of time and to a marked degree that adversely affects educational performance:

    (A) an inability to learn that cannot be explained by intellectual, sensory, or health factors;

    (B) an inability to build or maintain satisfactory interpersonal relationships with peers and teachers;

    (C) inappropriate types of behavior or feelings under normal circumstances;

    (D) a general pervasive mood of unhappiness or depression; or

    (E) a tendency to develop physical symptoms or fears associated with personal or school problems.

(ii) The term includes schizophrenia. The term does not apply to children who are socially maladjusted, unless it is determined that they have an emotional disturbance (Code of Federal Regulation, Title 34, Section 300.7(b) (9)).

The federal law definition includes five main characteristics of emotional disturbance, identified in sections (A) through (E). An identified student must exhibit at least one, but may exhibit more, of these characteristics in order to be identified as emotionally disturbed.

Cullinan and Sabornie (2004), in a study of the five eligibility characteristics among 1,210 secondary students with or without EBD, found that adolescents with EBD exceed adolescents without this diagnosis on the five characteristics, providing some validation of their usefulness. However, this definition, while appearing superficially objective, is actually considerably subjective (Gresham, 2007; Merrell, 2003). Further, Cullinan and Sabornie found differential patterns of age, gender, and ethnicity on these five characteristics and concluded that more research is needed regarding developmental and multicultural influences on the expression of EBD. For example, these authors found that when examining middle school and high school students with EBD, only middle school students had higher scores than non-EBD students on the characteristics of unhappiness/depression and physical symptoms or fears. They also noted category-by-gender patterns specific to each race-ethnic group (European Americans, African American, and Hispanics). Further, they found specific racial/ethnic group-by-category interactions, including the finding that European Americans exhibited greater physical symptoms or fears than African Americans, while Hispanics did not differ from either of the other two groups on this characteristic.

Even if one or more of the five characteristics is met, there are other qualifiers inherent in this definition, including "over a long period of time," "to a marked degree," and "adversely affects educational performance." Because all individuals may exhibit characteristics of emotional distress, sometimes severe, it is necessary to distinguish emotional disturbance that requires special education intervention from more transient negative emotional or behavioral states. The severity of emotional and behavioral problems must be such that they are persistent over time, exceed the norm for peers in terms of severity, and, as a result, negatively affect performance in school.

Each of these three qualifiers has provoked debate with respect to their meaning. Operationalization of duration, severity, and negative educational impact is not provided in federal law; therefore, across states, and even across individual school districts, guidelines and practices for identification vary. Although some states mandate specific assessment procedures, such as rating scales or behavioral observations, other states may require that a psychiatrist or other medical doctor evaluate the child before allowing classification (Merrell, 2003).

The specification in the federal definition that "socially maladjusted" children are not included unless they also have an emotional disturbance has also created confusion and debate, particularly since individuals with socially maladjusted behaviors typically have impaired relationships with peers and other adults (one of the IDEA qualifiers). Individuals determined to be socially maladjusted, a term which is not concretely defined in the law, are excluded from eligibility as EBD unless they also exhibit at least one of the five main characteristics over a long period of time, to a marked degree, and with adverse effects on educational performance (Epstein, Cullinan, Ryser, & Pearson, 2002). Traditionally, the term social maladjustment has been used to describe a pattern of behavioral problems that are thought to be goal-oriented, volitional, and often reinforced by a student's peer reference group (Merrell, 2003). However, the distinction between EBD and social maladjustment implies that the assessment provides insight into the intent, feelings, and thoughts associated with socially unacceptable behaviors, which may or may not be the case depending on student responses to selected assessment techniques. Federal law does not exclude students who are socially maladjusted from eligibility for special education under the classification of EBD; the determination of EBD is, however, more difficult (Gresham, 2007).

Procedural Requirements under IDEIA

The basic elements required for eligibility as EBD for special education services have been presented in the IDEIA definition. In order to ensure a comprehensive evaluation process involving multiple decision makers, the law also mandates that specific procedures be followed to ensure accuracy and fairness.

Parent consent provisions require that informed parent consent be obtained before the evaluation is conducted. Infrequently, school personnel may seek a due process hearing if parents refuse to consent to assessment for a child who is clearly in need of assistance to progress in school. Consent for special education placement, should the child be eligible, is a separate process.

Full Individual Evaluation by the IEP team means that eligibility must be determined by a *multidisciplinary team* based on information from an individualized evaluation in a number of areas such as language, cognitive-intellectual, adaptive behavior, academic, emotional, medical-physical, and behavioral, with specific areas of formal and informal assessment determined by the IEP team. Multidisciplinary teams were mandated to ensure that different perspectives from diverse groups were considered, to limit the decision-making authority of any one individual, and to involve parents.

According to the 2004 reauthorization of IDEA, the multidisciplinary team must include the parents, not less than one general education teacher of the child (if the child is or may be participating in the general education environment), not less than one special education teacher, the person responsible for assessment who can interpret the instructional implications of evaluation results, an administrator (or other representative who has knowledge of instruction in special and regular education and the availability of resources of the school), any other persons with knowledge or special expertise as appropriate, and, whenever appropriate, the student.

Parental involvement on IEP team ensures that parents have the right to participate in making decisions regarding the education of their child, including placement decisions and development of the individualized education plan (IEP). Over the past several decades since the passage of P.L. 94-142, the emphasis on family involvement in school – decision making has increased in response to federal mandates, and also because research supports that home–school collaboration yields positive results for children (Elizalde-Utnick, 2002; Hubbard & Adams, 2002). In a discussion of techniques to increase home–school collaboration, Esler, Godber, and Christenson (2002) observe that such positive partnerships are correlated with higher school achievement. Further, parents must be provided with a copy of the evaluation report and the documentation of eligibility determination, provisions which imply that assessment personnel are obligated to provide understandable results in written reports.

Nondiscriminatory testing means that state and local education agencies (LEAs) must establish guidelines to ensure that identification procedures are not culturally or racially biased. The child must be evaluated in the language and form most likely to yield accurate information on what the child knows and can do academically, developmentally, and functionally, unless it is not feasible to provide testing in such form or language.

Multitrait/multimethod assessment techniques are encouraged so that no single test or criterion is used in making placement decisions. This provision in the law is intended to ensure that no child is placed in special education without a comprehensive assessment; the IEP team must concur that criteria for eligibility are met. Merrell (2003) outlines methods for assessment to include direct observation, behavior rating scales, interviews, records reviews, sociometric assessment, and self-report measures.

Toffalo and Pederson (2005) conducted an investigation of the identification of EBD among 215 school psychologists in Pennsylvania. The school psychologists reviewed hypothetical referral forms and vignettes for children who did or did not meet federal eligibility criteria for EBD. They found that school psychologists in the study were just as likely to recommend children as eligible for classification when they carried a psychiatric diagnosis, but did not meet eligibility criteria, as when they met criteria but had no psychiatric diagnosis. The authors concluded that when a psychiatric diagnosis is available in the referral information, the child has a greater likelihood of being classified as EBD and in need of special education services. In other words, the school psychologists who are most often conducting the evaluation may be prone to view externally provided psychiatric diagnosis as acceptable confirmation for the presence of EBD. This implied power of one external diagnosis contradicts the IDEA provisions which require that the identification process include a full individual evaluation using multiple sources of information, whether or not there is a psychiatric diagnosis.

Appropriate test selection and administration is required so that tests are reliable and valid for the purposes for which they are used, and that they are administered by trained and knowledgeable personnel in accordance with the procedures provided by the test authors and publishers. The child must be assessed in all areas of suspected disability. Further, any assessment tools employed must directly assist the team in determining the educational needs of the child. In other words, the assessment techniques must be selected so that results are reliable, valid, and useful for designing practical interventions based on the child's educational needs.

Reevaluation provisions require that the child identified as EBD and placed in special education must be reevaluated at least once every three years, although the evaluation does not have to involve formal assessment (may be limited to review of records and current behavior and performance) unless it is suspected that the child's disability condition has changed. The IEP team is responsible for determining the specific reevaluation techniques that are needed. This reevaluation provision is of obvious importance with developing children for whom emotional and behavioral problems may change in nature, severity, and impact on education over time. It should be assumed that individualized interventions based on reliable and valid assessment will be effective in improving emotional and behavioral adjustment, so reevaluation at more frequent intervals may be needed in some cases.

From these basic mandates, state education agencies have adopted regulations and guidelines to assist local school districts in devising appropriate identification procedures. Although specific regulations vary from state to state, a few commonalities exist. In the case of a student to be considered for services under the category EBD, many states require that a licensed or certified mental health professional (e.g., psychologist, school psychologist, or psychiatrist) be responsible for the evaluation.

Merrell (2003), in a more conceptual discussion of assessment for EBD, points out that professionals involved in such assessment should approach their roles as data-oriented problem solvers, with assessment as part of a broad problems-solving process rather than a set of tests. This process should include identification and clarification of the referral source and purpose, data collection considerations, analysis of assessment information, and solution and evaluation regarding intervention. Although it is tempting to focus on legal regulations and procedural guidelines for assessment of EBD, professionals must select techniques that will guide identification, intervention, and evaluation of effectiveness.

Clinical Diagnosis

Although professionals practicing in school settings must abide by the federal definition of EBD, mental health professionals in other settings typically employ a manual for diagnostic decision making, the *Diagnostic and Statistical Manual of Psychiatric Disorder-Fourth Edition-Training Revision,* (DSM-IV-TR) (American Psychiatric Association (APA), 2000). The DSM-IV-TR does not specifically address EBD; rather, this manual provides criteria for specific types of disorders that may or may not directly impact school functioning. For example, under the heading of "Disorders First Diagnosed in Infancy, Childhood or Adolescence" (pp. 13–14), there are 10 different diagnostic categories, with more than 30 specific diagnoses. Included in this section are developmental disorders, such as mental retardation (intellectual impairment), pervasive developmental disorders and learning disabilities; disruptive behavioral disorders (often termed externalizing disorders), such as oppositional defiant disorder, attention-deficit/hyperactivity disorder and conduct disorder; feeding and eating disorders; tic disorders; elimination disorders, such as enuresis and encopresis; and disturbances of emotion and behavior, such as reactive attachment disorders, separation anxiety disorder, and selective mutism. Elsewhere in the DSM-IV-TR, diagnostic criteria for a range of mood and anxiety disorders are provided, along with criteria for impulse control disorders, substance-related disorders, adjustment disorders, obsessive-compulsive disorders, sexual and gender identity disorders, and disorders of personality, that may affect children and adolescents among others.

These diagnostic formulations from the DSM-IV-TR take into account the possibility that some disorders are developmental in nature, many disorders share similar symptoms, multiple factors can contribute to the manifestation of a disorder, and issues of duration, severity, and environment must be considered. In short, while the IDEA definition for EBD suggests that the classification is a "yes or no" decision, the DSM-IV-TR system assumes that individuals may exhibit symptoms characteristic of one or more diagnoses that exist on a continuum and may not fit neatly into the IDEA framework. For this reason, among others, there is disagreement among school professionals and mental health providers outside of schools regarding the identification of children with EBD. It is incumbent upon school professionals, and upon outside mental health professionals who work with school-age populations, to understand each other's classification systems and the implications for services. The DSM-IV diagnostic criteria can be helpful to school assessment personnel in considering whether, for example, adjustment disorders, characterized by time-limited emotional and behavioral reactions to specific environmental stressors, may provide better explanations for observed problems than a chronic and severe disturbance indicative of EBD. For outside mental health professionals, a child's school adjustment and progress is essential information for diagnosis and treatment.

Revisions in the DSM-V

As the revised manual, the DSM-V, nears publication, debate regarding the nature of and criteria for specific diagnoses can be followed online (APA, 2010). Of interest is proposed inclusion of the heading "Neurodevelopmental Disorders," which would contain many of the diagnoses listed in the DSM-IV-TR under the heading of "Disorders First Diagnosed in Infancy, Childhood or Adolescence." The change would appear to reflect greater attention to the brain–behavior relationships in manifest disorders, which would have implications for training of school professionals involved in diagnosis and intervention.

Diagnoses proposed for inclusion under the heading "Child and Adolescent Disorders" include several that could be related to EBD diagnoses in schools: disruptive mood dysregulation disorder, reactive attachment disorder, and disinhibited social engagement disorder, among others. Other proposed headings, each of which includes numerous disorders that may lead to an EBD classification in school settings, are "Schizophrenia Spectrum and Other Psychotic Disorders," "Bipolar and Related Disorders," "Depressive Disorders," and "Anxiety Disorders." Although DSM-V changes have not been finalized, these examples underscore the complexity of diagnosing disorders of emotions and behaviors, especially when multiple professional disciplines with different training models, both within and outside the school setting, are involved.

Co-morbidity of Other Disorders with EBD

The issue of social maladjustment as distinct from EBD leads to discussion of the larger issue of co-morbidity. Co-morbidity refers to the coexistence of two or more diagnosable disorders in the same individual. As anyone who works in school settings can attest, emotional and behavioral disorders often occur in conjunction with other disabilities. Further, both internalizing (e.g., depression or anxiety) and externalizing (e.g., oppositional-defiant disorders and attention deficit-hyperactivity disorder, ADHD) features may be present in the same individual. EBD is very commonly associated with the diagnostic categories of oppositional defiant and conduct disorders, ADHD, autistic disorder, mental retardation, and depression and anxiety disorders (Mash & Dozois, 1996). Similarly, children with ADHD and learning disabilities frequently display emotional and behavioral problems (Fessler, Rosenberg, & Rosenberg, 1991); it may be difficult or impossible to determine which disorder, if any, is primary and what symptoms have developed as complications of a pre-existing disorder. For example, in the federal definition of autism, emotional disturbance cannot be the primary cause of the autistic symptomatology. Within school systems, this criterion is often interpreted as meaning that autism spectrum disorders and EBD cannot be co-morbid, which is a misinterpretation likely intended to reduce diagnostic complexity. Children with acute or chronic medical conditions, such as traumatic brain injury, diabetes, or seizure disorders, may also present with emotional/behavioral problems (McConaughy & Ritter, 2002) as well as disorders of learning, memory, cognition, and/or impulse control. Unfortunately, children with more than one coexisting disorder are more likely to continue to have longer lasting and more severe problems than those with only one diagnosed disorder (Webber & Plotts, 2008). Development of substance abuse disorders, which is more likely among individual with disturbances of emotion and behavior, can greatly complicate the diagnostic and treatment formulation. However, as previously stated, the presence of a medical or psychiatric diagnosis in the context of emotional/behavioral problems does not necessarily indicate that a child should be identified as EBD for special education purposes.

Interface between Educational and Clinical Diagnostic Classification
Although frequent co-morbidity of disorders has been well established among children classified as EBD, it is not necessarily the case that a clinical psychiatric diagnosis justifies identification as EBD and placement in special education (Toffalo & Pederson, 2005). Often, children have been assessed by mental health professionals such as psychiatrists, psychologists, counselors, and social workers outside the school setting. In these cases, records with psychiatric diagnoses may be submitted to school personnel when a child is referred for special education. Such information should be considered by the IEP team, but the team is not required to base special education eligibility on the presence or absence of a psychiatric diagnosis.

In some school settings, the school psychologist is expected to provide a DSM-IV diagnosis when identifying a student as EBD, even though this practice is discouraged in other school settings because of the overreliance on the medical model (internal causation for psychopathology) and the weak link from a medical model to educational intervention. Such a model might be inconsistent with the data-based decision-making model that emphasizes collection of objective data over a period of systematic intervention (Gresham, 2007). Merrell (2003) cautions that pathologizing young children by assigning DSM-IV diagnoses should be avoided since many of the diagnostic categories are not appropriate for them. On the contrary, a large number of children have psychiatric diagnoses, often for which they are getting treatment such as medication or psychotherapy, and the proposed structure of the DSM-V suggests that disorders of childhood and adolescence, including developmental considerations, will receive considerable attention. Parents rightly express frustration when disagreement or poor communication among mental health professionals affects their child's access to or the consistency of services. For this reason, collaborative efforts to communicate and understand diagnostic and treatment formulations are essential among professionals within and outside of the school setting. Ideally, outside professionals would be invited to participate in the IEP team process.

Children and adolescents who have emotional and behavioral disorders are a heterogeneous group, with unique histories, family and social circumstances, temperaments, personality traits, cognitive skills, and social and adaptive skills. Consequently, the assessment process for these children requires an approach that views each child as a unique individual and not as a child who only represents a psychological disorder (Sattler, 2006). Further, the need to evaluate a unique individual in every case necessitates the use of a comprehensive evaluation model, with tests and techniques selected to assess all relevant factors. Professionals may differ in their selection of tests and techniques, depending on the unique history and problem presentation of each child, as well as upon differences in professional training. A goal of all techniques should be the determination of convergent data that lead to valid and defensible conclusions regarding diagnosis, classification, and intervention.

Although consideration of the uniqueness of the individual can contribute to personalization of the assessment process, it may also lead to a frustrating lack of consistency in the approach to identification of EBD. Diagnostic guidelines have been proposed by various professional groups to address this need for consistency. The guidelines proposed by the National Association of School Psychologists (NASP) are presented below.

National Association of School Psychologists (NASP) Guidelines

Given the lack of clarity in the federal definition of EBD and complications of frequent co-morbidity of disorders, the National Association of School Psychologists has provided a position statement on students with EBD (National Association of School Psychologists, NASP, 2002). NASP has adopted the definition proposed by the National Mental Health and Special Education coalition. The major elements of this definition of EBD are:

(1) EBD is a condition in which an individual's emotional or behavioral responses in school settings are markedly different from generally accepted, age appropriate, ethnic, or cultural norms and that they adversely affect performance in areas including self-care, social relationships, personal adjustment, academic progress, classroom behavior, or work adjustment.
(2) EBD is more than a transient and expected response to stressors and would persist even with individualized interventions.
(3) Eligibility for special education must be based on multiple sources of data and the associated behaviors must be exhibited in at least two different settings, at least one of which is school-related.
(4) EBD can exist with other handicapping conditions.
(5) EBD may include children with schizophrenia, affective disorders, anxiety disorders, or persistent disturbances of conduct, attention, or adjustment.

NASP's position statement also specifies that assessment identify both the strengths and weaknesses of the individual and of the systems (e.g., school and home) with which the student interacts. Results should describe the student's difficulties in a functional, objective, and observable fashion, with consideration of environmental and personal history variables that may relate to the student's school difficulties. The intensity, pervasiveness, and persistence of emotional and behavioral problems must be assessed, and the response to well-organized, empirically based and individualized intervention efforts documented. Developmental and behavioral status with respect to expectations for children of the same age, culture, and ethnic background must also be addressed.

These guidelines, along with federal definitions and mandates, provide a framework within which a child's unique needs can be considered with regard assessment for EBD. School professionals must ensure that an appropriate and thorough evaluation, including a pre-referral process, is completed with every child who is referred before decisions are made regarding eligibility and interventions through special education.

ASSESSMENT FOR EBD: A TIERED PROCESS

Consistent with the problem-solving process advocated by Merrell (2003), the identification of EBD can be conceptualized as occurring in three phases: (1) early identification of children at risk and provision of pre-referral interventions; (2) formal assessment for EBD; and (3) placement and provision of special education intervention services, if the child qualifies. Early identification and intervention is essential, whether or not a child is ultimately placed in special education, because, as observed by Lane, Gresham, and O'Shaughnessy (2002), intervention is more effective before maladaptive behavior has become firmly entrenched in a child's behavioral repertoire. Educators may be uncertain about how to best intervene with children with emotional and behavioral problems and may pursue referral to special education before alternative interventions have been tried. Severson and Walker (2002) note that early proactive screening and detection can help save the lives of children who are at high risk for developing serious emotional and behavioral problems; for this reason, they advocate for a formal universal screening process early in every child's school career.

Pre-referral interventions are based on the ecological or systems premise that learning and behavior problems should be viewed within the larger context of the classroom, school, home, and community. Goals include providing general education teachers with assistance and support, reducing inappropriate referrals for testing and special education placement (Graden, Casey, & Christenson, 1985), and reducing the emotional and behavioral interference that may lead to poor school outcomes as early as possible (Council for Exceptional Children [CEC], 2011). According to Gresham (2007), pre-referral interventions often lack an evidence base and thus are frequently ineffective in resolving problems.

Response to Intervention (RTI) and School-wide Positive Behavioral Supports (SWPBS, often referred to as PBS) are currently popular models of the tiered problem-solving approach in pre-referral intervention. These approaches operate under the risk model, in which all students are screened for potential behavior problems early in school, with supplemental positive behavioral supports (PBS) provided to students determined to be at risk (Gresham, 2007). With respect to EBD, both models have potential to aid in the prevention, early identification, and treatment of emotional/behavioral problems that, if not recognized and addressed, may result in chronic emotional/behavioral disorders.

Response to Intervention

Kovaleski (2002) noted that determination of whether or not a child should be placed in special education should also depend in part on RTI efforts implemented before assessment for special education. RTI interventions, which are intended to be evidence-based, are designed to be implemented through general education, often in collaboration school psychologists or behavior specialists, so that it can be determined if the child's problems are modifiable through carefully selected, implemented, monitored, and titrated interventions (CEC, 2011; Gresham, 2007). If a student shows inadequate response to the best intervention that is available, feasible, and implemented with integrity, then that child should be eligible for more intensive intervention. If the student still displays emotional and/or behavior problems that interfere with educational progress following increasing intervention intensity, then a referral to special education should be initiated and a full individual evaluation conducted, with eligibility for special education and related services determined by the IEP team. As pointed out by Gresham (2007), effective RTI programs are based on objective data collected continuously over a period of time (data-based decision making). Further, interventions must be implemented with integrity, meaning that they are implemented consistently as designed with relation to the identified problem.

Although not required by federal law for EBD identification or consistently implemented across states or schools, pre-referral interventions should be a precondition for referral for a comprehensive evaluation for special education eligibility and may be considered as part of the assessment process. Gresham advocates for RTI in the identification of students as ED using a multitiered system of interventions, which typically occur in three levels: universal, selected, and intensive interventions. A current problem in the formulation of RTI relates to the duration of services before a referral for special education assessment is made. With reference to EBD, there are no firm guidelines for duration of pre-referral interventions given the range of individual needs (CEC, 2011); however, assessment for a child with severe emotional/behavioral problems, for example for a child with a suspected psychotic disorder, should not be postponed if the child's well-being and educational progress are obviously threatened.

Positive Behavioral Supports

PBS (sometimes referred to Positive Behavioral Interventions and Supports or School-Based Positive Behavioral Supports) have been a fixture in special education literature for more than a decade. PBS is popular pre-referral intervention model based on a three-tiered approach to discipline and the prevention of problem behavior and shares many elements with RTI. PBS is based on the premise that if students are taught specific behavioral expectations and reinforced for meeting those expectations, then problem behavior will be prevented. PBS is a systems model requiring school district leadership, data collection and analysis, along with school-wide teams, behavior expectations, and promotion through encouragement and reinforcement. Teachers are expected to implement effective, consistent, research-based classroom management practices. Small group and individual supports for those relatively few students who, under such a system, still display problem behavior, are provided (Scott & Nelson, 1999; Sprague, Sugai, Horner, & Walker, 1999; Sugai & Horner, 1999). PBS might be especially effective in providing structures to support students in high-stress or high-risk situations who, while not chronically emotionally disturbed, may be at risk for self-defeating behaviors such as, truancy, disengagement, substance abuse, or other forms of self-harm, if problems are not recognized and addressed.

PBS and RTI share the foundation of a tiered approach to identification, assessment, and intervention, beginning at the systems level with appropriate supports for positive learning environments (tier 1 and moving to more specific interventions for groups and individuals determined to be at risk for development of more severe problems (tier 2 and tier 3). Although much discussion about empirically based academic interventions for RTI purposes has become common in school settings since IDEA 2004 specified RTI as a consideration for LD classification, fewer specific and research-validated techniques have been disseminated for EBD. Much of the school psychology and special education literature focuses on the procedures for tiered assessment and intervention; specific techniques (e.g., effective interventions for specific problem behaviors or classes of disorders) have yet to be integrated into school-based RTI models.

SPECIFIC TESTS AND TECHNIQUES FOR ASSESSMENT OF EBD

As noted previously, a full individual evaluation is required by IDEA for every child referred for special education services. Although the *specific* tests to be given are typically left to the discretion of assessment personnel, most of whom are school psychologists trained at the masters, specialist, or doctoral level, and who should be able to look at the technical features of available instruments and techniques, the following elements should be formally assessed in the initial evaluation of children suspected of having severe EBD that has not responded adequately to typically effective pre-referral interventions:

(1) Developmental history to establish risk factors, duration, chronicity, and possible sources for emotional and behavioral problems.
(2) Emotional/behavioral functioning, including behavioral observations, behavior rating scales and checklists, student and teacher interviews, and in some cases projective techniques to explore the nature and severity of problems relative to peers in school settings.
(3) Academic achievement levels to establish educational competencies and clarify educational need.
(4) Cognitive functioning to gauge patterns of learning abilities and to identify potential factors in academic underachievement and/or behavioral problems.
(5) Adaptive behavior to address issues of personal and social sufficiency in everyday environments, which can help to clarify educational need.

Other areas that may require formal or informal assessment, depending on referral questions, include speech, language, vision, hearing, and motor skills. The IEP team must ensure that all areas of suspected disability are assessed and that results can be used to plan the educational program. Various professionals, including speech/language pathologists, occupational or physical therapists, and other educational or medical specialists, in addition to parents and teachers, may be involved in portions of the full evaluation; however, the school psychologist or other licensed or certified mental health professional will typically complete the personality and emotional portions of the full individual evaluation. Teachers, parents, the referred child, and others may complete various behavior checklists and rating scales, although their interpretation is usually made by the assessment professional.

Rationales for and brief descriptions of commonly used techniques for identification of EBD, ranging from more structured, direct measures such as behavioral observations and rating scales, to more subjective and indirect measures, such as projective techniques are presented below.

Developmental History

Given the co-morbidity issues involved in EBD, and the need to document duration, severity, chronicity, and effects on school progress, it is essential to gain a thorough understanding of developmental history as part of the assessment process. Since early medical, developmental, or family problems may contribute to later school difficulties, including learning and behavior problems, a careful history-taking is an integral component of assessment for EBD. Unfortunately, this process is frequently undermined by the use of forms completed by parents or caretakers without the formal interviews needed to clarify and explore related history.

The developmental history is ideally obtained from the parents or other caretakers in the context of a face–face interview. Schools often employ background information forms that can serve as a guide, but not as a substitute for the interview, since parents may inadvertently leave out important information if responses are not probed. Typically, the interview to obtain developmental history will be conducted by the school psychologist, psychological examiner, or other mental health professional trained in interview procedures.

Essential elements of the developmental history include gathering historical and current functioning information in the following general areas:

(1) Medical (including gestation and birth history, pregnancy complications, maternal health, significant illnesses, head injuries, and hospitalizations);

(2) Developmental (motor and language milestones, emotional attachment, eating and sleeping habits, and toilet training);

(3) School (attendance at daycare or preschool, any prior group or individual educational assessments, grades, tutoring or interventions, and frequent moves);

(4) Family history (psychiatric, genetic, or other disorder among family members, including extended family; separation, divorce, death, or other family stressors such as military deployment that may affect adjustment; disciplinary techniques and their effectiveness); and

(5) Social (peer relationships, family relationships, interactions with teachers and other adults, extracurricular activities).

Another important component of background information is the collection of any relevant medical, psychological, psychiatric or other evaluation or treatment reports that may relate to the referral problem. Unless parents or prior school districts are specifically asked to provide prior reports of assessment or intervention, they may not realize such records are pertinent to accurate diagnosis. A further complication is that if prior records are not gathered, testing may be unnecessarily duplicated that was completed in another school district or setting. Assessment professionals should also be informed if a child is taking psychotropic medication (or has recently stopped taking medication) before initiating testing.

Examples of interview formats and forms that can be used to gather developmental history are available in commonly used behavior checklists such as the Behavior Assessment System for Children-2 (BASC-2) (Reynolds & Kamphaus, 2004) and the Child Behavior Checklist (CBCL) (Achenbach & Rescorla, 2001), as well as in reference texts, such as Sattler (2006).

Behavioral Observations

Observation of serious problem behavior by parents and/or teachers is the typical reason for referral for EBD assessment. It follows that structured and deliberate observation of a referred child's behavior in various settings is a cornerstone tool. Direct behavioral observation involves procedures in which observers develop operational descriptions of behaviors of concern, observe the behaviors in everyday settings, and record their observations. These techniques stem from behavioral psychology theory and have the advantage of identifying important antecedent stimuli and controlling consequences of behavior, which takes into account the system in which a child functions, rather than focusing on the internal pathology. Another advantage of behavioral observations is that they can be directly linked to the development of individualized interventions (Merrell, 2003).

Specific behavioral observation techniques are reviewed in Sattler (2006) and Merrell (2003) as well as in other sources. At this point, it is important to remember that behavioral observations are an essential element of comprehensive assessment designed to yield practical and effective educational programs. Teachers are particularly well-positioned to complete formal behavioral observations in natural settings as part of the identification process; other professionals, such as school psychologists, educational diagnosticians, counselors, or administrators may also participate in the observation process.

A *functional behavioral assessment* (FBA) is often considered part of the intervention after classification as EBD and placement in special education; however, preferred practice would be to conduct an FBA on every child who is considered for referral with the expectation that appropriately individualized interventions may preclude worsening of symptoms. Such an assessment may also shed light on the context of problem behavior, such as setting factors and reinforcing factors, so that intervention can be strategically designed to address behaviors of concern (Gresham, 2007). Along these lines, *applied behavior analysis*, a model which applies principles of learning to understanding of specific behaviors, has gained in popularity as a technique for both assessment and intervention with EBD as well as with other populations. Advantages include the establishment of baseline data from which change can be measured, the focus on specific behaviors of concern in everyday contexts, and amenability to a wide range of empirically based intervention strategies. Possible disadvantages of behaviorally focused assessment techniques are the likelihood of multiple behaviors of concern in EBD and the possibility that internalizing disorders have less obvious measureable manifestations of disturbed functioning. Further, altering specific behaviors may or may not significantly reduce degree of emotional distress so that educational impact of EBD continues even though specific behaviors may be ameliorated or improved.

Behavior Checklists and Rating Scales

Many behavior checklists and rating scales are available for completion by parents, teachers, and in some cases, the referred child. These measures assume that emotional disorders can best be understood through a careful evaluation of current behavioral symptoms, their duration, and intensity from the perspective of individuals most closely involved with the child. Although some of the measures are broad and encompass a wide range of behavioral symptoms, others are more specific to certain disorders, such as anxiety, depression, or attention-deficit hyperactivity disorder. In this chapter, several major broad-spectrum checklists will be discussed, followed by a listing of several disorder-specific techniques.

The use of rating scales to assist in determining behavioral pathology has increased in popularity since about the mid-1980s. Behavior rating scales provide a standardized format for judgments regarding behavioral characteristics by informants, including teachers or other school personnel and parents, who are familiar with the child. Items are usually rated on a continuum of frequency or severity, and the rater is asked to compare the student to average or typical students of the same age for normative comparisons. Behavior rating scales are less direct than behavioral observations because they measure perceptions of behaviors rather than the behaviors themselves; however, they are fairly objective measures and thus may yield more reliable data than unstructured interviews or projective techniques. Another advantage of behavior rating scales is that they are cost-efficient with respect to amount of professional time involved and amount of training needed to use such techniques (Merrell, 2003).

However, there are some potential limitations to the validity and reliability of behavior rating scales. Sattler (2006) cautions that judgments about a child's functioning can be subject to informant bias and distortion. Informants may differ in their familiarity with a child and in their sensitivity to and tolerance for behavior problems, or in their opportunities to observe behaviors across settings. It is not unusual to find that parents and teachers disagree on the severity of a student's behavior. Similarly, differences between parents or among teachers on the same behavior scales frequently occur for a variety of reasons, including respondent tolerance for the behavior, degree of the student's frustration in various settings, personal feelings about stigma associated with labeling, and agendas for identification and placement among respondents. Another potential problem is that rating scale items, no matter how clearly stated, may be misinterpreted. These potential problems can be controlled to some extent by the inclusion of validity scales that attempt to take into account respondents' tendencies to answer items in either a socially desirable manner or to rate the child in an overly critical manner.

Best practices in using behavior rating scales require seeking input from multiple informants across multiple settings and interpreting the findings with respect to information gathered from other techniques, including interviews, behavioral observations, and other tests. As with all tests, assessment personnel should consider the representativeness of the norm group and the reliability and validity of the measures. Norms are best when the test has been standardized on a large, nationally stratified sample that includes equal numbers of males and females. It is also preferable if gender and age norms, in addition to combined sample norms, are provided. Assessment personnel must also ensure that respondents understand the directions and are able to read and comprehend test items.

Teachers are often the best source of information regarding a child's behavior since they have the opportunity to observe students in situations under various circumstances and contexts and they have a developmental framework for age-typical behavior. However, the usefulness of teacher information varies according to the age of the child. Elementary school children frequently have one teacher who makes observations across several class periods and frequently throughout the entire day. High school teachers often have students for one class during the day. Therefore, the amount of information that a teacher can provide regarding a child's behavior decreases at the secondary level (Taylor, 1997). Another factor that influences teacher ratings is the frame of reference, or standard, that teachers use to make behavioral ratings. Teachers often rate behaviors based on a comparison to other children in their classroom or in their previous experience. Consequently, teacher ratings may be related to the teacher's own world view and not be an adequate representation of the sample population. Despite the limitations, behavior rating scales by teachers are a critical element of a comprehensive assessment of children's emotional and behavioral functioning.

Many behavior checklists and rating scales are available for assessing emotional/behavioral disorders in schools (see Sattler, 2002, 2006). Selected measures will be briefly reviewed, based on their relatively prominent use in the field and the availability of reviews in the relevant literature. Specific critiques are beyond the scope of this discussion, but can be referenced in the *Mental Measurements Yearbook with Tests in Print* online database and in relevant journals.

Rating Scales Based on IDEA Criteria
Several scales have been developed that are based specifically upon the federal definition of emotional disturbance. The Social–Emotional Dimension Scale (SEDS), developed by Hutton and Roberts (1986), is a 32-item scale with six factors that relate directly to components of the federal definition (1) avoidance of peer interaction, (2) avoidance of teacher interaction, (3) aggressive interaction, (4) inappropriate behavior, (5) depressive reaction, and (6) physical-fear reaction. The SEDS total score can be used to identify levels of risk for a student when compared to "typical" children his age.

The Behavior Evaluation Scale-2 (BES-2) (McCarney & Leigh, 1990) is another rating scale based on the federal definition. The BES-2 is composed of 76 items and five subscales: learning problems, interpersonal difficulties, inappropriate behavior, unhappiness-depression, and physical fears symptoms. Problem areas correlating to those outlined in the definition can be identified from the subscales.

The Scale for Assessing Emotional Disturbance (Epstein & Cullinan, 1998) contains 52 items comprising seven subscales: (1) inability to learn, (2) relationship problems, (3) inappropriate behavior, (4) unhappiness or depression, (5) physical symptoms or fears, and (6) social maladjustment. Interestingly, the SAED operationally defines socially maladjustment as comprised of antisocial acts occurring outside of school, thus distinguishing it from inappropriate in-school behavior. Whether or not child has a high socially maladjusted subscale score is irrelevant to the decision as to whether that student meets criteria to be classified as EBD. In addition to subscales matching the five federal criteria, there is a subscale for overall competence. One item is included that assesses whether identified problems adversely affect the student's educational performance.

The most recent rating scale based on IDEA criteria is the *Emotional Disturbance Decision Tree* (Euler, 2007). The EDDT is intended to offer a standardized approach to be completed by teachers or other professionals who have had substantial contact with the student. Euler describes this measure as mapping onto the IDEA criteria and as including inclusionary criteria (supporting eligibility) and exclusionary criteria (may rule out eligibility). Inclusionary criteria are the federal criteria (categories of eligibility), whereas exclusionary criteria are educational impact, severity, duration, and causation primarily from intellectual, sensory, or health deficits, or social maladjustment.

Scores from measures such as these are helpful to the team who must make eligibility decisions for several reasons. First, ratings on the same student from several teachers or school personnel may be obtained, thereby satisfying one requirement for multiple sources of information. Second, when discrepancies occur among these multiple ratings, then assessment personnel can observe and/or interview the individual whose rating was discrepant. Students who pose a problem for only one teacher or only in one class would not be considered EBD. Third, behavior rating scales focus primarily on observable behavior rather than inferred characteristics, thereby lending some degree of objectivity to the process, although ratings by individuals about other individuals always retain a degree of subjectivity. The link between these measures and the federal definition of EBD make them useful screening tools for addressing specific criteria.

General Purpose Behavior Rating Scales

Currently a number of multidimensional behavior rating scales that assess a wide range of potential problems are available. Four widely available and frequently employed scales are briefly reviewed.

The *Conners Comprehensive Behavior Rating Scales* (CBRS) (Conners, 2008) is a measure of emotional, behavioral, academic, and social functioning among children and adolescents ages 6–18 years. The purpose is to facilitate decision making with respect to diagnosis, special education classification, intervention planning, progress monitoring, and research. The CBRS includes a parent rating scale, teacher rating scale, and self-report scale, with number of items on each scale ranging from 179 to 204, so it is a relatively long measure. The CBRS yields 40 scales, including validity scales.

The parent, teacher, and self-report versions may be used independently or in conjunction with one another. Therefore, the format of the CBRS provides for input about a child's behavior from multiple informants across multiple settings. The scales included in this measure are discussed with reference to DSM and IDEA criteria, a desirable feature in light of the differing diagnostic models discussed previously.

The *Behavior Assessment System for Children -2* (BASC-2) (Reynolds & Kamphaus, 2004) is a comprehensive system for assessing child and adolescent behavior. This system includes parent and teacher rating scales for children ages 4–18 years. There are also comprehensive self-report forms for children (ages 6–11 years) and adolescents (ages 12–18 years). The various checklists are relatively long, ranging from 105 to 186 items. Also included in the system are a structured developmental history form and a student observation system. The BASC-2 assesses the child's strengths, or adaptive behaviors, as well as maladaptive behaviors. Composite scales can be useful in determining if IDEA criteria for EBD are met, including internalizing problems, externalizing problems, school problems, atypicality, withdrawal, and adaptive skills. There is also an overall Behavioral Symptoms Index, which is a composite problem behavior total score. The BASC-2 provides an integrative approach to assessment, with multiple informants. Standard scores are reported by gender and age for the general population and for a clinical population.

The *Child Behavior Checklist* (CBCL), *Teacher's Report Form* (TRF), and *Youth Self Report* (YSR) are incorporated into the Achenbach System of Empirically Based Assessment (ASEBA) (Achenbach & Rescorla, 2001). The ASEBA is a collection of several rating scales, self-report forms, semistructured interview forms, and observation forms for children, adolescents, and adults. Of interest here are the measures suitable for use with school-age children (ages 4–18 years). The CBCL (completed by parents), TRF, and YSR are designed for assessment of internalizing and externalizing problems in children and adolescents. The measures include 112–120 items and yield standard scores on 9 scales. A semistructured clinical interview (SCICA), test observation form, and direct observation form, are also available. Sattler (2002) notes that strength of this system is the emphasis on cross-informant assessment of child and adolescent behavior. According to Merrell (2003), the CBCL and TRF seem to have considerable clinical utility and may be powerful predictors of present and future behavioral disorders of children and adolescents.

The *Personality Inventory for Children-2* (PIC-2) (Wirt, Lachar, Seat, & Broen, 2001) is a parent-completed survey of children's behavior (ages 5–19 years). The 275 items (standard form) address behavior, emotional, cognitive, and interpersonal adjustment. There is also a 96-item brief form. The PIC-2 has 3 validity scales, 9 adjustment scales, and 21 adjustment subscales, so it covers a wide range of psychological and adjustment problems. There is also a *Personality Inventory for Youth* (Lachar & Gruber, 2005), which is a self-report measure for ages 10–18 years. Standard scores are reported by age and gender. This instrument provides useful interpretive guidelines, but may be used less frequently in the schools because of its length.

Advantages of these measures are their comprehensive structure, clear procedures for administration and scoring and reports of at least adequate reliability and validity. For the ASEBA and the BASC-2, the inclusion of multiple informants, as well as formats for interviews and observations, heighten the appeal for school professionals conducting comprehensive assessments. Other instruments that may be employed in schools, but are more typically used in clinical settings, include the *Minnesota Multiphasic Personality Inventory-Adolescent* (MMPI-A) (Butcher et al., 1992) and the *Millon Adolescent Personality Inventory* (MAPI) (Millon, Green, & Meagher, 1982). Both are self-report inventories for adolescents.

Specific Purpose Rating Scales
When referral problems include clear symptoms of particular types of emotional/behavioral disorders, the assessment professional may select rating scales that are designed to assess more specific behaviors, thoughts, and feelings. Many such scales are available and are beyond the scope of this discussion. Checklists have been published to assess anxiety, depression, social skills, self-esteem, self-concept, hyperactivity, inattention, and antisocial behavior. Some of the more commonly used self-report checklists include the *Children's Depression Inventory-2* (Kovacs, 2003), the *Children's Depression Rating Scale-Revised* (Posnanski & Mokros, 1995), the *Reynolds Adolescent Depression Scale-2* (Reynolds, 2002), the *Revised Children's Manifest Anxiety Scale* (Reynolds & Richmond, 1985), and the *Manifest Anxiety Scale for Children* (March, 1997).

Child Interviews
Face-to-face child interviews can build rapport while allowing children to convey their own perceptions of school, relationships, significant events, and coping strategies. Further, these interviews can provide opportunity for direct observations of behavior and interaction style that can be compared to the reports of other informants, such as parents and teachers

(McConaughy & Ritter, 2002). Areas to be covered in the child interview include perceptions of school, social activities, friends, family relationships, fantasies, self-perceptions and feelings, and the child's view of the problems leading to referral. When adolescents are interviewed, somatic complaints, use of alcohol or drugs, and problems with the law should also be explored.

Although a variety of child interview formats are available, and assessment professionals may develop their own formats, use of standardized interview instruments offers the advantages of consistency and comparability across assessments. An example of such an interview is the Semistructured Clinical Interview for Children and Adolescents (SCICA) (Achenbach & Edelbrock, 2001) for children ages 6–18 years. This instrument includes structured rating scales for scoring the interviewer's observations of the child's behavior and of problems reported by the child.

Projective Techniques
Projective techniques refer to procedures and tests in which ambiguous stimuli, such as inkblots or picture of situations or people, are presented and the child's response is interpreted as a "projection" of inner feelings and conflicts that may not be readily accessed through more direct measures, such as self-report inventories and behavior checklists. Examples include the Rorschach Inkblot Test (Exner & Weiner, 1994), the Thematic Apperception Test (TAT) (Murray, 1943), the Children's Apperception Test (CAT) (Bellak & Bellak, 1949), the Roberts Apperception Test for Children-2 (RATC-2), (Roberts, 2005), sentence completion techniques, and drawings generated by the child, such as human figure and family drawings. Although some of these techniques will be briefly described, the Rorschach, for which administration, scoring, and interpretation requires extensive training, is rarely used in school settings and thus will not be discussed here.

These techniques, many which stem from psychodynamic theory of emotional/behavioral functioning that is usually studied in the context of graduate training in psychology, must be used only by qualified professionals trained in their administration and interpretation, such as clinical psychologists and school psychologists. Because interpretation of projective measures involves subjective judgment and validity and reliability may be difficult to establish, their use to identify EBD in school settings has long provoked debate, even though these tests continue to be widely used as psychological assessment techniques (Merrell, 2003). McConaughy and Ritter (2002) caution that even when qualified professionals administer and interpret these measures, subjective judgment is involved and normative data, reliability, and validity are often limited. However, as noted previously, even more direct techniques such as behavior ratings and checklists, involve subjective variables that may affect reliability and validity. Findings from projective measures often seem mysterious to other educators; when they are used by psychology professionals, it is incumbent upon those individuals to use other more direct techniques as well and to gauge the convergent validity, or consistency of findings, across measures. Assessment professionals also have the ethical obligation to make the findings understandable and meaningful to parents, teachers, and other team members.

The TAT, CAT, and RATC-2 are all considered thematic approaches, in which the examinee is presented with a series of cards with pictures or drawings of ambiguous characters or situations and is asked to tell a story about each picture. The examinee is expected to project his or her emotions, needs, and conflicts into the resulting story. Because the pictures and stories are indirectly associated with the individual's real life, there may be less resistance to disclosure than sometimes encountered in self-report and interview techniques. Evidence regarding reliability and validity is mixed and interpretative conclusions should be made only with additional supporting evidence.

Drawing techniques, such as the human figure drawing and kinetic family drawing, enjoy wide use as personality assessment techniques in school settings, despite limited evidence of reliability and validity (Merrell, 2003). In particular, while scoring for such drawings may be reliable across raters, test-retest reliability (stability in features of drawings over time) is more problematic. Further, validity findings, with respect to whether emotional indicators differ significantly between emotionally disturbed and normal children, are mixed. Human figure drawings were initially used in assessment as measures of intellectual and developmental functioning, but have evolved into personality assessment techniques as qualitative differences in the drawings of children have been observed and reported (Cummings, 1986). Kinetic family drawings, in which children are asked to draw a picture of everyone in their family doing something, have been used as a means to assess the child's perception family dynamics, emotional relationships, and position within the family. In assessment for EBD, when projective drawings are employed, they may often be used as techniques to build rapport, with interpretations made cautiously and in conjunction with other findings from more direct measures.

In sentence completion tasks, the child is presented with sentence stems (the beginning of a potential sentence) and asked to complete the sentence, either orally or in writing. Systematic inspection of the responses may provide insight into; for example, the child's self-image, relationships with peers, teachers, and family members, mood states, and needs. Inferences and interpretations are usually made based on clusters of items rather than on responses in isolation (Merrell, 2003).

Although these projective techniques remain in wide use, they have been associated with longstanding controversy with respect to use in schools because of limited psychometric properties and subjective interpretation. When used in EBD assessment, these techniques may be helpful in establishing rapport and communication with children who have difficulty verbally conveying thoughts and feelings. They may also generate hypotheses about social and emotional functioning that can be further assessed with more direct and objective approaches. McConaughy and Ritter (2002) caution that projective techniques should not be used as the primary or only sources of data for assessment of EBD. Mental health professionals who use projective techniques are obligated to make the findings useful and understandable to other members of the assessment team.

ACADEMIC ASSESSMENT AND DETERMINATION OF EDUCATIONAL NEED

To qualify for special education services, it is not sufficient that a child meet criteria for a specific disability category, such as EBD. The IEP team must also document need for special education services, including specially designed instruction or other interventions that cannot be accomplished in the general education program. If pre-referral interventions have been tried and have been minimally effective in reducing the problems or improving school performance, then this resistance to intervention may be evidence of the need for special education (McConaughy & Ritter, 2002).

Since all special education evaluations involve assessment of a child's current academic achievement, the data gathered in this phase of the evaluation should be used to document underachievement that may be related to emotional/behavioral factors. Although wide variation exists among individuals, in general students with EBD as a group score lower than average on both intelligence and achievement measures, so academic difficulties are often identified. Learning disabilities may also coexist with emotional/behavioral disorders, so thorough assessment of learning abilities and academic skills is essential. Although a discussion of achievement tests is outside the scope of this chapter, examples of techniques to assess academic achievement include standardized, norm-referenced individually administered tests such as the *Wechsler Individual Achievement Test-3* (WIAT-3) (The Psychological Corporation, 2009), the *Woodcock-Johnson Tests of Achievement–III* (WJ-III) (Woodock, McGrew, & Mather, 2001), and the *Kaufman Tests of Educational Achievement-2* (KTEA-2) (Kaufman & Kaufman, 2004a, 2004b), among many others. Curriculum-based methods, criterion-referenced tests, report cards, work samples, and standardized group achievement tests mandated by states or local school districts can also provide evidence regarding academic achievement. These measures, depending on the type of test and training required, may be administered by school psychologists, other educational appraisal staff, general education teachers, or special education teachers. All measures of achievement, including classroom-based measures, group achievement tests, and formal individual testing, should be considered together in determining academic functioning, both in terms of achievement levels and in motivation and study skills. Standardized teacher rating scales, such as the BASC-2, the TRF, and the CBRS (reviewed previously) also provide scales for academic performance and school adaptive functioning and can be considered along with academic achievement levels on tests.

The NASP position statement on EBD discussed earlier suggests a broader perspective on educational need than just academic achievement. In an individual with EBD, emotional or behavioral responses in school settings would be expected to adversely affect performance in a variety of areas, including self-care, social relationships, personal adjustment, academic progress, and/or classroom behavior. In the actual practice of EBD assessment, consideration of overall school adjustment and day-to-day classroom performance should be taken into account, along with achievement levels on standardized tests. Tests of adaptive behavior can be useful in this regard; The *Adaptive Behavior Assessment System, 2nd Edition* (Harrison & Oakland, 2002-2003) and the *Vineland Adaptive Behavior Scales, 2nd Edition* (Sparrow, Cicchetti, & Balla, 2005) are examples of comprehensive scales that measure everyday communication, personal care, social behavior, and school/community adjustment with reference to an age-based national normative sample. Caretaker and teacher formats are available for comparison across informants and settings.

In order to gauge the degree of educational need, IEP teams typically need a measure of cognitive functioning to examine with respect to academic achievement and patterns of cognitive information processing. This information can help the team to determine if current instructional content and strategies are appropriate for the child's needs and abilities. Other considerations might be determining a baseline for measuring change or improvement in cognitive processing with intervention. For example, processing speed, memory, attention, and concentration, all of which are measured on tests of cognitive processing, may be negatively impacted by depression and can improve with treatment. Commonly used standardized tests of intelligence include the *Wechsler Intelligence Scale for Children-IV* (Wechsler, 2003), the *Kaufman Assessment Battery for Children-2* (Kaufman & Kaufman, 2004a, 2004b), the *Woodcock-Johnson Tests of Cognitive Abilities-III* (Woodock, McGrew, & Mather, 2001), and the *Differential Abilities Scales-2* (Elliott, 2007). These tests, among others, will typically be administered by the school psychologist on the IEP team as part of the Full Individual Evaluation.

LINKING ASSESSMENT TO INTERVENTION

If assessment is to be useful to children, parents, and teachers, then the findings must extend beyond identification and placement in special education. The link between assessment findings and interventions must be considered when the assessment plan is designed by the IEP team. Too often, a disconnect occurs between the results of the assessment and the initiation of special education services, so that the IEP is developed and implemented distinct from the assessment process. Lack of treatment validity of assessment data is addressed by Shinn (2002) in a discussion of curriculum-based measurement and by Gresham (2007), in a discussion of RTI for EBD. The link between assessment and intervention can be strengthened through (1) selection of appropriate assessment tools that have strong ties to intervention strategies and (2) dissemination of results and recommendations in a manner that is understandable to teachers, parents, and others who will be implementing interventions.

The pre-referral intervention models (e.g., RTI, PBS, consultation and collaboration among professionals) serve as a blueprint for the design of effective assessment to intervention links. If assessment is done with ecological validity (consideration of the whole system in which the child functions), collaborative problem-solving between teachers, parents, and assessment personnel, and regular monitoring and evaluation of the intervention, then the relationship between data gathering and intervention is strengthened (Gresham, 2007). Even if a pre-referral intervention is insufficient to ameliorate serious emotional and behavioral problems, the foundation will have been laid for collaborative problem-solving, including teamwork in identification of intrapersonal, interpersonal, and environmental variables contributing to the child's difficulties in school. Numerous school consultation models exist, but most emphasize collabora- tive problem-solving for effecting behavioral change (Allen & Graden, 2002); such techniques may focus on instructional needs or behavioral needs, depending on the teacher's perception and the outcome of observations and other assessment data.

In the domain of externalizing disorders, characterized by acting-out, aggressive, disruptive, oppositional, defiant, and hyperactive behaviors, research suggests that direct behavioral techniques that take into account environmental variables and interpersonal interactions are most productive for generating effective intervention (Hoff, Doepke, & Landau, 2002; Lane, Gresham, & O'Shaughnessy, 2002). In other words, functional behavioral assessments (FBAs) can be very effective with children who exhibit primarily externalizing problem behaviors.

In contrast, internalizing disorders are characterized by over-control of behavior and may be harder to detect. This domain includes symptoms such as depressed mood, social withdrawal, anxiety, and somatic complaints. Because the associated behaviors are less likely to be directly observable and noxious to the classroom teacher, it may be harder to identify antecedents and cues, or consequences that can be modified. Nevertheless, there are effective interventions available for internalizing disorders when a com- prehensive, individualized assessment has been completed. Cognitive- behavioral interventions receive the most support in the literature for internalizing disorders. Careful study of student responses to self-report checklists and interview questions can help guide the selection of intervention techniques that can be highly effective. As stated previously, however, many students exhibit symptoms of both internalizing and externalizing disorders, so initial intervention efforts may target most troublesome symptoms with respect to profit from school.

In summary, the development of the intervention plan, usually in the form of an IEP for children identified as having EBD, should represent a collaborative effort of the multidisciplinary team in which assessment findings are used to design practical and realistic interventions. Before placement in special education, the RTI and PBS models inform increasingly intensive and data-based interventions that target specific behaviors of concern.

MULTICULTURAL CONSIDERATIONS

According to Ortiz and Flanagan (2002), the foremost principle for using best practices in working with culturally diverse children and families is that "any individual's own culture greatly affects the way they view the world and others, including people from both within and outside the culture" (p. 337). Attention to cultural diversity within educational and psychological assessment has only fairly recently become a focus of professional preparation and practice. As noted by Baker, Kamphaus, Horne, and Winsor (2006), diversity in American schools is increasing, resulting in increasing variability in academic as well as inter- and intrapersonal behavior of children in classrooms.

The terms *test bias* and *assessment bias* refer to test instruments or methods that result in one group being systematically disadvantaged or yield group differences on characteristics other than those being measured by the test or technique. It is an ethical violation to use tests or methods that are not appropriate for the purpose of the assessment or that unfairly discriminate against any group (American Educational Research Association [AERA], American Psychological Association [APA], National Council on Measurement in Education [NCME], 1999). Ortiz (2002) has observed that since complete elimination of every potential source of bias is unrealistic, the goal of nondiscriminatory assessment should be to reduce it to the maximum extent possible.

Nondiscriminatory assessment requires that other sources, including nonstandardized methods and information, be included. Further, all information gathered in an assessment should be considered with respect to the individual's unique experience and background (Ortiz, 2002). Gresham (2007) points out that the use of an RTI approach in the referral process reduces the likelihood of disproportionate overrepresentation of certain minority groups in special education that may result from the traditional refer, test, and place process.

Merrell (2003) offers further recommendations for culturally competent assessment practice. Some of these recommendations are: (1) obtaining sufficient cultural background information before planning and conducting assessment; (2) using a multimethod, multisource, multisetting approach to minimize culturally limiting factors of any one method; (3) being flexible in the design and implementation of the assessment; (4) striving for honesty and open communication regarding cultural issues with students and their families in both the assessment and feedback process; (5) developing awareness of individual as well as group cultural differences; and (6) examining one's own cultural background, values, beliefs, and assumptions. All of these suggestions underscore the need to view any student's behavior from within the student's own cultural context, and with recognition of one's own cultural perspective.

CONCLUSIONS

In summary, the assessment procedures associated with identification of students with EBD are complex and vary across practitioners, school districts, states, and the nation, although federal law mandates the general criteria to be addressed and procedures to be followed. Recommended techniques for assessment and identification include employment of screening techniques and pre-referral interventions, developmental histories, interviews, behavior checklists and rating scales, and intellectual and achievement testing. Multimethod, multisource, and multisetting approaches are essential for valid and culturally fair assessment. Projective techniques continue to be used in school-based assessment for EBD, although problems exist with reliability and validity. The link between assessment and intervention is strengthened when there is collaborative problem-solving among the multidisciplinary team, including the parents and community professionals and when assessment and associated interventions have ecological validity. All children's behavior should be viewed within each individual's own cultural context, so that assessment and placement bias is reduced.

REFERENCES

Achenbach, T. M., & Edelbrock, C. (2001). *Semistructured clinical interview for children and adolescents.* Burlington, VT: Achenbach System of Empirically Based Assessment.

Achenbach, T. M., & Rescorla, L. A. (2001). *Manual for ASEBA school-age forms & profiles.* Burlington, VT: University of Vermont, Research Center for Children, Youth, & Families.

Allen, S. J., & Graden, J. L. (2002). Best practices in collaborative problem solving for intervention design. In A. Thomas & J. Grimes (Eds.), *Best practices in school psychology IV* (pp. 565–582). Bethesda, MD: National Association of School Psychologists.

American Educational Research Association, American Psychological Association, & National Council on Measurement in Education. (1999). *Standard for educational and psychological testing.* Washington, DC: American Educational Research Association.

American Psychiatric Association. (2000). *Diagnostic and statistical manual of mental disorders, Fourth Edition, Text Revision.* Washington, DC: American Psychiatric Association.

American Psychiatric Association. (2010). *DSM V: The future of psychiatric diagnosis.* Retrieved from http://www.dsm5.org/Pages/Default.aspx. Accessed on April 30, 2011.

Baker, J. A., Kamphaus, R. W., Horne, A. M., & Winsor, A. (2006). Evidence for population-based perspectives on children's behavioral adjustment and needs for service delivery in schools. *School Psychology Review, 35,* 31–46.

Bellak, L., & Bellak, S. (1949). *The children's apperception test.* New York: C.P.S.

Butcher, M. N., Williams, C. L., Graham, J. R., Archer, R. P., Tellegan, A., Ben-Porath, Y. S., & Kaemmer, B. (1992). *Minnesota multiphasic personality inventory–adolescent: Manual for administration, scoring, and interpretation.* Minneapolis, MN: University of Minnesota Press.

Conners, K. (2008). *The conners comprehensive behavior rating scales.* Tonawanda, NY: Multi-Health Systems, Inc.

Council for Exceptional Children. (2011). *RTI for emotional/behavioral disorders shows promise.* Retrieved from http://www.cec.sped.org/AM/Template.cfm?Section=Home& TEMPLATE=/CM/ContentDisplay.cfm&CONTENTID=11297&CAT=none. Accessed on May 28.

Cullinan, D., & Sabornie, E. J. (2004). Characteristics of emotional disturbance in middle and high school students. *Journal of Emotional and Behavioral Disorders, 12*(3), 157–167.

Cummings, J. A. (1986). Projective drawings. In H. M. Knoff (Ed.), *The assessment of child and adolescent personality* (pp. 199–244). New York: Guilford Press.

Elizalde-Utnick, G. (2002). Best practices in building partnership with families. In A. Thomas & J. Grimes (Eds.), *Best practices in school psychology IV* (pp. 413–429). Bethesda, MD: National Association of School Psychologists.

Elliott, C. D. (2007). *Differential abilities scales-2nd edition (DAS-2).* San Antonio, TX: Pearson.

Epstein, M. H., & Cullinan, D. (1998). *Scale for assessing emotional disturbance.* Austin, TX: PRO-ED.

Epstein, M. H., Cullinan, D., Ryser, G., & Pearson, N. (2002). Development of a scale to assess emotional disturbance. *Behavioral Disorders, 28*(1), 5–22.

Esler, E. N., Godber, Y., & Christenson, S. L. (2002). Best practices in supporting home-school collaboration. In A. Thomas & J. Grimes (Eds.), *Best practices in school psychology IV* (pp. 389–411). Bethesda, MD: National Association of School Psychologists.

Euler, B. L. (2007). *Emotional disturbance decision tree.* Lutz, FL: Psychological Assessment Resources, Inc.

Exner, J. E., Jr., & Weiner, I. B. (1994). *The rorschach: A comprehensive system, Vol. 3: Assessment of children and adolescents* (2nd ed). New York: Wiley.

Fessler, M. A., Rosenberg, M. S., & Rosenberg, L. A. (1991). Concomitant learning disabilities and learning problems among children with behavior/emotional disorders. *Behavioral Disorders, 16*(2), 97–106.

Graden, J. L., Casey, A., & Christenson, S. (1985). Implementing a prereferral intervention system: Part II the data. *Exceptional Children, 51,* 377–384.

Gresham, F. (2007). Response to intervention and emotional and behavioral disorders: Best practices in assessment for intervention. *Assessment for Effective Intervention, 32*(4), 214–222.

Harrison, P., & Oakland, T. (2002–2003). *Adaptive behavior assessment system.* Los Angeles: Western Psychological Services.

Hoff, K. E., Doepke, K., & Landau, S. (2002). Best practices in the assessment of children with attention deficit/hyperactivity disorder: Linking assessment to intervention. In A. Thomas & J. Grimes (Eds.), *Best practices in school psychology IV* (pp. 1120–1150). Bethesda, MD: National Association of School Psychologists.

Hubbard, D. D., & Adams, J. (2002). Best practices in facilitating meaningful family involvement in educational decision making. In A. Thomas & J. Grimes (Eds.), *Best practices in school psychology IV* (pp. 377–387). Bethesda, MD: National Association of School Psychologists.

Hutton, J. B., & Roberts, T. (1986). *Social-emotional dimension Scale-2nd edition.* Austin, TX: Pro-Ed.

Individuals with Disabilities Education Improvement Act of 2004, 20 U.S.C. § 1400 et seq. (2004) (reauthorization of the Individuals with Disabilities Education Act of 1990).

Kaufman, A. S., & Kaufman, N. L. (2004a). *Kaufman assessment battery for children-second edition (KABC-II).* San Antonio, TX: Pearson.

Kaufman, A. S., & Kaufman, N. L. (2004b). *Kaufman tests of educational achievement-second edition (KTEA-II).* San Antonio, TX: Pearson.

Kovacs, M. (2003). *Children's depression inventory (2003 update).* North Tonawanda, NY: Multi-Health Systems.

Kovaleski, J. F. (2002). Best practices in operating pre-referral intervention teams. In A. Thomas & J. Grimes (Eds.), *Best practices in school psychology IV* (pp. 645–655). Bethesda, MD: National Association of School Psychologists.

Lachar, D., & Gruber, C. P. (2005). *Personality inventory for youth.* Los Angeles: Western Psychological Services.

Lane, K. L., Gresham, F. M., & O'Shaughnessy, T. E. (2002). Serving students with or at-risk for emotional and behavioral disorders: Future challenges. *Education and Treatment of Children, 25*(4), 507–521.

March, J. (1997). *The multidimensional anxiety scale for children (MASC).* North Tonawanda, NY: Multi-Health Systems, Inc.

Mash, E. J., & Dozois, D. J. (1996). Child psychopathology: A developmental systems perspective. In E. J. Mash & A. Barkley (Eds.), *Child psychopathology* (pp. 3–60). New York: Guilford.

McCarney, S. B., & Leigh, J. E. (1990). *The behavior evaluation scale-2 (BES-2).* Columbia, MO: Hawthorne Educational Services.

McConaughy, S. H., & Ritter, D. R. (2002). Best practices in multidimensional assessment of emotional or behavioral disorders. In A. Thomas & J. Grimes (Eds.), *Best practices in school psychology IV* (pp. 1303–1320). Bethesda, MD: National Association of School Psychologists.

Merrell, K. W. (2003). *Behavioral, social and emotional assessment of children and adolescents.* Mahwah, NJ: Lawrence Erlbaum Associates.

Millon, T., Green, C. J., & Meagher, R. B. (1982). *Millon adolescent personality inventory.* Minneapolis, MN: National Computer Systems.

Murray, H. A. (1943). *Thematic apperception test manual.* Cambridge, MA: Harvard University Press.

National Association of School Psychologists. (2002). *Position statement of students with emotional and behavioral disorders.* Retrieved from http://www.nasponline.org/information/pospaper_sebd.html. Accessed on August 2, 2005.

Ortiz, S. O. (2002). Best practices in nondiscriminatory assessment. In A. Thomas & J. Grimes (Eds.), *Best practices in school psychology IV* (pp. 1321–1336). Bethesda, MD: National Association of School Psychologists.

Ortiz, S. O., & Flanagan, D. P. (2002). Best practices in working with culturally diverse children and families. In A. Thomas & J. Grimes (Eds.), *Best practices in school psychology IV* (pp. 337–351). Bethesda, MD: National Association of School Psychologists.

Posnanski, E., & Mokros, H. (1995). *Children's depression rating scales/revised CDRS/R.* Los Angeles: Western Psychological Services.

Reynolds, C. R., & Kamphaus, R. W. (2004). *Behavior assessment for children-second edition.* Circle Pines, MN: American Guidance Service.

Reynolds, C. R., & Richmond, B. O. (1985). *Revised children's manifest anxiety scale.* Los Angeles: Western Psychological Services.

Reynolds, W. M. (2002). *Reynolds adolescent depression scale-2.* Lutz, FL: Psychological Assessment Resources.

Roberts, G. E. (2005). *Roberts appreciation test for children: 2nd edition (RATC-2).* North Tonawanda, NY: Multi-Health Systems, Inc.

Sattler, J. M. (2002). *Assessment of children: Behavioral and clinical applications* (4th ed). La Mesa, CA: Sattler.

Sattler, J. M. (2006). *Assessment of children: Behavioral, social, and clinical applications* (5th Ed). La Mesa, CA: Sattler.

Scott, T. M., & Nelson, C. M. (1999). Universal school discipline strategies: Facilitating positive learning environments. *Effective School Practices, 17*(4), 54–64.

Severson, H. H., & Walker, H. M. (2002). Pro-active approaches for identifying children at risk for socio-behavioral problems. In K. L. Lane, F. M. Gresham & T. E. O'Shaughnessy (Eds.), *Interventions for students with or at-risk for emotional and behavioral disorders* (pp. 33–53). Boston, MA: Allyn & Bacon.

Shinn, M. R. (2002). Best practices in using curriculum-based measurement in a problem-solving model. In A. Thomas & J. Grimes (Eds.), *Best practices in school psychology IV* (pp. 671–697). Bethesda, MD: National Association of School Psychologists.

Sparrow, S., Cicchetti, D., & Balla, D. (2005). *Vineland adaptive behavior scales-2nd ed.* San Antonio, TX: Pearson.

Sprague, J. R., Sugai, G., Horner, R., & Walker, H. M. (1999). Using office discipline referral data to evaluate school-wide discipline and violence prevention interventions. *Oregon School Study Council Bulletin, 42*(2), 1–18.

Sugai, G., & Horner, R. (1999). Discipline and behavioral support: Practices, pitfalls, and promises. *Effective School Practices, 17*(4), 10–22.

Taylor, R. L. (1997). *Assessment of exceptional students: Educational and psychological procedures* (4th ed). Boston: Allyn & Bacon.

The Psychological Corporation. (2009). *Wechsler individual achievement test: 3rd edition (WIAT-III).* San Antonio, TX: Pearson.

Toffalo, D. A. D., & Pederson, J. A. (2005). The effect of a psychiatric diagnosis on school psychologists' special education eligibility decisions regarding emotional disturbance. *Journal of Emotional and Behavioral Disorders, 13*(1), 53–60.

Webber, J., & Plotts, C. (2008). *Emotional and behavioral disorders: Theory and practice.* Boston: Pearson, Allyn & Bacon.

Wechsler, D. (2003). *Wechsler intelligence scale for children: 4th edition (WISC-IV).* San Antonio, TX: Pearson.

Wirt, R. D., Lachar, D., Seat, P. D., & Broen, W. E., Jr. (2001). *Personality inventory for children – second edition.* Los Angeles: Western Psychological Services.

Woodock, R. W., McGrew, K. S., & Mather, N. (2001). *The woodcock-Johnson III.* Itasca, IL: Riverside.

CHAPTER 4

PLACEMENT OF STUDENTS WITH EMOTIONAL AND BEHAVIORAL DISORDERS

Sarup R. Mathur and Kristine Jolivette

ABSTRACT

Students with emotional and behavioral disorders (E/BD) receive educational and related services within a continuum of placement options per the Individual with Disabilities Education Act. The continuum of placement options ranges from fully included general education type classrooms to more restrictive environments such as alternative education settings, residential facilities, and schools within secure juvenile justice facilities. A specific placement option is based on the individualized academic and social needs of the student and includes the least restrictive environment to meet those needs. After the IFSP or IEP team develops a student's IFSP or IEP, then the team makes a placement decision. Multiple factors influence initial placement decisions including an overall reluctance to identify students with E/BD, false positives and negatives, co-morbidity, and disproportionality. Other factors may influence a temporary or long-term change in placement such as inappropriate student behavior and/or academic failure. No matter the placement, the educational services provided within each should be evidence-based, implemented with fidelity, be individualized, and be socially valid.

Behavioral Disorders: Identification, Assessment, and Instruction of Students with EBD
Advances in Special Education, Volume 22, 87–105
Copyright © 2012 by Emerald Group Publishing Limited
All rights of reproduction in any form reserved
ISSN: 0270-4013/doi:10.1108/S0270-4013(2012)0000022007

Keywords: Placement options; emotional and behavioral disorders; restrictive placement; least restrictive placement; alternative placements; co-morbidity

Placement generally refers to a decision of serving a student with a disability in an educational environment where instructional processes are most likely to meet the student's specific learning and/or behavioral needs and produce long-term positive educational outcomes. The main purpose of placement is to develop social ecologies that are conducive to student learning and behavior (Kauffman, 2010). Placement is a critical component in the discussion of the types of educational services that students with emotional and behavioral disorders (E/BD) receive. Students with E/BD demonstrate significant behavioral challenges, interpersonal problems, and emotional issues that interfere with their and others learning. Due to chronic behavioral difficulties and disciplinary challenges associated with students with E/BD, educational placement is one of the most controversial issues (Hayling, Cook, Gresham, State, & Kern, 2008).

According to the Individual with Disabilities Education Act (IDEA, 2004), the specific placement option, setting, or facility is determined based on the goals from the student's individual family service plan (IFSP) or individual education plan (IEP). More specifically, IDEA requires that students with E/BD: (a) have access to a full continuum of placement options ranging from general education to residential treatment settings depending on their needs, (b) are placed in a least restrictive environment (LRE) to receive an appropriate education, and (c) have a placement that is individualized based on the appropriate education described in the student's IFSP or IEP (Yell & Katsiyannis, 2004). Technically, placement decisions can only be made after the development of the IFSP/IEP (IDEA Regulations, 300.552(b)(2)); however, educational practice does not follow this consistently in many cases.

Despite specific guidance from IDEA, controversies continue to appear in many due process hearings and court cases involving students with E/BD, where placement decisions of IFSP/IEP teams have been questioned (Bartlett, Weisenstein, & Etscheidt, 2002). Such placement controversies for students with E/BD, can be linked to (a) the federal definition of emotional disturbance which may be considered vague, contradictory, arbitrary, and ambiguous (Cullinan, 2004; Gresham, 2005; please see the Identification chapter for full details of the definition), (b) the notion that a large number of students are not identified as being E/BD even though they present characteristics similar to students E/BD; thus, there are concerns of underserving these students (Gresham, 2005; Kauffman, 2010), and (c) the influences of advocacy and political changing viewpoints on what the continuum of placement options should be for students with disabilities in general as well as those with E/BD (Kauffman & Hallahan, 2005). In this chapter, placement options are presented from less to more restrictive, the prevalence of students with E/BD in various placement options are discussed, factors which influence placement of students with E/BD are described, and future trends in placement are presented.

PLACEMENT OPTIONS FOR STUDENTS WITH E/BD

Students with E/BD present many complex behavioral and academic challenges throughout their educational careers to teachers which may create difficulties in providing them with effective practices, fidelity of implementation of such practices, and practices addressing both behavioral and academic areas. The placements in which these students receive their educational services are critical in positioning the student for improved outcomes. Two important principles that should be adhered to when making decisions regarding student placement are: (a) the principle of individualization and (b) the principle of appropriate education. Placement decisions for students with E/BD must be individualized to meet his/her unique educational needs and must provide meaningful educational benefits (Yell & Katsiyannis, 2004).

Placement Options

There are numerous educational placement options afforded to students with E/BD depending on what is most appropriate to meet their unique academic and/or social needs. These placements may be accessed at any time given the students current academic and social needs; thus, a student's educational placement may change throughout their educational career. Placement decision making may be influenced by two perspectives that have been stretched to the extreme. First, one perspective is that all students, no matter if they have a disability or not, should be taught in a *fully included environment*. According to this view, all students should be placed in general education classes in their neighborhood school regardless of their emotional disabilities and specific IFSP/IEP needs. Researchers indicate that basing all services for all students with E/BD in their neighborhood schools where they live may neither be possible nor beneficial for some students (Kauffman & Hallahan, 2005; Kauffman & Landrum, 2009). Although in many cases, placement of a student with E/BD in a general education classroom may not be the most appropriate placement but due to lack of other options and supports, it becomes the only possible option. In times of budgetary constraints, educational placements and their respective evidence-based and specialized programs for students with E/BD may be viewed as expensive. As such, special education placements show a trend toward inclusionary programs and community-based services despite limited research on their effectiveness on student outcomes (Kauffman & Landrum, 2009). Facilities, such as hospitals, behavioral health day treatment settings, and residential placements for students with severe E/BD are equally important to provide services to many students with E/BD, who experience internalizing disorders and other psychiatric and mental health issues (Kauffman & Landrum, 2009) but may not be considered given the current economic landscape.

Second, the other perspective is that due to their significant behavioral challenges, students with E/BD should receive all their educational services in *specialized environments* away from the general education setting including peers and curriculum. Many students with E/BD do benefit from specialized environments, where they are taught by specially trained special educators and receive individualized attention to benefit them academically and behaviorally (Landrum, Tankersley, & Kauffman, 2003). Some students with E/BD do need individualized attention, intensive supports, and a teacher who has received comprehensive training in intensive academic and behavioral interventions and supports provided separately from the general education classroom (Kauffman, 2010). No matter the perspective taken, all placement options should be considered, since students with E/BD are entitled to a free and appropriate public education aligned with their individual education plan and behavior intervention plan goals and objectives as per the IDEA (2004). These options include a continuum of placements from less to more restrictive which may differ according to physical locale of the placement as well as be influenced by student age. A continuum of placements is discussed below in light of the least restrictive environment options put forth by IDEA with the intent for students with E/BD to have access to their typical peers and general education curriculum to the extent appropriate.

Early Childhood Placements
Children birth to three who display challenging behaviors typically are not found eligible for services under IDEA in the emotional disturbance

category, instead they may receive educational services with a developmental delay label. Most of these children are in *inclusive early childhood settings* (e.g., HeadStart, and preschool, early intervention programs) which provide services to the child directly within the classroom setting alongside their peers. It is common to observe multiple adults within these settings such as teachers, instructional assistants, speech and language pathologists, occupational therapists, physical therapists, and behavior specialists all of whom work directly with the children with challenging behaviors as they engage in typical classroom activities and routines. For children with more complex and chronic challenges, they also may receive additional services by these adults outside the natural occurring classroom and schedule through a *pull-out* model. In this model, specialized and individualized services are provided to the child outside the purview of the classroom typically one-on-one for a set period of time per day or week. However, some young children with challenging behaviors may be found ineligible for specific programs and/or schools due to failing to meet the eligibility requirements for the particular placement (e.g., privately managed), in which case, their educational needs may not be met (Conroy, Hendrickson, & Hester, 2004).

Traditional Elementary, Middle, and High School Placements
Within these schools there are four placement options for students with E/BD. First, a student with E/BD may be placed alongside their peers within *general education classes* with few to no supports (e.g., case manager or behavior specialist checks in with student or works "behind the scenes" with the general education teacher to make adaptations and accommodations to the curriculum and behavior management system). However, for many students with E/BD this placement option may not be the best to meet their complex and intertwined academic deficits and/or social excesses/deficits. If this placement option is considered, then the general education settings in which the student with E/BD is placed must be continually monitored for its ability to meet the needs of the students. A second option, is for the student with E/BD to be provided services alongside their peers within an *inclusive/collaborative class* in which both a general education teacher and a special education teacher provides continuous academic and social support related to the general education curriculum and the student's IEP. In this placement, the general education curriculum is adapted to meet the student's needs and re-teaching/remediation can occur in real-time within the context of the ongoing instruction. Third, a student with E/BD may attend a combination of general education classes and/or inclusive/collaborative classes along with a portion of the day being spent in a

resource classroom. A resource classroom is typically staffed by a special education teacher and one other instructional assistant depending on the number of students in the class and state policies. In this type of class, individualized and small group instruction is provided to the student to (a) build on the academic instruction and content provided in the student's other classes and (b) promote more social competence through social skill instruction and other behavioral strategies. Fourth, some students with E/BD are best served within traditional schools but in a *self-contained classroom* within the school. Those who attend a self-contained classroom are usually provided with all academic coursework within this class by a special education teacher and instructional assistant with consultation by content area general education teachers. These students typically have access to the general education curriculum and their peers during nonacademic class periods (e.g., art, music, physical education, lunch, homeroom, and special assemblies) throughout each day per their IEP. In all of these placement options, students with E/BD also may be provided with additional services (e.g., counseling, speech, and language therapy) to meet their individualized IEP needs.

Alternative Education (AE) Placements
AE settings typically serve a plethora of students at-risk whether due to inappropriate behavior and/or academic failure. For those students with E/BD in districts which have AE options, there are at least five different AE placements which may be available whether selected through voluntary (e.g., self-referral or family-referral) or nonvoluntary (e.g., due to disciplinary action, by a juvenile judge, and by a social agency) means. In addition, the duration of a student's stay within any of these options may be based on student characteristics (e.g., behavioral improvement and academic improvement), temporal characteristics (e.g., a specified length of time for those court ordered), and/or other factors (e.g., insurance approval). Researchers (Carver & Lewis, 2010; National Center on Education Statistics, 2001) have found that those most at-risk for placement in an AE setting include those who live in a district which are large and urban within the Southeast and have large concentrations of poverty and minority populations. In fact, when compared to all other disability groups, students with E/BD are the most likely to receive educational services in AE settings (Wagner & Davis, 2006). From less to more restrictive, they include (a) alternative schools, (b) day treatment schools, (c) residential schools, (d) hospital schools, and (e) juvenile justice facility schools.

Alternative Schools. There are two different types of alternative school models, a school-within-a-school and as a separate school, in which students with E/BD may be placed. A *school-within-a-school* means that a classroom, portion of the building, or a space on the campus of a regular school (e.g., middle or high school) is designated for the AE program. Both general and special education teachers staff these classes while permitting the student to still have physical access to their peers without challenges as well as participate in non-AE classes. This placement may be used for students with E/BD who are in the process of transitioning from a more restrictive AE environment to a less restrictive environment. An AE *separate school* operates as a stand-alone educational center staffed by general and special education teachers. In this placement option, the students are provided with all their educational needs alongside other students with similar academic and behavioral challenges whether they have a disability or not. Both of these placements may be an interim alternative education setting for those with E/BD who committed an egregious act while at school. Also, the services provided within these two placement options usually mirror that of typical elementary, middle, high school programming with more of an emphasis on social development and regulation.

Day Treatment Schools. Students with E/BD who receive their education within day treatment schools typically have complex mental health issues which must be addressed alongside their academic and social needs. Services are provided to the students by general and special education teachers, mental health staff, social workers, and other medical personnel; and services are provided to the student's family as needed. Placement within a day treatment school may be for a short-period or an extended period of time and is typically on a nonvoluntary basis.

Residential Schools. Residential schools are for those students with E/BD whose academic, social, and mental health needs cannot be appropriately met in an outpatient setting. AE schools within residential facilities function similarly to a typical school in terms of appearance, general and special education staffing, and academic and nonacademic course offerings. Students within this placement option receive a comprehensive set of individualized services 24/7 from a diverse and specialized staff. Some residential facilities, and thus the AE school, only serve students with E/BD.

Hospital Schools. Similar to a residential school, hospital schools are appropriate for students with E/BD who require medical evaluations and/or treatment services under the direct care of a physician 24/7. For these students, it may be a temporary placement to assess pharmacological medication changes, to address an acute medical issue, or for a psychological evaluation beyond the scope and expertise found within a typical school. The students would attend classes during the day staffed by educators. The coursework may be that from the student's regular school or that used by the local school district.

Juvenile Justice Facility Schools. Students with E/BD may be placed by a juvenile judge within the custody of a secure juvenile justice facility due to serious offenses committed within the community at-large. In fact, almost half of youth in secure care are those with disabilities (Gagnon, Barber, Van Loan, & Leone, 2009) with the most prevalent disability being those with E/BD (U.S. Department of Education, 2009). Although incarcerated, all school-age youth attend school during school hours usually on a year round calendar. These students are offered (a) courses with credit earned being transferable to their neighborhood school, (b) curricula where they may earn a high school diploma and/or a general equivalency diploma, and (c) technical or vocational certification programs. A school within a juvenile justice facility operates same as any other school with general and special education teachers and is either under the governance of the state department of juvenile justice or the local school district. One difference between a school within a juvenile justice facility and a traditional non-AE school is the presence of correctional officers who are in proximity for the safety and wellbeing of all youth and adults.

Home-Based Education

Some students with E/BD may receive their educational services through home-based instruction provided by a family member or via internet school program. Others may participate in community-based educational programs through a charter organization.

No matter the educational placement location, all students with E/BD are to be afforded evidence-based practices by highly skilled teachers and offered the same opportunities and experiences as their peers without disabilities (Cook, Landrum, Tankersley, & Kauffman, 2003). In addition, these students will require tiered support that encompasses school-wide, classroom, and individual behavioral strategies, especially if placed within general education and inclusive/collaborative classes (Hieneman, Dunlap, & Kincaid, 2005).

Prevalence of Placement Options

The estimates of prevalence for students with E/BD receiving educational services in the various placement options need to be interpreted with caution. Since the enactment of the IDEA, the number of students found eligible for special education services has declined to 6.48 million students in 2009–2010 which is 13.1% of all students nationwide including 0.8% being students with E/BD. In addition, E/BD has been reported as one of the shrinking disability categories with 480,000 students with E/BD in 2001 to 407,000 in 2010 (1.0–0.8%: Scull & Winkler, 2011). However, data from the U.S. Department of Health and Human Services (1999) as well as from other studies (e.g., Costello, Egger, & Angold, 2005; Kauffman & Landrum, 2009) suggest the actual prevalence rate of E/BD to be at least five times greater or at about 5%. Other estimates indicate that almost 20% of the school-age population could qualify for a behavioral or psychiatric diagnosis per the *Diagnostic and Statistical Manual of Mental Disorders* (Gresham, 2005). Also, for some educational placements (e.g., juvenile justice school facility) the prevalence for E/BD is predicted at even higher percentages (Quinn, Rutherford, Leone, Osher, & Poirier, 2005).

Although there is no agreement on the actual number of students who should be receiving services under IDEA for E/BD, there are numbers provided for these students currently being served in various educational placement options. A large percentage of students with E/BD spend less than 50% of the day in a general education classroom. Specifically, 25% of students with E/BD spend about 80% of their school day in general education classrooms (Wagner et al., 2006). Differences in how much time students with E/BD spend in special education class placements as compared to students with other disabilities are evident. For example, 30% of elementary school students with E/BD and 33% of middle school students with E/BD spend time in special education classes as compared to 14% of elementary and 18% of middle school students having other disabilities (Bradley, Doolittle, & Bartolotta, 2008).

Students with E/BD are more likely than students with other disabilities (e.g., learning disabilities) to be served in self-contained classrooms with other students with E/BD. Most of the students (82%) with E/BD are served in their neighborhood schools with the remaining 18% of students with E/BD served in separate public or private facilities, residential facilities, or home/hospital environments (U.S. Department of Education, 2009). Students with E/BD are three times more likely than their peers with other disabilities to be educated in placements outside their neighborhood school.

A significant number of these students with E/BD are being placed in AE schools, which is a more exclusionary placement for those who have externalizing conduct disorders, aggressive, and violent behaviors (Furney, Hasazi, Clark/Keefe, & Hartnett, 2003). In a longitudinal study of 3,066 participants from 5 to 18 years of age, Farmer, Mustillo, Burns, and Holden (2008) found that youth with more behavioral problems had fewer academic and behavioral strengths, and those who were male 15 years or older were more likely to be placed in more restrictive placements out of the home (e.g., group homes, residential treatment, or juvenile corrections) than in less restrictive placements (e.g., foster care or therapeutic foster care). Farmer et al. (2008) suggest additional research to better understand (a) how placement decisions are made, (b) the extent to which capacity, options, or quality of services may influence more restrictive placements, and (c) the degree to which such placements influence behavioral and academic outcomes for students with E/BD and behavioral challenges.

WHO MAKES PLACEMENT DECISIONS AND REASONS WHY PLACEMENTS MAY CHANGE

For young children with behavioral challenges, a variety of persons may contribute to the discussion and decision related to placement. If the young child has not been identified as having a disability, then family members, agency personnel, and/or medical staff may suggest and select specific early childhood intervention programs, centers, or facilities for the child. If the child has been identified with E/BD, then the IFSP team makes the decision and recommendation of where best to serve the child. The IFSP team is interdisciplinary in nature and typically consists of teachers, parents, related services staff (e.g., speech and language pathologists, behavioral specialist, physical therapist, and occupational therapists), and school administrator as well as an advocate if the parents request one. For older students with E/BD, the IEP team makes the decision and recommendation for placement. Like the IFSP team, team membership is very similar with the inclusion of the student, if appropriate. Placement decisions typically happen at various points of time. These may include: (a) when the child or student is first found eligible for services under E/BD and (b) when the child or student is transitioning from preschool to kindergarten, from elementary to middle school, and from middle to high school, and between educational placements (e.g., juvenile justice facility to an AE school, or AE school to neighborhood school). The student's academic and social functioning (e.g., grades, office discipline referrals, and behavioral incidents) also may trigger the team to make new placement recommendations at any point in time.

Making a placement recommendation for a student with E/BD is a daunting task which the IFSP and IEP teams do not take lightly. As they decide which placement is the best match for the student and their current academic, social, and mental health needs per the IFSP or IEP or behavioral intervention plan, they need to think through contextual factors of existing placement options that may help or hinder the student's growth. For example, the team will want to consider placements which will provide a positive host environment to the student with E/BD. Such a positive host environment would be one whose mission and philosophy is proactive and preventative behaviorally not reliant on reactive and punitive practices (Hieneman et al., 2005). Also, the team needs to consider the educational services and practices as well as staff expertise provided within the specific placement. In addition, the team may be looking for a placement which would help break or minimize the negative cycle and influence of a deviant peer group.

As stated earlier, a student's placement is not necessarily held constant over their educational career. There may be circumstances in which the IFSP and IEP teams are reconvened to make a recommendation for a placement change. One of the most common reasons a student with E/BD placement may be changed is due to their behavior. Three behavioral scenarios may warrant a change in placement, whether temporary or more long-term, and include (a) student inappropriate behavior that is ongoing and has not positively responded to current behavioral strategies as monitored by the team, (b) inappropriate behavior which is increasing in severity, chronicity, and/or intensity across the educational and home environments, and (c) egregious behavioral incidents such as when students inflict bodily harm to another individual in school, possess drugs or alcohol on school grounds, or bring weapons to school. In addition, a student's academic status may influence placement changes like adding resource room assistance for an academic area in which the student is not passing.

FACTORS THAT INFLUENCE PLACEMENT DECISIONS

Multiple factors may negatively influence the placement decisions of the IFSP and IEP team and thus, the delivery of efficacious interventions for students with EBD. These include: (a) overall reluctance to identify students with E/BD, (b) false positive and false negative, (c) co-morbidity, and (d) disproportionality. Each factor is described below.

Overall Reluctance to Identify Individuals with E/BD

As indicated by recent prevalence data, it is clear that students with E/BD are underidentified/underserved per the identification process. For example, in Mississippi only about 600 students in the state received services under the E/BD category, whereas another 27,000 students were estimated to have mental health concerns (Judge David Bazelon Center for Mental Health Law, 2003). Since schools have the freedom to operationalize, as they deem appropriate, the specific eligibility criteria for E/BD, it is likely that students with E/BD in one state may no longer qualify for services if they move to another state or if their placement changes. Also, the social stigma attached to being identified as having EBD (Kauffman, 2010) has been considered the most common reason for underidentification and underservicing for many students with E/BD (Kauffman et al., 2009). However, research supports the significant costs connected to failure to serve students who actually have E/BD (Quinn & Poirier, 2004).

False Positive False Negative

There are two issues related to identifying students under the E/BD eligibility criteria that may lead to inappropriate placement decisions. These include: (a) false positive decisions or a Type I error, which is when a student is identified as having E/BD when in reality he/she does not have E/BD and (b) false negative or a Type II error, which is when a student is found not eligible for E/BD services when in reality he/she actually does have E/BD. False negatives (Type II errors) are more common than false positives (Type I errors) for students with challenging behaviors (Kauffman, 2010). This error leads to underservicing students who actually need individualized and specialized services to address their E/BD needs. Steps to minimize both types of errors include: (a) promoting more awareness and a better understanding of the complex nature and intertwined characteristics of E/BD, (b) facilitating a set of appropriate "best practice" assessment strategies for those students and who are presenting characteristics of one with E/BD, and (c) reviewing placement options and selected in relation to a student's social, emotional, and behavioral functioning on an ongoing, regular basis to determine whether a change in placement is warranted or not.

Co-morbidity

One of the most complex aspects presented by students with E/BD are that multiple other identifiable conditions (e.g., mood disorder, attention and activity disorder, obsessive-compulsive disorder, learning disabilities, or substance abuse) may be co-occurring during the assessment and/or placement process which may make it more difficult for an IFSP/IEP team to make appropriate placement decisions. Prevalence rates for students with E/BD who have co-morbid challenges vary, ranging from 25% to 97% (Reid, Gonzalez, Nordness, Trout, & Epstein, 2004). In recent years, there has been a significant increase in the number of students needing interventions, such as psychiatric medication or cognitive-behavioral therapy (Forness, Freeman, & Paparella, 2007; Silverman, Pina, & Viswesvaran, 2008) who display characteristics of E/BD along with other behavioral, learning, or mental health challenges. No matter the specific co-morbid challenges, IFSP and IEP teams more frequently are concerned with determining placement options for students with E/BD who display externalizing behaviors (e.g., noncompliance, disruption, or aggression) as compared to those who present internalizing behaviors (e.g., sleeping in class or shyness). Although studies do occasionally distinguish between internalizing and externalizing disorders, most use that distinction to focus on students who exhibit disruptive behavior (Gresham & Kern, 2004; Trout, Nordness, Pierce, & Epstein, 2003). As a result, students with E/BD and externalizing behaviors receive higher rates of services and alternate placement options than those students with internalizing behaviors (Bradshaw, Buckley, & Ialongo, 2008). However, many students with internalizing disorders (anxiety and fear) are encompassed within the federal definition of emotional disturbance (Gresham & Kern, 2004) but schools are still not equipped to provide such services in less restrictive environments. Clearly, schools have a responsibility to consider all appropriate placement options to meet a student's emotional needs but many of these students with E/BD and co-morbid conditions fail to receive appropriate services, falling through the cracks with no provision of evidence-based interventions causing further escalation of risks and outcomes during post-school.

TOURO COLLEGE LIBRARY

Disproportionality

Minority disproportionality has been viewed as a major concern as it relates to placement decisions for students with E/BD. Asians and Latinos are less likely to be identified as having E/BD than Caucasians (Parrish, 2002); however, the risk ratios for African-Americans have been reported higher than other groups (Cartledge & Dukes, 2009). For example, African-American students with E/BD are 1.2 times more likely than their white peers to be taught in self-contained settings and much less likely to be educated in settings where they may access general education environments and curriculum (Fierros & Conroy, 2002; Skiba, Poloni-Staudinger, Gallini, Simmons, & Feggins-Azziz, 2006). As compared with their white counterparts, African-American students with E/BD were (a) found to receive fewer appropriate supports and related services such as counseling (Osher, Woodruff, & Sims, 2002) and (b) be more likely referred to the juvenile justice system (Parrish, 2002).

These factors influence prevalence data, and placement decisions and options for students with E/BD. Maintaining accuracy in data collection, using reliable and valid tools of assessment, and following the eligibility criteria for students with E/BD consistently across states, are a few suggestions to improve placement decisions and options.

FUTURE TRENDS IN PLACEMENT

There are several trends within the field of E/BD which may influence IFSP and IEP teams when making placement recommendations for students with E/BD. One is the emergence and application of tiered frameworks of prevention, including *Response to Intervention (RtI) and school-wide positive behavioral interventions and supports (SW-PBIS)*. Tiered supports are provided to all students within an educational setting before making an eligibility determination for E/BD. These frameworks emphasize the steps of pre-referral interventions before assessing a student for E/BD eligibility and subsequent placement. The underlying assumption is that when students who are at-risk for E/BD are exposed to systematic, evidence-based interventions before eligibility determination, they are likely to develop a more adaptive repertoire preventing further escalation of emotional or behavioral challenges. According to Kauffman, Simpson, and Mock (2009), "Response to intervention may be a good idea for finding a better match of child characteristics and teaching, but it is not a good idea for defining disability" (p. 178). In respect to SW-PBIS, research has shown it to be adaptable based on student characteristics and performance provided in a consistent, proactive, and supportive environment (Lewis, Jones, Horner, & Sugai, 2010). Additional research is warranted to determine SW-PBIS and its effects on students already receiving E/BD services.

A second trend in the field of E/BD which may influence placement recommendations for students with E/BD is *emerging research as to the effectiveness of such placements* in terms of student academic, social, and behavioral growth. IFSP and IEP teams may be swayed by data if they indicate that some placements are more effective than others or if some placements produce similar results whether positive, neutral, or negative. As more and more students with E/BD are educated across the continuum of least restrictive environments, research on outcomes related to specific placements or comparisons on varying placements and all services provided will emerge in the literature. For example, Lane, Wehby, Little, and Cooley (2005) compared the academic and social progress of students with E/BD whose placements were either in a self-contained classroom or a self-contained school; and found that neither group of students made academic, social, or behavioral progress during the year. Also minimal, neutral, or worsening outcomes for students with E/BD in more restrictive placements have been documented before (e.g., Reid et al., 2004). As more is known about the effectiveness of the practices and services afforded to students with E/BD in the various placement options, IFSP and IEP teams can make better decisions related to placement and better meet the unique needs of the student in their charge.

A third trend is an awareness, based on data, about the *school-to-prison pipeline phenomenon* which may influence placement decisions. This phenomenon refers to "the national trend of criminalizing, rather than educating, our nation's children" (ACLU, 2008, p. 1). For students with E/BD who display externalizing behaviors, many are forced out of school and into the juvenile justice system. Amending the No Child Left Behind Act (NCLB, 2002) to minimize reasons for schools to push students with EBD out of school could make a significant difference in the experiences of youth returning to school from juvenile justice placements.

CONCLUSION

Placement decisions need to be relevant for the student with E/BD in accordance to the services outlined in their IFSP/IEP. This means that a continuum of placement options be considered and the less restrictive environment appropriate for the individual be selected. Placements should include: (a) a range of practices demonstrated to be effective with students with E/BD (evidenced-based), (b) implementation of effective practices with fidelity (treatment fidelity), and (c) practices that are unique to the needs of the student (individualized) that need to be implemented sufficiently or satisfactorily (social validity) (Cook & Schirmer 2003). These essentials cannot be compromised in any placement option for students with E/BD (Kern, Hilt-Panahon, & Sokol, 2009).

REFERENCES

American Civil Liberties Union. (June 6, 2008). *School to prison pipeline: Talking points.* Retrieved from http://www.aclu.org/racial-justice/school-prison-pipeline-talking-points

Bartlett, L. D., Weisenstein, G. R., & Etscheidt, S. (2002). *Successful inclusion for educational leaders.* Upper Saddle River, NJ: Merrill/Prentice-Hall.

Bradley, R., Doolittle, J., & Bartolotta, R. (2008). Building on the data and adding to the discussion: The experiences and outcomes of students with emotional disturbance. *Journal of Behavioral Education, 17*(1), 4–23.

Bradshaw, C. P., Buckley, J. A., & Ialongo, N. S. (2008). School-based service utilization among urban children with early onset educational and mental health problems: The squeaky wheel phenomenon. *School Psychology Quarterly, 23,* 169–186.

Cartledge, G., & Dukes, C. (2009). Disproportionality of African American children in special education. In L. Tilman (Ed.), *Current issues: Theory and research on the participation of African Americans in U.S. education.* Thousand Oaks, CA: Sage.

Carver, P. R., & Lewis, L. (2010). *Alternative schools and programs for public school students at risk of educational failure: 2007–08* (NCES 2010–026). U.S. Department of Education, National Center for Education Statistics. Washington, DC: Government Printing Office.

Conroy, M. A., Hendrickson, J. M., & Hester, P. P. (2004). Early identification and prevention of emotional and behavioral disorders. In R. B. Rutherford, M. M. Quinn & S. R. Mathur (Eds.), *Handbook of research in emotional and behavioral disorders* (pp. 199–215). New York: Guilford.

Cook, B. G., Landrum, T. J., Tankersley, M., & Kauffman, J. M. (2003). Bringing research to bear on practice: Effecting evidence-based instruction for students with emotional and behavioral disorders. *Education and Treatment of Children, 26,* 345–361.

Cook, B. G., & Schirmer, B. R. (2003). What is special about special education? Overview and analysis. *Journal of Special Education, 37,* 200–205.

Costello, E. J., Egger, H. H., & Angold, A. (2005). One-year research update review: The epidemiology of child and adolescent psychiatric disorders. *Journal of the American Academy of Child and Adolescent Psychiatry, 44,* 972–986.

Cullinan, D. (2004). Classification and definition of emotional and behavioral disorders. In R. B. Rutherford, M. M. Quinn & S. R. Mathur (Eds.), *Handbook of research in emotional and behavioral disorders* (pp. 32–53). New York: Guilford.

Farmer, E. M. Z., Mustillo, S., Burns, B. J., & Holden, E. W. (2008). Use and predictors of out-of-home placements within systems of care. *Journal of Emotional and Behavioral Disorders, 16,* 5–14.

Fierros, E. G., & Conroy, J. E. (2002). Double jeopardy: An exploration of restrictiveness of race in special education. In D. Losen (Ed.), *Minority issues in special education* (pp. 39–70). Cambridge, MA: The Civil Rights Project, Harvard University and the Harvard Education Publishing Group.

Forness, S. R., Freeman, S., & Paparella, T. (2007). Recent randomized clinical trials comparing behavioral interventions and psychopharmacologic treatments for school children with EBD. *Behavioral Disorders, 31,* 284–296.

Furney, K. S., Hasazi, S. B., Clark/Keefe, K., & Hartnett, J. (2003). A longitudinal analysis of shifting policy landscapes in special and general education reform. *Exceptional Children, 70,* 81–94.

Gagnon, J. C., Barber, B. R., Van Loan, C. L., & Leone, P. E. (2009). Juvenile correctional schools: Characteristics and approaches to curriculum. *Education and Treatment of Children, 32,* 673–696.

Gresham, F. M. (2005). Response to intervention: An alternative means of identifying students as emotionally disturbed. *Education and Treatment of Children, 28,* 328–344.

Gresham, F. M., & Kern, L. (2004). Internalizing behavior problems in children and adolescents. In R. B. Rutherford, M. M. Quinn & S. R. Mathur (Eds.), *Handbook of research in emotional and behavioral disorders* (pp. 262–281). New York: Guilford.

Hayling, C. C., Cook, C., Gresham, F. R., State, T., & Kern, L. (2008). An analysis of the status and stability of the behaviors of students with emotional and behavioral difficulties: A classroom direct observation study. *Journal of Behavioral Education, 17,* 24–42.

Hieneman, M., Dunlap, G., & Kincaid, D. (2005). Positive support strategies for students with behavioral disorders in general education settings. *Psychology in the Schools, 42,* 779–794.

IDEA Regulations, 300.552(b)(2). Retrieved from http://cfr.vlex.com/vid/300-552-placements-19759690. Accessed on 11 February 2011.

Individuals with Disabilities Education Act (IDEA) of 2004, Pub. L. NO. 108–446.

Judge David L. Bazelon Center for Mental Health Law. (2003). *Recovery in the community (Vol. II): Program and reimbursement strategies for mental health and rehabilitative approaches under medicaid.* Washington, DC: Judge David L. Bazelon Center for Mental Health Law.

Kauffman, J. M. (2010). Commentary: Current status of the field and future directions. *Behavioral Disorders, 35,* 180–184.

Kauffman, J. M., & Hallahan, D. P. (Eds.). (2005). *The illusion of full inclusion: A comprehensive critique of a current special education bandwagon* (2nd ed.). Austin, TX: PRO-ED.

Kauffman, J. M., & Landrum, T. J. (2009). *Characteristics of emotional and behavioral disorders of children and youth* (9th ed.). Upper Saddle River, NJ: Prentice Hall.

Kauffman, J. M., Simpson, R. L., & Mock, D. R. (2009). Problems related to underservice: A rejoinder. *Behavioral Disorders, 34,* 172–180.

Kern, L., Hilt-Panahon, A., & Sokol, N. G. (2009). Further examining the triangle tip: Improving support for students with emotional and behavioral needs. *Psychology in the Schools, 46,* 18–32.

Landrum, T. J., Tankersley, M., & Kauffman, J. M. (2003). What is special about special education or students with emotional or behavioral disorders? *Journal of Special Education, 37,* 148–156.

Lane, K. L., Wehby, J. H., Little, M. A., & Cooley, C. (2005). Academic, social, and behavioral profiles of students with emotional and behavioral disorders educated in self-contained classrooms and self-contained schools: Part I – are they more alike than different? *Behavioral Disorders, 30,* 349–361.

Lewis, T. J., Jones, S., Horner, R. H., & Sugai, G. (2010). School-wide positive behavior support and students with emotional/behavioral disorders: Implications for prevention, identification and intervention. *Exceptionality, 18,* 82–93.

National Center on Education Statistics. (2001). *Public alternative schools and programs for students at risk of education failure: 2000-01.* Washington, DC: National Mental Health Advisory Council.

No Child Left Behind (NCLB) Act of 2001, Pub. L. No. 107-110, § 115, Stat. 1425 (2002).

Osher, D., Woodruff, D., & Sims, A. (2002). Schools make a difference. The relationship between education services for African American children and youth and their overrepresentation in the juvenile justice system. In D. Losen (Ed.), *Minority issues in special education* (pp. 93–116). Cambridge, MA: The Civil Rights Project, Harvard University and the Harvard Education Publishing Group.

Parrish, T. (2002). Racial disparities in the identification, funding, and provision of special education. In D. J. Losen & G. Orfield (Eds.), *Racial inequity in special education* (pp. 15–37). Cambridge, MA: Harvard Education Press.

Quinn, M. M., & Poirier, J. M. (2004). Linking prevention research with policy: Examining the costs and outcomes of the failure to prevent EBD. In R. B. Rutherford, M. M. Quinn & S. R. Mathur (Eds.), *Handbook of research in emotional and behavioral disorders* (pp. 78–97). New York: Guilford Press.

Quinn, M. M., Rutherford, R. B., Leone, P. E., Osher, D. M., & Poirier, J. M. (2005). Youth with disabilities in juvenile corrections: A national survey. *Exceptional Children, 71,* 339–345.

Reid, R., Gonzalez, J. E., Nordness, P. D., Trout, A., & Epstein, M. H. (2004). A meta-analysis of the academic status of students with emotional/behavioral disturbance. *Journal of Special Education, 38,* 130–143.

Scull, J., & Winkler, A. M. (2011). Shifting trends in special education. Retrieved from http://www.edexcellence.net/publications-issues/publications/shifting-trends-in-special.html

Silverman, W. K., Pina, A. A., & Viswesvaran, C. (2008). Evidence-based psychosocial treatments for phobic and anxiety disorders in children and adolescents. *Journal of Clinical Child and Adolescent Psychology, 37,* 105–130.

Skiba, R. J., Poloni-Staudinger, L., Gallini, S., Simmons, A. B., & Feggins-Azziz, L. R. (2006). Disparate access: The disproportionality of African American students with disabilities across educational environments. *Exceptional Children, 74,* 411–424.

Trout, A. K., Nordness, P. D., Pierce, C. D., & Epstein, M. H. (2003). Research on the academic status of children with emotional and behavioral disorders: A review of the literature from 1961 to 2000. *Journal of Emotional and Behavioral Disorders, 11,* 198–210.

U.S. Department of Education. (2009). *28th annual report to congress on the implementation of the Individuals with Disabilities Education Act.* Washington, DC: U.S. Department of Education.

U.S. Department of Health and Human Services. (1999). *Mental health: A report of the surgeon general*. Rockville, MD: U.S. Department of Health and Human Services.

Wagner, M., & Davis, M. (2006). How are we preparing students with emotional disturbances for the transition to adulthood? Findings from the National Longitudinal Transition Study-2. *Journal of Emotional and Behavioral Disorders, 14*, 86–98.

Wagner, M., Friend, M., Bursuck, W. D., Kutash, K., Duchnowski, A. J., Sumi, W. C., & Epstein, M. H. (2006). Educating student with emotional disturbances: A national perspective on school programs and services. *Journal of Emotional and Behavioral Disorders, 14*, 12–30.

Yell, M. L., & Katsiyannis, A. (2004). Placing students with disabilities in inclusive settings: Legal guidelines and preferred practices. *Preventing School Failure, 49*, 28–34.

CHAPTER 5

PLACEMENT OF CULTURALLY AND LINGUISTICALLY DIVERSE STUDENTS IN PROGRAMS FOR STUDENTS WITH EMOTIONAL AND BEHAVIORAL DISORDERS: CONTEMPORARY TRENDS AND RESEARCH NEEDS

Alfredo J. Artiles, Aydin Bal, Stanley C. Trent and Kathleen King Thorius

ABSTRACT

Little research has been conducted regarding the disproportionate representation of minority learners in programs for students with Emotional/Behavioral Disorders (E/BD). To date, the majority of the disproportionality literature examines multiple eligibility categories, most frequently the high incidence disabilities of Mild Intellectual Disabilities, E/BD, and Learning Disabilities. This chapter narrows analytical attention to a single category to add specificity and depth to

Behavioral Disorders: Identification, Assessment, and Instruction of Students with EBD
Advances in Special Education, Volume 22, 107–127
Copyright © 2012 by Emerald Group Publishing Limited
All rights of reproduction in any form reserved
ISSN: 0270-4013/doi:10.1108/S0270-4013(2012)0000022008

disproportionality knowledge through a review of the E/BD literature between 2000 and 2010. Of the 16 studies reviewed, we found 11 socio-demographic, quantitative studies that analyzed E/BD special education placement patterns or office discipline referrals for students with E/BD. Two quantitative studies explored ecological conceptualizations of behavioral problems to understand interactions between institutions' special education eligibility processes, and socio-cultural and spatial contexts of schools. Finally, we located three studies that targeted families' perceptions of student behavior, and professionals' biases related to disproportionality. We conclude with reflections about what the current literature suggests as necessary for the next generation of research on this important topic.

Keywords: Emotional and behavioral disorders; minority students; disproportionality; research trends; systemic literature review

This chapter covers contemporary trends on placement patterns that affect culturally and linguistically diverse (CLD) students in emotional/ behavioral disorders (E/BD) programs. The problem space with which we are concerned is generally defined as research on the disproportionate representation of diverse students in special education (Skiba et al., 2008). Surprisingly, although there has been an increase in the number of studies on this topic, the bulk of this research is relatively recent (Waitoller, Artiles, & Cheney, 2010). The majority of studies as well as the reviews and critiques of this knowledge base examine multiple categories, most frequently the high incidence disabilities (i.e., mild intellectual disabilities [MID], E/BD, and learning disabilities [LD]) (e.g., Artiles, Trent, & Palmer, 2004; Trent, 2010). LD and African American students have received the most attention in this literature (Waitoller et al., 2010). Analytic attention to a single disability category would enable researchers to scrutinize specific aspects and dimensions of a particular disability (e.g., definitional issues, etiological debates, and intervention designs). It would also add specificity and depth to the study of this problem. This chapter represents a first step in this direction. First, we contextualize E/BD disproportionality with discussions about why this is a problem and how it has been studied. Next, we discuss the contemporary evidence on this topic. We conclude with reflections about the next generation of research on this important topic.

WHY IS DISPROPORTIONALITY A PROBLEM?

The struggle for the passage of a federal special education law gained momentum, in part, in the aftermath of civil right victories for African Americans. The 1975 federal law granted rights, and thus, access to services and entitlements to children and youth with disabilities. Ironically, the problem of racial disproportionality in disability identification patterns lies at the heart of struggles that have defined and shaped the identity of the special education field. Specifically, special education was created out of equity concerns for the rights of people with disabilities, but even before 1975, the special education field and advocates for CLD learners were mindful of inequities linked to social, cultural, linguistic, and racial differences as reflected in the law's inclusion of nondiscriminatory clauses.

Over time, the special education field's equity struggles moved from a concern with educational *rights and access* for this population to deliberations about *reproduction* of historical inequities for certain subgroups (e.g., racial minorities), and to reforms and debates about *participation and outcomes* for students with disabilities (e.g., access to the general education curriculum, academic outcomes, and post-secondary outcomes).[1] The controversy about the reproduction of inequities for racial minorities as indexed by the disproportionate placement in certain disability categories has increased in the past decade, and culminated in the inclusion of monitoring and intervention mandates to address this problem in the 2004 re-authorization of IDEA. First, this re-authorization requires that each state determine the level of significant disproportionality based on a technical assistance guide furnished by the U.S Department of Education. Second, if significant disproportionality exists in a school district, the district must review identification policies and practices to ensure that they are in compliance with IDEA and make these revisions accessible to the public. Third, states are now required to monitor each local educational agency's (LEAs) level of disproportionality annually under its 6-year State Performance Plan (SPP). Lastly, states may require LEA's to use 15% of Part B of IDEA funds to develop interventions to address disproportionality (U.S. Department of Education, 2007).

A central concern in this debate and part of the reason for monitoring has been the specter of false positives. That is, to what extent are racial minority students misidentified? Attention to false negatives, which is equally problematic, has been negligible. On the one hand, the evidence on the disproportionate representation of these students is compelling; members of racial minority groups have a significantly higher chance to be identified in the high incidence disability categories (Donovan & Cross, 2002). The evidence on misidentification, on the other hand, is mixed, and theoretical and methodological considerations bear on this evidence (Artiles, Kozleski, Trent, Osher, & Ortiz, 2010). Not surprisingly, social class has often been blamed for the disproportionate number of CLD students in special education. There is evidence, nevertheless, that suggests race can play a key role in placement practices, sometimes even after statistically controlling for student social class (Skiba et al., 2008). For instance, student racial minority status is a significant special education placement predictor; racial minority students receive fewer related services, and are placed in more segregated programs than White students with the same diagnosis (Skiba et al., 2008). Moreover, special education placement has lasting consequences for students that include higher risk for school dropout, lower graduation rates, and more negative post-school outcomes than students without disabilities. For these reasons, it has been argued that racial disproportionality tends to reproduce (if not compound) inequities for minorities that are observed in other areas of their educational and societal experiences such as lower quality schools and teachers, and limited access to labor and housing opportunities (Artiles, 2011).

The last consideration in addressing the question, why is disproportionality a problem?, is related to opportunity to learn and educational progress. In other words, disproportionality constitutes a problem if special education placement is due to poor instruction in general education and if special education program quality interferes with student educational progress (Heller, Holtzman, & Messick, 1982).

Overview of the Problem

Disproportionate representation is defined as "the extent to which membership in a given [racial, ethnic, linguistic] group affects the probability of being placed in a specific disability category" (Oswald, Coutinho, Best, & Singh, 1999; p. 198). The problem has been present in the special education literature for at least 43 years (Artiles et al., 2010). It entails over- and under-representation of racial minority students, particularly boys; the former in high incidence disabilities, and the latter in gifted and talented programs. There is a slow growth in studies that examine this problem as it affects English language learners (ELLs) (Artiles, Waitoller, & Neal, 2011). *At the national level*, African Americans are most affected particularly in the E/BD and MID categories. Native American students are the second most affected group in LD programs. Other disproportionality patterns are observed by racial or linguistic group and by disability category when the placement data are examined *at the regional, state, or district levels* (Artiles et al., 2004).

The available disproportionality research evidence paints a complex picture in which interactional effects are the norm. Investigators have pursued at least three kinds of explanations for this problem, namely the role of professional practices (e.g., bias), the effects of socio-demographic factors (e.g., poverty and race), and a sociological/critical model in which the role of power in racial inequities is examined (Waitoller et al., 2010). The model that has informed the majority of studies is related to professional practices. Specifically, this line of inquiry was concerned with "professional practices carried out to determine a child's disability diagnosis. These studies addressed individuals' biases in referrals and student perceptions, assessment issues, other beliefs, and decision-making processes in eligibility team meetings" (Waitoller et al., 2010, p. 39). In turn, the socio-demographic model aims to identify "a set of factors, such as environmental, socio-demographic, health, economic, and academic variables, that relate to children's educational outcomes and special education placement" (p. 36). Socio-demographic factors in previous studies include poverty levels of schools and communities, families and student traits (e.g., number of parents, social class, and level of education). An example of a sociological approach is a study that examined whether a history of school desegregation court orders in a district was associated with disproportionality patterns (Eitle, 2002).

E/BD Disproportionality: A Closer Look

We review in this section recent evidence on E/BD disproportionality. Before we summarize this research, however, we outline the methods used to locate this work.

Article Selection
The literature review focused on disproportionality studies in the field of E/BD published between 2000 and 2010. We followed a two-step process in the selection of articles, namely preliminary selection and criteria-based selection. The term "disproportionality" referred to practices and referral processes in both special education and discipline programs (i.e., office discipline referrals [ODRs]). ODRs were included because discipline

interventions (e.g., the use of in-and-out-of-school suspension and expulsion) are used to a significant degree to address rule infractions and, "this practice often has a disproportionate impact on Black, Latino, and American Indian students" (Gregory, Skiba, & Noguera, 2010, p. 59). Gregory et al. suspect that high rates of suspensions and expulsions may contribute to the gaps in academic achievement for CLD learners. To be able to understand the extent of CLD disproportionality in E/BD more comprehensively, we chose to include studies on racial disparities in ODRs for CLD students with E/BD identification. The term "CLD" refers to non-White students.

Preliminary Selection
The first phase of the review included a search for general disproportionality studies in peer-reviewed journals. To conduct the literature search, we used three databases: Web of Science, Psych Info, and Google Scholar. To identify disproportionality studies during this time period, these electronic databases were searched by using keywords with the following combinations: (emotional behavioral disability *or* emotional disorder *or* behavioral disorder *or* EBD) *and* (disproportionality *or* overrepresentation *or* special education, office discipline referral *or* referral) *and*, (minority *or* African American, *or* Native American *or* American Indian, *or* Asian American *or* Latino *or* Hispanic). Studies were selected provisionally if the study was related to disproportionality. The studies ranged in scope and included those that focused on different special education subgroups (e.g., LD and MID), different geographic areas (e.g., suburban and rural), and multiple racial categories (e.g., African American and Latino). Next, we conducted reference and footnote searches in the most recent systematic literature review on empirical studies on minority overrepresentation by Waitoller et al. (2010). References were crosschecked with the articles we located through our systematic search to ensure all current studies were included. The preliminary selection phase resulted in 83 studies that focused on disproportionality.

Criteria-Based Selection
For the second step of article selection, we established four criteria to select studies for this review. In the criteria-based selection phase, we selected articles if they:

1. reported primary or secondary data analysis on CLD students' disproportionate representation in either (a) special education referral or placement in the E/BD category or (b) ODRs;
2. used quantitative, qualitative, or mixed research methods;

3. were published between 2000 and 2010; and
4. were published in peer-reviewed journals.

Each study identified in the initial search was examined against these criteria to determine, for example, if students with E/BD were included in the sample or if the issues addressed in the study were directly and explicitly related to the E/BD category. For example, we eliminated three studies (Klingner & Harry, 2006; Skiba, Michael, Nardo, & Peterson, 2002; Skiba, Poloni-Staudinger, Gallini, Simmons, & Feggins-Azziz, 2006a). Although those studies investigated the role of race or language status of CLD students with academic and behavioral difficulties in special education referral or in ODRs, they did not directly study CLD students with E/BD. For example, Klingner and Harry studied the special education referral and identification processes in urban schools, especially for ELLs who were struggling to read. Although 4 of the 12 ELLs whom they worked with were identified with some behavioral problems, their unit of concern was the workings of the Child Study Teams in ELL identification with LD.

On the contrary, in this review, we selected two articles from the same authors who used the data from the same large ethnographic study they conducted. As a result, we selected 16 studies that met these criteria and sorted them into three categories (see the references section for the selected studies with an asterisk). The first category of studies represents a socio-demographic approach ($n = 11$). This category includes disproportionality studies that analyzed students' special education placement in the E/BD category or ODRs. These studies used socio-demographic characteristics of individuals and the environments and families from which those individuals came as independent variables. The second category represents an ecological approach. It consists of studies ($n = 2$) focusing on socio-cultural processes from an ecologically situated perspective to understand how those processes reproduce patterns of minority disproportionality in LEAs. The last set includes studies on school professionals' and caregivers' beliefs and perspectives regarding etiology of students' behavioral problems as well as school professionals' biases in EBD referral, identification, and placement practices ($n = 3$).

The selected studies were further categorized to code descriptive methodological characteristics. For this purpose, an excel file was created that contained the following categories: methodology, participants, sample size range, racial groups, unit(s) of concern (i.e., dependent variables in quantitative studies such as special education placement), type of data (e.g., student scores on normative academic tests or interview transcripts), level of analysis, and data analysis methods (Table 1).

Table 1. Descriptive Features of Selected E/BD Disproportionality Studies.

Descriptive Feature	All Studies (n = 16)	Socio-Demographic (n = 11)	Ecological (n = 2)	Perceptions/ Biases (n = 3)
Methodology				
QUAL	3		2	1
QUAN	13	11		2
MIXED				
Sample				
Students with E/BD	10	10		
Students with E/BD and school professionals	1			1
Care givers	1			1
Child study teams	1			1
Students with E/BD and care givers	1	1		
Students with E/BD, caregivers, and school professionals	2		2	
Sample range				
Students with E/BD	4 – all students federal level in a given school year	234 – all students federal level in a given school year	4	769
School professionals	24–769		24	769
Care givers	4–1,019		4	1,019
Child study teams	2 teams (8–16 people)			2 teams (8–16 people)
Schools	12		12	
District	1–14,645	1–14,645		
Racial group				
AA, Latino, and White	3	1	2	
AA and White	1			1
AA and all other federal racial categories	3	3		
AA, Latino, Asian American, and White	1			1
All federal racial categories	8	8		
Unit of concern				
SPED referral for E/BD	1			1
SPED placement for E/BD	8	7		1
SPED referral for E/BD and SPED placement for E/BD	3		2	1
SPED placement for E/BD and ORDs	2	2		
SPED placement for E/BD and access to LREs	2	2		
Type of data				
SD and SE	4	4		
SD, SE, and academic data	2	2		
SD, SE, academic data, and behavioral data	1	1		

Table 1. (*Continued*)

Descriptive Feature	All Studies (n = 16)	Socio-Demographic (n = 11)	Ecological (n = 2)	Perceptions/ Biases (n = 3)
SD, SE, and surveys	1			1
SD, SE, and behavioral data	1	1		
SD, behavioral data, and surveys	1			1
Field notes, interviews, meeting transcripts, and documents	3		2	1
SD, SE, and access to LREs	2	2		
SD, SE, academic, and behavioral data, access to LREs, interviews, and survey	1	1		
Variables included				
Student level and family level	2	2		
Student level and school level	1	1		
Student, family, and school level	2		2	
Child study team level	1			1
District level	2			2
County level	1	1		
Student level and school professional level	1	1		
Student level and district level	1	1		
State level and district level	1	1		
Individual state level	2	2		
State level and regional	2	2		
Methods of analysis				
Inferential statistics	6	5		1
Grounded theory	2		2	
Discourse analysis	1			1
Descriptive statistics and inferential statistics	5	5		
Inferential statistics and interview analysis	1	1		
Descriptive statistics, inferential statistics, and longitudinal analysis	1	1		

Notes: QUAL, qualitative research methodologies; QUAN, quantitative research methodologies; MIXED, mixed or multiple research methodology; E/BD, emotional or behavioral disorder; AA, African-American; SPED, special education; LRE, least restrictive environment; SD, socio-demographic; SE, socioeconomic; behavioral data: Data on E/BD symptomatology and/or behavioral difficulties; academic data: Data on normative test scores and/or grades.

E/BD Interventions

Because this volume covers the current status of various topics related to E/BD, as well as solutions, the final phase of the search focused on major literature reviews on interventions for children and youth with E/BD. This search was limited to literature reviews and studies that included meta-analyses. Google Scholar was used for this portion of the literature review. The search terms "intervention," *and* (EBD, *or* emotional disability, *or* disorder) *and* review *or* meta-analysis were used. This search yielded an additional 20 systematic reviews of E/BD interventions. We examined these reviews to identify interventions conducted to prevent, address, and/or change disproportionality in the E/BD category. We found only one review (Serpell, Hayling, Stevenson, & Kern, 2009) that focused on racial minority students (i.e., African American learners).

E/BD DISPROPORTIONALITY RESEARCH: CONTEMPORARY TRENDS

Fig. 1 presents the frequency of research articles on E/BD disproportionality published between 2000 and 2010. Notice the number of publications per year is very low, with a maximum of four studies published in 2005. We also identified an upward trend in publications between 2000 and 2005, which then changed to a noticeable decline in publication output for the next three years (until 2008). A small upward trend is observed in the past two years of the period under review. The overall pattern in the number

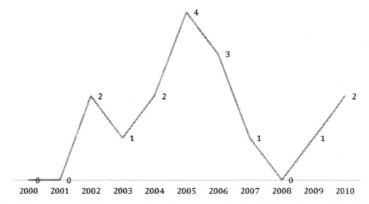

Fig. 1. Frequency of Disproportionality Research Articles by Year of Publication.

of disproportionality studies published in the past decade has been twofold. First, we found a small research output on this topic, and second, the research community's attention to this problem has been unstable with alternating increases and decreases in the number of publications.

The identified research on racial disparities in the E/BD category aligns in some respects to the broader disproportionality literature in the high incidence disability categories. For instance, most studies ($n = 11$) are grounded in a socio-demographic model, though we also found a small number of studies categorized as ecologically oriented ($n = 2$), and studies focusing on perceptions/biases ($n = 3$).

Socio-Demographic Studies

Socio-demographic research aims to analyze students' special education placement in the E/BD category or ODRs for students with E/BD. The socio-demographic studies were grounded in a quantitative paradigm (with a reliance on descriptive and inferential statistical methods) (see Table 1). Among them, seven studies used multilevel analyses. Socio-demographic study had a wide range of sample sizes – i.e., from 234 students to all students with E/BD in the nation in a given school year (e.g., 2000–2001 school year). The majority of studies relied on secondary analyses on national data sources such as the U.S. Department of Education Office for Civil Rights (Coutinho & Oswald, 2005; Coutinho, Oswald, Best, & Forness, 2002; Hosp & Reschly, 2004), multiple reports of the federal government (Zhang & Katsiyannis, 2002) as well as the data drawn from individual states, more specifically Indiana and Maryland (Krezmien, Leone, & Achilles, 2006; Skiba et al., 2006b), San Diego county (Gudino, Lau, Yeh, McCabe, & Hough, 2009), and district (De Valenzuela, Copeland, Qi, & Park, 2006; Skiba, Poloni-Staudinger, Simmons, Feggings-Azziz, & Chung, 2005). The range in districts involved in these studies also varied widely from 1 to over 14,000. For instance, De Valenzuela et al. (2006) studied the relationship between student race/ethnicity and language proficiency and special education placement and services provided within a large urban school district of a Southwestern state. The majority of these studies focused on student characteristics with E/BD, though the socio-economic and demographic characteristics of caregivers, school professionals, and child study teams were also included. Only one selected study included students, caregivers, and school professionals as participants. Most studies included student socio-economic (e.g., eligibility for free and reduced lunch and household income) and socio-demographic (e.g., race/ethnicity) variables, as well as student behavior and academic-related variables. For instance, in their data analysis of the Early Childhood Longitudinal Study, Hibel, Farkas, and Morgan (2010) used the average of a student's test scores in reading and math on a standardized kindergarten entry exam. From an analytical perspective, these studies focused on a variety of levels, though most were concerned with the individual student and their families or regional or state levels of analysis (see Table 1). Most research studies were comprehensive in the racial/ethnic groups included since eight encompassed all federal categories, and a few articles targeted several racial groups (e.g., White, African American, and Latino) (see Table 1).

Eight of the 11 socio-demographic studies were concerned with obtaining insights about the variables associated with minority students' E/BD identification rates. One socio-demographic study (Skiba et al., 2006a, 2006b) investigated what happens after minority students are identified with E/BD in terms of their access to least restrictive environments (LREs) as well as their disproportionate representation in the E/BD category. They found that in the state of Indiana, the risk of E/BD identification for African American students was more than twice that of all other students during the 2001–2002 school year. Moreover, African American students were disproportionally overrepresented (almost three times as likely) in more restrictive school settings (i.e., spending more than 60% of the school being excluded from social and learning opportunities in general education classrooms). Lastly, two studies (Achilles, McLaughlin, & Croninger, 2007; Krezmien et al., 2006) examined the disparities in schools' disciplinary exclusion practices (suspension and expulsion) for minority students and students with disabilities, including E/BD. Achilles and colleagues found that African American students and students with E/BD and ADHD disproportionately face disciplinary exclusion. Their findings complemented the findings of the other socio-demographic studies and further demonstrated the complexity in unequal identification and placement patterns for CLD students, specifically for African American students in urban educational settings where the majority of CLD students are educated.

The picture that emerges from these studies is complex with numerous interactions among school location, student race, and socio-demographic factors such as the representation of racial or socio-economic groups in schools. For instance, Coutinho et al. (2002) found that African American and Latino male students were at a lower risk for E/BD identification in schools with a high CLD enrollment compared to those enrolled in schools with a high White student enrollment. On the other hand, the higher levels of non-White student enrolment (i.e., 60% and up) dramatically increased Native American students risk for E/BD identification.

Ecological Studies

The E/BD disproportionality research coded as ecological included only two studies (Harry, Klingner & Hart, 2005; Hart, Cramer, Harry, Klingner, & Sturges, 2010). Both articles are based on a large qualitative study conducted in 12 schools in the Southeastern U.S. The articles included four students with E/BD and their families, and White, Latino, and African American students were represented in the sample. A wide range of evidence was collected that included field notes, interviews, school records, meeting transcripts, etc. A grounded theory approach was used to analyze the data and the analytic process focused on students and families as well as the school level. Overall, these studies suggest an ecological conceptualization of behavioral problems to understand the dynamic interactions between the institutional decisions of special education referral and identification, and the socio-cultural and spatial contexts where social representation, power/privilege, and the educational ideologies of the medical paradigm pervade. It was argued that complex culturally situated processes influence disproportionate representation of CLD students in remedial and special education programs, as well as the opportunities and outcome gaps between CLD students and their counterparts. Although the number of studies framed from this perspective is small, they had important implications for ontology and epistemology in the E/BD field. Hart et al. (2010) proposed E/BD disproportionality research should move from "decontextualized" approaches to study the disruptive behaviors of students interpreted on a troubling to troubled continuum in the natural environments where those behaviors occur.

Studies Focusing on Perceptions/Biases

The last group of studies ($n = 3$) targeted perceptions or beliefs of students and families, and biases of professionals. One study addressed beliefs of caregivers about the cause of their children's impairments (Yeh, Forness, Ho, McCabe, & Hough, 2004) to explore the relationship between caregivers' explanatory etiologies and minority disproportionality in E/BD service use for a group of students identified as "at-risk." The study included four racial groups (White, African American, Latino, and Asian) and the evidence used included socio-demographic factors (e.g., age, gender, and family income) and two parent-report surveys (the Child Behavior Checklist and the Beliefs About the Causes of Child Problems). The study showed that parental beliefs about personality and the child's difficulty with relationships may explain minority children's enrollment in E/BD programs in this study when controlling for symptom severity and socio-demographic factors.

The two other studies examined bias in assessment and eligibility decisions (Cullinan & Kauffman, 2005; Knotek, 2003). The former study examined whether professionals ratings of children's behavioral character- istics would be moderated by child's race. They found teachers' perceptions of behavioral problems varied depending on the five characteristics of the children's emotional and behavioral difficulties (inability to learn, relation- ship problems, inappropriate behaviors, unhappiness or depression, phy- sical symptoms or fears and socially maladjusted). Overall, Cullinan and Kauffman found that student race and the race of the professionals who rated students' behavior did not have any significant effects on African American students' identification with any of the E/BD characteristics. Yet, in a micro-ethnographic analysis of fairness and objectivity among members of multidisciplinary problem-solving teams in two rural schools, Knotek (2003) documented the complexity of the social construction of difference at the intersections of race, income, and disorder. The Knotek study showed how biases covertly "creep into" the problem-solving processes even though racial biases were not apparently visible. This was found to be the case specifically when students were from low-income families and socially positioned as "at-risk" of having E/BD.

STUDIES ON INTERVENTIONS FOR MINORITY STUDENTS WITH OR AT-RISK FOR E/BD

Very little research has been conducted to reduce the disproportionate representation of minority learners in programs for students with E/BD. We found one literature review focused on this issue. In this article, Serpell et al. (2009) reviewed the research to determine what school-based interventions had been developed to address the needs of African American adolescent boys with E/BD. These authors found one intervention study that was designed to increase the rate of school completion among urban high school students with E/BD (Sinclair, Christenson, & Thurlow, 2005). Of the African American students in the sample, 82% were male. Students were randomly assigned to a treatment or control group and the majority of them were followed for four years. In addition, a subsample was followed for five years. The intervention, called "check and connect," maximizes student contact with monitors who check their success indicators (e.g., attendance and assignment completion) and collaborate with school personnel to help students connect with the school experience in meaningful and relevant ways. Over time, students in the treatment group had lower rates of transience and dropout than their counterparts in the control group. Also treatment group students attended school more regularly and their transition plans were more comprehensive.

Serpell et al. recommended that, "interventions, supports, and services address both socio-demographic factors and contextual variables in order to adequately address the needs of African American males with EBD" (p. 325). These recommendations were based on research that focused on teacher bias and perceived discriminatory encounters among African American males. They also recommended the development, implementation, and study of interventions that incorporated activities and themes emanating from, "African American meaning systems" (p. 326). Other researchers have echoed such recommendations to address the disproportionate representation of minority students in E/BD programs and high incidence programs in general. For example, Harris-Murri, King, & Rostenberg (2006) recommended that culturally responsive instructional practices be incorporated into RTI models designed to reduce the disproportionality of minority students in E/BD programs. However, the message from the review of the disproportionality intervention literature is clear: this line of inquiry has been neglected, largely due to missed opportunities. As Serpell et al. explained (see also Donovan & Cross, 2002; Waitoller et al., 2010),

> Intervention studies of children with EBD often include a relatively large sample of African Americans, but results are rarely disaggregated by race or ethnicity [...] A recent review of over 40 journals examining intervention outcomes for adolescents with EBD [...] yielded 160 studies, none of which included measures related to racial or ethnic identity, in spite of the fact that 72 studies reported having African American adolescents in the sample. (Serpell, Hayling, Stevenson, & Kern, 2009; p. 324)

CONCLUSION

Our findings reveal that since 2000, few studies have addressed the disproportionate placement of minority students in E/BD programs. However, the number of studies addressing this issue has been on the upswing since

2008. A socio-demographic model was used to frame 11 of the studies, 2 were ecologically oriented, and 3 focused on student and family perceptions and biases.

Quantitative methods were used in the socio-demographic studies and studies that addressed student and family perceptions (e.g., descriptive and inferential statistics, surveys, and checklists). In general, we found missed opportunities in this work since many studies included culturally diverse samples, though most research questions and data analysis procedures did not advance our understanding about cultural processes or influences that mediated the disproportionality problem. We refer to "cultural processes or influences" from a socio-cultural perspective in which the notion of culture transcends people's backgrounds or traits, and stress instead everyday practices of communities and institutions. An implication of adopting this theoretical perspective is to transcend the search for (racial-ethnic-linguistic) group-specific interventions and methods. Instead, a socio-cultural perspective focuses on the ways in which groups' cultural practices intersect/interact with the cultural practices of institutions and classrooms.

In addition, the multiple interactions identified in this emerging work affirm the need to study disproportionality with designs that enable researchers to delve into the complexities of this problem (e.g., multilevel designs and ethnographic studies). Moreover, it is urgent that this research offer more detailed information about the students' needs and disabilities included in these studies since little information was provided about the E/BD of these students. Attention to these aspects promises to enhance discussions in the E/BD field about definitional and etiological considerations as they intersect with cultural forces (both group- and institutionally based).

Qualitative methods were used in the two studies that were designed to explore the complexities of disproportionality from an ecological perspective. Data collected in these studies included field notes, interviews, school records, and meeting transcripts. The designs of these studies were informed by culture theory and represent an attempt to transcend a deficit model when addressing disproportionality. Overall, however, the bulk of the research reported in this review tends to rely on a more static view of students' experiences, institutional processes, and cultural practices. Furthermore, the sample sizes of studies that explored disproportionality from an ecological perspective were small, making it difficult to generalize results to the population of minority students with E/BD.

Our results have led us to ask the question, What changes do we need to make in the research questions asked, instruments created, and designs used to study the disproportionality of minority students in E/BD programs in ways that might lead to more positive outcomes? We have concluded that all of the categories of studies that we analyzed in this review are necessary to paint a clearer picture of this problem and to address it in a comprehensive manner. There continues to be a need for studies that explore the relationship between socio-demographic factors and E/BD placement. Studies that examine perceptions and beliefs among students, parents, and teachers are also warranted. Studies that explore disproportionality from an ecological/contextual perspective are needed as well. In this vein, we propose that a cultural ecological approach be used as an overarching framework to guide future disproportionality studies in the area of E/BD. Within this context, minority students are not seen as the primary unit of analysis. Instead, these students are placed within the context of schools and the unit of analysis is the interplay between the students and everyone who has been charged to meet their educational needs (e.g., parents, educators, and other agencies). As Trent (2010) stated:

> Learning does not occur in a vacuum, but within situated contexts; and these contexts shape how students view themselves and how others view them. If others' acknowledged or unacknowledged beliefs about students are adversely influenced by culturally based constructs grounded in pathology, their experiences in school may lead to less than desired results. In fact, results may be injurious. (p. 777)

These types of studies would move the field beyond deficit and cultural incongruity theories and lead to a deeper understanding of how societal factors (e.g., prevailing social norms) may influence school practices with minority students with or at risk for E/BD placement. Researchers using a cultural-ecological approach, which would include components of all three categories identified in this review, might ask the following research questions (see also Artiles, Kozleski, Waitoller, & Lukinbeal, in press):

1. How are students viewed by educators?
2. How are educators viewed by parents and students?
3. How do educators' beliefs about students and parents influence student behavioral and academic outcomes?
4. Conversely, how do student and parent beliefs about educators influence student behavioral and academic outcomes?
5. What are the levels of risk for the students in the home, school, and community contexts?
6. Do these risk factors influence students' behavior in school and if so, how?
7. How do educators interpret and respond to these behaviors?

8. What are alternative reasons that might explain student behaviors?
9. What antecedents precede these behaviors?
10. In what ways do parents, community leaders, and governmental agencies interact with the school?
11. What are the desired outcomes for all members of the system?
12. What instructional tools and processes are used to accomplish these outcomes?
13. What instruments are used to measure student and teacher outcomes?

Data would be collected longitudinally using both quantitative and qualitative methods. For example, quantitative instruments for students might include measures to assess how their behavior across different contexts is affected by their self-reported coping strategies (Spencer, Fegley, Harpalani, & Seaton, 2004). Qualitative measures might include video of students across settings (e.g., school, afterschool programs, and home) to confirm or disconfirm self-report data. An intervention might include discussions with students about their perceived coping strategies and review of video data to identify the antecedents and consequences of behavior across settings and their perceptions about their behaviors and the behaviors of their students, educators, siblings, and/or parents. Students and educators could then use results to develop more efficient coping strategies that would be monitored and generalized across settings.

Concurrent with this research would be individual and collective self-study among educators to recursively assess effectiveness of instructional methods and processes and their self-efficacy related to teaching students from minority backgrounds with behavior problems. Regular recorded study group sessions would be analyzed to determine patterns in discourse and activities that lead to or thwart improvements in behavioral and academic outcomes. Standardized scales could be administered to teachers to determine if their beliefs about students and their perceived efficacy to teach them influences behavioral and academic outcomes (Pigott & Cowen, 2000). Triangulation of student and teacher data over time, especially if desirable outcomes ensue, may mediate educators' thinking and activities in schools and classrooms. We contend that studies of this nature are needed if we believe that the disproportionality of minority students in E/BD programs is problematic. In taking this stance, we acknowledge the fact that many of these students live in environments that place them at risk for school failure. However, at the same time, we contend that cultural norms and practices within schools also place these students at risk. We agree with Harry et al. (2005) and Hart et al. (2010) that researchers must move beyond traditional inquiry methods that seek to control for context and begin to study disruptive student behaviors within the contexts where they occur. In so doing, we may be able to unravel the complexities of educating these students and create, implement, replicate, and sustain interventions that result in higher levels of achievement and success beyond the K-12 experience.

NOTE

1. A discussion about equity debates in the special education field on participation and outcomes is beyond the scope of this chapter (see McLaughlin, 2010 for a discussion on this topic); we focus instead on the debates germane to racial disparities.

ACKNOWLEDGMENT

The first author acknowledges the support of the Equity Alliance at ASU under the Office of Elementary and Secondary Education's grant #S004D080027. Funding agency's endorsement of the ideas expressed in this manuscript should not be inferred.

REFERENCES

* Studies selected for the literature review are identified with an asterisk.

Achilles, G. M., McLaughlin, M. J., & Croninger, R. G. (2007). Sociocultural correlates of disciplinary exclusion among students with emotional, behavioral, and learning disabilities in the SEELS national dataset. *Journal of Emotional & Behavioral Disorders, 15*(1), 33–45.

Artiles, A. J. (2011, April). *Toward an interdisciplinary understanding of educational inequity and difference: The case of the racialization of ability.* Wallace Foundation Distinguished Lecture. Annual meeting of the American Educational Research Association. New Orleans, LA.

Artiles, A. J., Kozleski, E., Trent, S., Osher, D., & Ortiz, A. (2010). Justifying and explaining disproportionality, 1968–2008: A critique of underlying views of culture. *Exceptional Children, 76,* 279–299.

Artiles, A. J., Kozleski, E. B., Waitoller, F., & Lukinbeal, C. (in press). Inclusive education and the interlocking of ability and race in the U.S.: Notes for an educational equity research program. In A. J. Artiles, E. B. Kozleski, & F. Waitoller (Eds.), *Inclusive education: Examining equity on five continents.* Cambridge, MA: Harvard Education Press.

Artiles, A. J., Trent, S. C., & Palmer, J. (2004). Culturally diverse students in special education: Legacies and prospects. In J. A. Banks & C. M. Banksm (Eds.), *Handbook of research on multicultural education* (2nd ed, pp. 716–735). San Francisco, CA: Jossey Bass.

Artiles, A. J., Waitoller, F., & Neal, R. (2011). Grappling with the intersection of language and ability differences: Equity issues for Chicano/Latino students in special education. In R. R. Valencia (Ed.), *Chicano school failure and success: Past, present, and future* (3rd ed, pp. 213–234). London: Routledge/Falmer.

*Coutinho, M. J., & Oswald, D. P. (2005). State variation in gender disproportionality in special education. *Remedial & Special Education, 26*(1), 7–15.

*Coutinho, M. J., Oswald, D. P., Best, A. M., & Forness, S. R. (2002). Gender and socio demographic factors and the disproportionate identification of culturally and linguistically diverse students with emotional disturbance. *Behavioral Disorders, 27*(2), 109–125.

*Cullinan, D., & Kauffman, J. M. (2005). Do race of student and race of teacher influence ratings of emotional and behavioral problem characteristics of students with emotional disturbance? *Behavioral Disorders, 30*(4), 392–402.

*De Valenzuela, J. S., Copeland, S. R., Qi, C. H., & Park, M. (2006). Examining educational equity: Revisiting the disproportionate representation of minority students in special education. *Exceptional Children, 72*(4), 425–441.

Donovan, M. S., & Cross, C. T. (Eds.). (2002). *Minority students in special and gifted education.* Washington, DC: National Academies Press.

Eitle, T. M. (2002). Special education or racial segregation: Understanding variation in the representation of Black students in educable mentally handicapped programs. *Sociological Quarterly, 43*(4), 575–605.

Gregory, A., Skiba, R. J., & Noguera, P. A. (2010). The achievement gap and the discipline gap: Two sides of the same coin? *Educational Leadership, 39*(1), 59–68.

*Gudino, O. G., Lau, A. S., Yeh, M., McCabe, K. M., & Hough, R. L. (2009). Understanding racial/ethnic disparities in youth mental health services: Do disparities vary by problem type? *Journal of Emotional and Behavioral Disorders, 17*, 3–16.

Harris-Murri, N., King, K. A., & Rostenberg, D. (2006). Reducing disproportionate minority representation in special education programs for students with emotional disturbances: Toward a culturally responsive response to intervention model. *Education and Treatment of Children, 29*(4), 779–799.

*Harry, B., Klingner, J., & Hart, J. (2005). African-American families under fire: Ethnographic views of families' strengths. *Remedial and Special Education, 12*(2), 101–112.

*Hart, J., Cramer, E., Harry, B., Klingner, J., & Sturges, K. (2010). The continuum of "troubling" to "troubled" behavior. *Remedial and Special Education, 31*(3), 148–162.

Heller, K. A., Holtzman, W. H., & Messick, S. (Eds.). (1982). *Placing children in special education: A strategy for equity.* Washington, DC: National Academy Press.

*Hibel, J., Farkas, G., & Morgan, P. (2010). Who is placed in special education? *Sociology of Education, 83*, 312–333.

*Hosp, J. L., & Reschly, D. J. (2004). Disproportionate representation of minority students in special education: Academic, demographic, and economic predictors. *Exceptional Children, 70*(2), 185–199.

Klingner, J. K., & Harry, B. (2006). The special education referral and the decision-making process for English language learners: Child study team meetings and placement conferences. *Teachers College Record, 108*(11), 2247–2281.

*Knotek, S. (2003). Bias in problem solving and the social process of student study team: A qualitative investigation. *Journal of Special Education, 37*(1), 2–14.

*Krezmien, M. P., Leone, P. E., & Achilles, G. M. (2006). Suspension, race, and disability: Analysis of statewide practices and reporting. *Journal of Emotional & Behavioral Disorders, 14*(4), 217–226.

McLaughlin, M. (2010). Evolving interpretations of educational equity and students with disabilities. *Exceptional Children, 76*, 265–278.

Oswald, D. P., Coutinho, M. J., Best, A. M., & Singh, N. (1999). Ethnic representation in special education: The influence of school- related economic and demographic variables. *Journal of Special Education, 32*, 194–206.

Pigott, R. L., & Cowen, E. L. (2000). Teacher, child race, racial congruence, and teacher ratings of children's school adjustment. *Journal of School Psychology, 38*, 177–196.

Serpell, Z., Hayling, C. C., Stevenson, H., & Kern, L. (2009). Cultural considerations in the development of school-based interventions for African American Adolescent boys with emotional and behavioral disorders. *Journal of Negro Education, 78*(3), 321–332.

Sinclair, M. F., Christenson, S. L., & Thurlow, M. L. (2005). Promoting school completion of secondary youth with emotional or behavioral disabilities. *Exceptional Children, 71*, 465–482.

Skiba, R. J., Michael, R. S., Nardo, A. C., & Peterson, R. L. (2002). The color of discipline: Sources of racial and gender disproportionality in school punishment. *Urban Review, 34*, 317–342.

*Skiba, R. J., Poloni-Staudinger, L., Gallini, S., Simmons, A. B., & Feggins-Azziz, R. (2006a). Disparate access: The disproportionality of African American students with disabilities across educational environments. *Exceptional Children, 72*, 411–424.

*Skiba, R. J., Poloni-Staudinger, L., Simmons, A. B., Feggings-Azziz, R., & Chung, C. G. (2005). Unproven links of poverty: Can poverty explain ethnic disproportionality in special education? *Journal of Special Education, 39*(3), 130–144.

Skiba, R. J., Simmons, A. B., Ritter, S., Gibb, A. C., Rausch, M. K., & Cuadrado, J. (2008). Achieving equity in special education: History, status, and current challenges. *Exceptional Children, 74*, 264–288.

Skiba, R. J., Simmons, A. B., Ritter, S., Kohler, K., Henderson, M., & Wu, T. (2006b). The context of minority disproportionality: Practitioner perspectives on special education referral. *Teachers College Records, 108*(7), 1424–1459.

Spencer, M. B., Fegley, S. G., Harpalani, V., & Seaton, G. (2004). Understanding hypermasculinity in context: A theory-driven analysis of urban adolescent males' coping responses. *Research in Human Development, 1*(4), 229–257.

Trent, S. C. (2010). Overrepresentation of culturally and linguistically diverse students in special education. In E. Baker, P. Peterson, E. Baker & B. McGaw (Eds.), *International encyclopedia of education* (pp. 774–779). Amsterdam, The Netherlands: Elsevier.

U.S. Department of Education, Office of Special Education Programs. (2007). *Disproportionality and overrepresentation.* Retrieved from http://nichcy.org/laws/idea/legacy/module5

Waitoller, F., Artiles, A. J., & Cheney, D. (2010). The miner's canary: A review of overrepresentation research and explanations. *Journal of Special Education, 44*, 29–49.

*Yeh, M., Forness, S. R., Ho, J., McCabe, K., & Hough, R. L. (2004). Parental etiological explanations and disproportionate racial/ethnic representation in special education services for youths with emotional disturbance. *Behavioral Disorders, 29*(4), 348–358.

*Zhang, D., & Katsiyannis, A. (2002). Minority representation in special education. *Remedial & Special Education, 23*(3), 180–187.

CHAPTER 6

PREVENTION OF AND EARLY INTERVENTION FOR STUDENTS WITH EMOTIONAL AND BEHAVIORAL DISORDERS: SYSTEMS TO SUPPORT DATA-BASED DECISION MAKING

Timothy J. Lewis and Barbara S. Mitchell

ABSTRACT

Students with emotional and behavioral disorders are at great risk for long-term negative outcomes. Researchers and practitioners alike acknowledge the need for evidence-based, preventive, and early intervention strategies. Accordingly, in this chapter an expanded view of prevention is presented as a series of data driven decisions to guide provision of supports that lessen the impact of emotional/behavioral disorders (EBD). Universal screening, use of a multitiered framework, delivery of increasingly intensive support prior to chronic and persistent patterns of behavior, and continuity of service across school, home, and community settings are discussed. Specific techniques for data

Behavioral Disorders: Identification, Assessment, and Instruction of Students with EBD
Advances in Special Education, Volume 22, 129–149
Copyright © 2012 by Emerald Group Publishing Limited
All rights of reproduction in any form reserved
ISSN: 0270-4013/doi:10.1108/S0270-4013(2012)0000022009

decision-making, use of a school-based team approach, and recommendations for future research are also provided.

Keywords: School-wide positive behavior support; three-tiered models; prevention/early intervention; data decision rules; social/emotional screening

Poor outcomes for the majority of children and youth identified with emotional/behavioral disorders (EBD) are well documented within the literature (e.g., Wagner, Kutash, Duchnowski, Epstein, & Sumi, 2005) and throughout this text. For example, half of students identified as having EBD drop out before completion of high school (U.S. Department of Education, 2004). Among those who remain in school, only 42% graduate with a diploma and overall demonstrate lower academic performance than any other group of students with disabilities (Wagner et al., 2005). Beyond the challenges associated with school dropout, students experiencing EBD are also at greater risk for incarceration (National Research Council and Institute of Medicine [NRC & IOM], 2009). Alarmingly, 20% of students with EBD are arrested at least once before they leave school and over half are arrested within a few years of leaving school. Among those who have dropped out, 70% have been arrested (VanAcker, 2004). Students with EBD are also more likely to experience disappointing post-school outcomes such as unemployment, substance abuse, homelessness, inadequate social supports, and difficulties initiating and maintaining satisfactory personal relationships (NRC & IOM, 2009; Wagner et al., 2005).

Given the poor within and post-school outcomes for students with EBD, researchers, practitioners, and service providers frequently highlight the need for an increase of proactive prevention strategies within schools, homes, and communities and for provision of high-quality, evidence-based early intervention for children who may be at-risk for developing an EBD (Conroy, Hendrickson, & Hester, 2004). One difficulty in prevention and early intervention research however is establishing a clear link from effort to impact. More specifically, an inherent challenge of prevention science is the ability to document risk factors and problem behavior that *did not occur* as a result of preventing or interrupting a negative trajectory. Further compounding the issue is a lack of consensus regarding the simple question of what exactly are we "preventing?" On one hand, the focus of prevention and early intervention might be the reduction in overall number of students served under the EBD label. However, schools currently identify less than 1% of the student population as meeting criteria for service eligibility within the EBD category (U.S. Department of Education, 2006). Considering consistently low identification rates juxtaposed with much higher prevalence estimates, it is expected 5–7% of school aged students will manifest emotional or behavioral issues that require individualized supports (Kauffman, 2005), serving fewer students is not a direction in which the field should be moving.

A more desirable direction is to view prevention and early intervention for EBD as a series of steps taken to lessen the potential impact EBD has on a child's functioning. At a minimum, advancement of prevention and early intervention efforts will require communication, agreement, and collaboration among family, school, and community stakeholders; implementation of practices that currently are not widespread; and ongoing, multisystemic support at school, district, state, and national levels. In addition, reframing the concept of prevention and early intervention from a generic set of practices designed for all to a series of data-decision rules used to guide intervention selection and drive the intensity of environmental supports will be a necessary starting point. Within this conceptual framework, prevention and early intervention would include (a) regularly scheduled universal screening to detect early signs of social, emotional, and/or behavioral risk; (b) a continuum of supports across general and special education placements that facilitates rapid and effective response at the first signs of risk; (c) provision of specialized, more intensive supports before the development of chronic, persistent problems; and (d) connection of supports across school, home, and community environments.

Consider the following analogy as an example of how preventive and early intervention supports could be designed and delivered. Regardless of why patients come into contact with a medical professional, a blood pressure reading is one routine screening data point all health care providers gather every time they interact with a patient. The reading does not provide guidance for course of action; rather, it simply indicates the presence or absence of potential risk. If the patient is identified as "healthy" in terms of weight, diet, exercise, and lack of family history for high blood pressure, a high reading may simply prompt the provider to collect additional readings on a more frequent basis. The condition would be monitored to determine if the high reading was a short-term issue or something that requires additional attention. However, if the patient has a family history of high blood pressure, but is otherwise healthy, the course of treatment might again be more frequent monitoring, a stricter diet, and exercise regiment, and at some point medication to keep blood pressure within the normal range – thereby preventing other related complications. Under different conditions if, for example, the individual is morbidly overweight, has a bad diet, does not exercise, but also has no family history of high blood pressure the course of treatment most likely would be to address the mitigating factors, diet and exercise, to bring the blood pressure down, and prevent other related possible health problems such as diabetes. When risk of family history is added to the above patient, additional supports such as medication, frequent pressure monitoring, and blood tests to check for related issues (e.g., kidney or liver damage) will likely be prescribed. In each case, the response can be viewed as prevention, diet, and frequent blood tests to check for kidney damage, and early intervention, no serious organ damage to date, but risk factors combined with lifestyle will likely lead to serious health problems, even though each case needs increasingly more environmental support and monitoring. For each patient, the course of treatment began as a result of one data point indicating possible "risk." The compilation of additional issues dictated next steps that lead to simple actions such as periodic monitoring or to more comprehensive treatment such as medication, change in diet, and ongoing monitoring for related health concerns. Considering schools as an optimal location for providing preventive and early intervening supports, educators need a system similar to the medical example described. Ideally, the system is created to guide and assist practitioners through a series of clear, data-based decision procedures that starts with a screening point, includes gathering of additional relevant information, and then provides treatment matched to the data regardless of eligibility for specialized services such as special education or mental health services.

PREVENTION OF WHAT?

As discussed above within the medical example, it is not sufficient to simply put in place a universal measure that then leads directly to a generic solution as a course of prevention. Prevention with respect to children and youth with EBD can be viewed in two ways. First, prevention should be considered in the traditional sense – when supports are put in place for young children, educators may reduce the likelihood for later displays of more intense emotional or behavioral concerns that require specialized instruction (Tolan & Guerra, 1994; Webster-Stratton & Hammond, 1998; Webster-Stratton, Reid, & Hammond, 2004; Ziglar, Taussig, & Black, 1992). For example, H. Walker et al. (1997) developed *First Step to Success* – packaged intervention that has been shown to reduce antisocial behavior among students in kindergarten through second grade. Webster-Stratton and colleagues using their program *The Incredible Years* (Webster-Stratton, 1984) have documented reductions in social behavior problems that maintained into school age years when provided during the preschool years.

While the "traditional" view of prevention (i.e., providing service early to young children as an effort to avoid what may later occur without those provisions) is critical and routinely called for in the related EBD literature (Conroy et al., 2004; Kupersmidt, Bryant, & Willoughby, 2000), a second more expansive view of prevention is equally important given the continued poor outcomes among students identified with EBD. Through this expanded lens, prevention should be viewed along a continuum with an eye toward *lessening the impact* of external risk factors and/or the child's emotional/behavioral patterns that can lead to increasing life difficulties over time. First, a percentage of children and youth will manifest issues related to a disability to the point where they could be eligible for specialized services within the "Seriously Emotionally Disturbed," or other category, under the Individual with Disabilities Education Act (IDEA) even when proven prevention strategies are in place. In this case, prevention and early intervention focuses on reducing the impact of the disability and/or preventing other disability related difficulties. Second, given that (a) less than 1% of students receive special education under the EBD category when it is expected 5–7% should be served and (b) some students eligible for EBD may be served within other categories (e.g., learning disabled (LD), other health impaired) and may not be receiving specific supports to address social/emotional needs, early intervention/prevention supports should be available to all students to address potentially underserved students. Taking an expanded perspective allows educators to continue to provide "traditional" prevention and early intervention supports during the early childhood and elementary school years while simultaneously addressing specific educational and emotional concerns among children who are already experiencing difficulty.

The purpose of this chapter is to outline a potential framework using the logic model of School-Wide Positive Behavior Supports (SW-PBS) and Response to Intervention (RtI) to create a viable, effective prevention and early intervention process. Specifically, this chapter will review (a) techniques for using data-based decision-making to identify which students may be at-risk, (b) a school-based system that teaches teams of educators to use data to guide decision-making linking risk to early intervention as well as placing prevention strategies in place school-wide, and (c) propose recommendations for additional research to continue to build more efficient and effective systems that support at-risk and identified students.

USING DATA TO IDENTIFY RISK

Within any discussion of prevention/early intervention, the starting point is always some marker of potential risk. In the health field, as discussed previously, one critical measure is blood pressure, in the stock market, it is a trend in reduction of dollar value, and in meteorology, it is a drop in barometric pressure. While none of these markers alone can predict what will happen, they all prompt related professionals to begin more comprehensive assessments to guide decision-making. Within schools, we provide students with vision and hearing tests; we gather and require certain health prevention measures such as vaccinations; we routinely test for academic aptitude. Unfortunately, educators rarely establish data collection strategies about possible social/emotional risk and/or provide systematic school-wide screening similar to other targets (e.g., all students get vision test and all take part in academic testing). If educators are to successfully provide early intervention and target specific prevention strategies, systemic data must be collected and reviewed on an ongoing and scheduled basis. Fortunately, the tools and measures do exist that can reliably flag students at risk. Unfortunately very few schools have system-wide strategies in place that can use or take advantage of these tools and measures.

One of the simplest strategies schools can put in place to assess risk is to engage in school-wide screening (Elliot, Huai, & Roach, 2007; Lane, Bruhn, Eisner, & Robetson-Kalberg, 2010; Severson, Walker, Hope-Doolittle, Kratochwill, & Gresham, 2007). Several screening instruments have been developed with proven psychometric properties to identify internalizing and externalizing social/emotional risk. The majority of instruments require informants, typically classroom teachers or parents, to be familiar with the child's social/emotional behavior patterns to the degree they can accurately respond to the screening tool items (see appendix for a sample list of social/emotional screening instruments). One example, the *Systematic Screening for Behavior Disorders* (Severson & Walker, 1992) asks classroom teachers to consider all students in their class and rank order up to 10 children who most match a given definition for internalizing characteristics and up to 10 with externalizing behavior concerns. The top three ranked students in each category move to the next stage. For these children, teachers are then asked to complete a short rating scale indicating the degree to which each nominated child displays behavioral problems. The scale is nationally normed and provides cut scores that indicate risk. Use of these scores guide school personnel to possibly proceed to the last and most intensive stage of the screening, which involves direct observation of the child. Regardless, if the child's score warrants additional screening steps or indicates significant risk is not present, use of the systematic process brings that child to the school's attention. Consideration of screening score results, along with additional information, can assist educators in making decisions long before intensive problems begin to occur. For example, if no or minimal risk is present, it may be determined the child does not need additional supports, but school personnel should continue to monitor the student's progress. However, if the screening results suggest the child is at risk, this information can be used to trigger a response by a designated team of educators and related school personnel to identify and implement the simplest support that is matched to child needs.

Educators should also consider using data that are commonly collected and readily available to assist in decision-making. All American public schools collect information such as attendance, work completion, behavioral infractions (often times referred to as office discipline referrals), detentions, and suspensions, which are all markers of existing or possible behavioral difficulties (Irvin et al., 2006; Irvin, Tobin, Sprague, Sugai, & Vincent, 2004; McIntosh, Campbell, Russell-Carter, & Zumbo, 2009). While measures such as office discipline referrals or behavioral infractions potentially represent variation across teachers within a single school, they do allow the school to answer such questions as where, when, what, and who are displaying problem behaviors allowing educators to intervene before patterns become chronic (Irvin et al., 2006). Such commonly collected data also allow educators to monitor progress and impact of in-place prevention/early intervention strategies. In addition, as Tobin and colleagues have reported, certain patterns of early behavioral infractions are often robust indicators of later more serious emotional/behavioral problems. For example, Tobin and Sugai (1999b) reported that students with high rates of office discipline referrals in the sixth grade had statistically significant higher rates of chronic discipline referrals and suspensions at the secondary level. Tobin and colleagues also report that students with high rates of office discipline referrals at the elementary school level had a higher risk of being identified with an EBD and subsequently placed in more restrictive placements (Tobin, Sugai, & Colvin, 1996; Tobin & Sugai, 1999a, 1999b).

One additional emerging measure of social behavior that shows potential for use as a screener and for progress monitoring is the development of Direct Behavior Ratings (DBR; Christ, Riley-Tillman, & Chafouleas, 2009; Christ, Riley-Tillman, Chafouleas, & Jaffery, 2011). DBRs have been developed through direct observation paired with rating scales to provide a snapshot of student performance within a given classroom or context.

Like direct observation, it is place and time specific unlike traditional rating scales that ask educators to assess overall level of appropriate or inappropriate behavior (Chafouleas, Christ, & Riley-Tillman, 2009). Work to date is promising in that DBRs show the potential to be as reliable as direct observation of student behavior in identifying risk. As data continue to emerge on the psychometric properties of DBRs, their use as a potential quick screener and as a progress-monitoring tool warrants consideration.

Beyond using data to flag individual students who may be at-risk, schools should also use data to guide whole-school preventive and early intervention efforts. Screening data and frequent systematic review of commonly collected school data can be useful for identifying the overall level of risk present across all students and/or school environments. When data indicate a large percentage of students display at-risk markers, rather than providing supports to each individual student, teaching and response strategies can be identified and implemented in specific settings where issues are noted or throughout the whole-school environment. For example, if 30% of students score as "high risk" on a screening instrument and 40–50% of all students have two or more office discipline referrals, the level of universal to individual supports will require much more intensity on the part of educators than a school where only 2% of students screened high risk and only 5% have two or more office referrals. In other words, in addition to using data to flag certain students who may be at-risk, schools should also use data to guide what supports should put in place across school environments if the data indicate a large percentage of students they serve display at-risk markers. If large percentages of students are indicated as at-risk, the school cannot and should not conduct business as usual and expect students to succeed. The same logic should also be applied at the district, region, or state level. In other words, if an individual school has a large percentage of students who are identified as at-risk, the intensity of resources and support should follow suit as opposed to the current model where all schools get the same amount of resources or maybe slightly more based on formula funding such as Title One, which are also typically limited in their target (e.g., math and reading only).

SYSTEMS TO FACILITATE DATA-BASED DECISIONS

While the advantages for use of screening and ongoing school data decision-making are easily evident, a more complicated issue is determining the details of how this information will be acquired, reviewed, and utilized. Use of screening and school data for efficient decision-making requires a clearly defined and organized system for (a) gathering the data, (b) making decisions about what additional information may be needed, (c) implementing supports based on student need with fidelity, and (d) monitoring impact and making adjustments if students are not responding. Unfortunately, as Kauffman pointed out directly within the title of his 1999 article, the field has a history of "prevent[ing] the prevention of emotional and behavioral disorders" (p. 448). Kauffman eloquently summarized the state of prevention efforts, which unfortunately continues to ring true:

> Prevention of emotional and behavioral disorders seems to be everyone's rhetorical darling, but I have come to the sad conclusion that most of our talk about prevention is of little substance. We often find ways to avoid taking primary or secondary preventive action, regardless of our acknowledgment that such prevention is a good idea. Other concerns take precedence, and as a result we are most successful in preventing prevention itself. (p. 448)

Special education has provided millions of children and youth with a free and appropriate public education; however, a continued challenge driven by the current federal statutes and regulations is the reliance on a "wait-fail" model to gain access to specialized instruction, while research continues to point to the need to intervene as soon as risk is evident. Under the current model, to provide individualized intensive educational supports, general educators must struggle with and allow students to display problem behavior "to a marked degree" and "over a long period of time" (U.S. Department of Education, 2006) before receiving specialized instruction. While no one would argue against the IDEA procedural safeguards provided to students and their families, including the prevention of providing special education without due process, the continued reliance on the current definition and evaluation paradigm will continue to put students who are in need of services further behind (Maag & Katsiyannis, 2008).

One encouraging note in a move to provide more early intervention and supports before identification for special education services was put in place with the reauthorization of IDEA in 2004. RtI (U.S. Department of Education, 2004) was introduced within the category of LD. Documentation of a discrepancy between cognitive ability and achievement is no longer required to find students eligible for special education. Instead, educators can document that the student is not benefiting from instruction even with additional supports and accommodations put in place within the general education setting (Gersten et al., 2008). Stated another way, student performance has repeatedly demonstrated they are "not-responding" to additional interventions beyond core instruction and common accommodations, suggesting that the student might have a disability and is therefore eligible for specialized instruction.

Before and parallel with the call for an RtI option in the identification of students with LD, the EBD field has also advocated for the use of "nonresponse" data within the eligibility process (e.g., Forness & Knitzer, 1992; Peacock Hill Working Group, 1991). Since 2004, an emerging call for the examination of a similar social behavior RtI protocol has been advocated (e.g., Barnett et al., 2006; Cheney, Flower, & Templeton, 2008; Fairbanks, Sugai, Guardino, & Lathrop, 2007; Gresham, 2005, 2007; Gresham et al., 2005; Hawken, Vincent, & Schumann, 2008; Maag & Katsiyannis, 2008). One of the more articulated systems on the social behavior side has been the development of SW-PBS (Sugai et al., 2000). SW-PBS provides a framework for school-based teams of educators to make data-based decisions about what behavioral supports should be introduced in the environment to address challenges.

The initial focus of SW-PBS starts with building universal-level supports that are implemented by all staff across all settings for all students. Key features of universal supports include specifically identifying appropriate social behaviors versus the traditional list of behavioral infractions, explicitly teaching the expectations, and providing feedback to students on mastery display of the skills. In addition to strategies to improve student behavior, systems of universal SW-PBS also serve to build fluency among educators in (a) using data to determine what practices should be in place to increase the likelihood of student success as well as to monitor progress and problem solve when students do not respond to current supports; (b) working across disciplines and traditional roles (e.g., special education, general education, administrator, and paraprofessional) in teams to provide a true multidisciplinary approach to addressing challenging behavior; and (c) building a school environment that will increase the likelihood of generalized responding when students require more intensive behavioral supports (Lewis, Jones, Horner, & Sugai, 2010). In essence, the SW-PBS systems approach builds fluency among all educators on the simple, yet fundamental premise that teaching and learning environments must change if behavior change is to take place (i.e., student behavior is functionally related to the school environment). Research to date has demonstrated that school teams can alter learning environments to reduce overall levels of problem behavior and increase social and academic success thereby creating a school environment focused on prevention of problem behavior (e.g.,

Bradshaw, Mitchell, & Leaf, 2010; Bradshaw, Reinke, Brown, Bevans, & Leaf, 2008; Horner et al., 2009).

More importantly, the SW-PBS/RtI logic provides teams of educators with a framework to support systematic use of data to identify students who are not successful with universal supports, or "non-responders," and to identify and implement contextually appropriate, research-based small group (i.e., Tier II) and individualized (i.e., Tier III) practices independent of current IDEA eligibility. Use of SW-PBS/RtI organizational structures creates an environment for providing "early intervention" along a continuum of increasingly intensive supports (Cheney et al., 2008). For example, Hawken and colleagues (2007) evaluated a Tier II self-monitoring process in which students used a central location to "check in and out" at the start and end of the school day with a designated staff member. In addition, classroom teachers provided specific feedback to students at regular intervals throughout the school day. Teacher feedback was documented daily and reviewed on a frequent basis to make decisions about student progress. Results from research on use of this strategy indicate decreases in problem behavior and increases in work completion and academic performance (e.g., Hawken, 2006; Hawken & Horner, 2003; Hawken, MacLeod, & Rawlings, 2007). While the logic and essential features of SW-PBS demonstrate a systemic framework for using data to identify students not responding to universal supports and matching them with supplemental interventions, additional data are needed to show the overall, long-term impact on risk as well as a seamless connection between school-wide prevention and early intervention and special education supports (Lewis et al., 2010).

CONCLUSION AND RECOMMENDATIONS

This chapter provided an overview of one facet to addressing the challenges found within the field of EBD; the provision of early intervention and building proactive preventative school environments. While "what" the field of special education should put in place for children and youth with EBD has been established over several decades (e.g., Epstein, Atkins, Cullinan, Kutash, & Weaver, 2008; Peacock Hill Working Group, 1991), the "how" continues to remain a challenge given the current special education eligibility determination process (Maag & Katsiyannis, 2008). Key to implementing such a system of prevention/early intervention is the ongoing and systematic collection of data to pinpoint "who" needs "what" as soon as risk is detected (Severson et al., 2007). Data should be easy to collect and collected over the entire school year. Data should be used to determine what additional supports a child or youth might need regardless of current special education or non-special education status; rather, any time risk is noted, a system should exist that allows educators to assess what additional supports, from universal to intensive, the student might need. Frameworks such as SW-PBS and RtI provide the field with an opportunity to build in preventative and early intervention strategies across a continuum of student need based on intensity of risk and/or identified disability. Use of a tiered framework that provides a continuum or SW-PBS teaches teams of educators to make data-based decision matching need to intervention. Although outcomes to date are encouraging, much work remains.

While several screeners are currently available, and schools have commonly collected measures at their disposal to assist in decision-making, a clearly established set of steps that leads to an efficient match between data and intervention is still needed. Both school data and screening instruments only provide an indicator the child might be at-risk. At present, most school teams rely on professional judgment regarding additional assessments and related interventions that may be needed. This model may suffice when expertise is present and readily available; however, few school districts have behavioral expertise that is not already dedicated to activities such as eligibility evaluations or crisis response. Additional research and demonstration is needed to develop a series of steps that can lead school teams through a process from noted risk, to collecting additional data, to matching data to supports that are most appropriate for each individual child within existing behavioral expertise and skill sets commonly found in schools.

A related challenge is to develop, or test, a set of easy to collect measures that allow educators to effectively monitor progress. While it is simple enough to make macro decisions such as the student is getting better, staying the same, or getting worse, educators also need tools that allow for decisions at the micro level, specifically what to do if behavior is not improving. In addition to the development of new measures, or the psychometric validation of current measures, related professional development and "user-friendly" guides are also needed. At present, most measures, even those recommended within this chapter, simply lack the sensitivity to lead to highly individualized intervention. Even strategies such as functional behavioral assessment (FBA), which is designed to match specific interventions to patterns of problem behavior including environmental changes, still lacks a commonly accepted standardized series of steps and ultimately continues to rely on highly skilled behavioral experts (Scott & Kamps, 2007; Scott et al., 2005).

As noted previously, the difficulty in prevention research is drawing clear causal conclusions linking prevention/early intervention efforts and student outcomes. If prevention is effective, the challenge becomes measuring the absence of behavior problems. While it is encouraging that SW-PBS prevention/early intervention efforts at the preschool level within high-risk classrooms have demonstrated that educators can put in positive practices that lead to decreases in problem behavior and increases in prosocial behavior related to later more intensive behavior problems (Covington-Smith, Lewis, & Stormont, 2011; Stormont, Covington-Smith, & Lewis, 2007), additional, large-scale longitudinal research is clearly needed. Specially, research should continue to focus on (a) screening methods and risk indicators, (b) additional needed assessments based on screening metrics and student school performance data, (c) processes that teams of educators engage in to link screening and broad assessment to school-wide and individual supports, and (d) sophisticated progress monitoring that allows educators to alter interventions based on data patterns.

In 1991, the Peacock Hill Working Group crafted an elegant and articulate discourse in response to criticisms against special education and disregard of existing effective practices for students with EBD. In addition, the group offered a list of recommendations for moving the field of special education toward an emphasis on consistent implementation of empirically tested approaches by way of changes in practice, policy, research and professional practice (Peacock Hill Working Group, 1991). Twenty years later, the promises of special education to improve outcomes for *all* students with EBD continue to be unfulfilled. Writing specifically about prevention/ early intervention, Kauffman (1999, p. 463) offered the following recommendations that provide a fitting conclusion to this chapter:

Establish common standards for judging evidence of the effectiveness of preventive interventions at all levels of a continuum of supports (primary, secondary, tertiary).

Abandon and publicly condemning interventions for which evidence clearly is not supportive or negative or that make tertiary prevention inevitable because primary and secondary prevention are highly unlikely if not impossible.

Increase our immediate positive attention to and, when possible, prompt financial and social support of primary and secondary preventive action, thereby creating a professional culture more supportive of prevention.

REFERENCES

Barnett, D. W., Elliott, N., Wolsing, L., Bunger, C. E., Haski, H., McKissick, C., & Vander Meer, C. D. (2006). Response to intervention for young children with extremely challenging behaviors: What it might look like. *School Psychology Review, 35*(4), 568–582.

Bradshaw, C. P., Mitchell, M. M., & Leaf, P. J. (2010). Examining the effectiveness of schoolwide positive behavioral interventions and supports on student outcomes: Results from a randomized controlled effectiveness trial in elementary schools. *Journal of Positive Behavior Interventions, 12*, 133–148.

Bradshaw, C. P., Reinke, W., Brown, L., Bevans, K., & Leaf, P. (2008). Implementation of school-wide positive behavioral interventions and supports (PBIS) in elementary schools: Observations from a randomized trial. *Education & Treatment of Children, 31*, 1–26.

Chafouleas, S. M., Christ, T. J., & Riley-Tillman, T. C. (2009). Generalizability and dependability of scaling gradients on direct behavior ratings. *Educational and Psychological Measurement, 69*, 157–173.

Cheney, D., Flower, A., & Templeton, T. (2008). Applying response to intervention metrics in the social domain for students at risk of developing emotional or behavioral disorders. *Journal of Special Education, 42*, 108–126.

Christ, T. J., Riley-Tillman, T. C., & Chafouleas, S. M. (2009). Foundation for the development and use of direct behavior rating (DBR) to assess and evaluate student behavior. *Assessment for Effective Intervention, 34*, 201–213.

Christ, T. J., Riley-Tillman, T. C., Chafouleas, S. M., & Jaffery, R. (2011). Direct behavior rating: An evaluation of alternate definitions to assess classroom behaviors. *School Psychology Review, 40*, 181–199.

Conroy, M. A., Hendrickson, J. M., & Hester, P. (2004). Early identification and prevention of emotional and behavioral disorders. In R. B. Rutherford, M. M. Quinn & S. R. Mathur (Eds.), *Handbook of research in emotional and behavioral disorders* (pp. 199–215). New York, NY: Guildford Press.

Covington-Smith, S., Lewis, T. J., & Stormont, M. (2011). The effectiveness of two universal behavioral supports for children with externalizing behavior in Head Start classrooms. *Journal of Positive Behavior Interventions, 13*, 133–143.

Elliot, S. N., Huai, N., & Roach, A. T. (2007). Universal and early screening for educational difficulties: Current and future approaches. *Journal of School Psychology, 45*(2), 137–161.

Epstein, M., Atkins, M., Cullinan, D., Kutash, K., & Weaver, R. (2008). *Reducing behavior problems in the elementary school classroom: A practice guide* (NCEE#2008-012). Washington, DC: National Center for Education Evaluation and Regional Assistance, Institute of Education Science, U.S. Department of Education.

Fairbanks, S., Sugai, G., Guardino, D., & Lathrop, M. (2007). Response to intervention: Examining classroom behavior support in second grade. *Exceptional Children, 73*(3), 288–310.

Feil, E. G., Walker, H. M., & Severson, H. H. (1995). The early screening project for young children with behavior problems. *Journal of Emotional and Behavioral Disorders, 3*(4), 194–202.

Forness, S., & Knitzer, J. (1992). A new proposed definition and terminology to replace "serious emotional disturbance" in Individuals with Disabilities Education Act. *School Psychology Review, 21*, 12–20.

Gersten, R., Compton, D., Connor, C. M., Dimino, J., Santoro, L., Linan-Thompson, S., & Tilly, W. D. (2008). *Assisting students struggling with reading: Reponses to intervention and multi-tier intervention for reading in the primary grades. A practice guide (NCEE2009-4045)*. Washington, DC: National Center for Education Evaluation and Regional Assistance, Institute of Education Science, U.S. Department of Education.

Goodman, R. (1997). The strengths and difficulties questionnaire: A research note. *Journal of Child Psychology and Psychiatry, 38*(5), 581–586.

Gresham, F. M. (2005). Response to intervention: An alternative means of identifying students as emotionally disturbed. *Education & Treatment of Children, 28*, 328–344.

Gresham, F. M. (2007). Response to intervention and emotional and behavioral disorders: Best practices in assessment for intervention. *Assessment for Effective Intervention, 32*, 214–222.

Gresham, F. M., & Elliot, S. (2007). *Social skills improvement system*. Minneapolis, MN: Pearson.

Gresham, F. M., Reschly, D. J., Tilly, W. D., Fletcher, J., Burns, M., & Prasse, D. (2005). A response to intervention perspective. *The School Psychologist, 59*, 26–33.

Hawken, L. S. (2006). School psychologists as leaders in the implementation of a targeted intervention: The Behavior Education Program (BEP). *School Psychology Quarterly, 21*, 91–111.

Hawken, L. S., & Horner, R. (2003). Evaluation of a targeted group intervention within a school-wide system of behavior support. *Journal of Behavioral Education, 12*, 225–240.

Hawken, L. S., MacLeod, K. S., & Rawlings, L. (2007). Effects of the Behavior Education Program (BEP) on problem behavior with elementary school students. *Journal of Positive Behavior Interventions, 9*, 94–101.

Hawken, L. S., Vincent, C. G., & Schumann, J. (2008). Response to intervention for social behavior. *Journal of Emotional and Behavioral Disorders, 16*, 213–225.

Horner, R., Sugai, G., Smolkowski, K., Todd, A., Nakasato, J., & Esperanza, J. (2009). A randomized control trial of school-wide positive behavior support in elementary schools. *Journal of Positive Behavior Interventions, 11*(3), 133–144.

Irvin, L. K., Horner, R. H., Ingram, K., Todd, A. W., Sugai, G., Sampson, N., & Boland, J. (2006). Using office discipline referral data for decision-making about student behavior in elementary and middle schools: An empirical investigation of validity. *Journal of Positive Behavior Interventions, 8*(1), 10–23.

Irvin, L. K., Tobin, T., Sprague, J., Sugai, G., & Vincent, C. (2004). Validity of office discipline referral measures as indices of school-wide behavioral status and effects of school-wide behavioral interventions. *Journal of Positive Behavior Interventions, 6*, 131–147.

Kamphaus, R. W., & Reynolds, C. R. (2007). *Behavioral and emotional screening system. Manual*. Minneapolis, MN: Pearson.

Kauffman, J. M. (1999). How we prevent the prevention of emotional and behavioral disorders. *Exceptional Children, 65*(4), 448–468.

Kauffman, J. M. (2005). *Characteristics of emotional and behavioral disorders of children and youth* (8th ed.). Upper Saddle River, NJ: Prentice Hall.

Kupersmidt, J. B., Bryant, D., & Willoughby, M. T. (2000). Prevalence of aggressive behaviors among preschoolers in Head Start and community child care programs. *Behavioral Disorders, 26,* 42–52.

Lane, K. L., Bruhn, A. L., Eisner, S. L., & Robetson-Kalberg, J. (2010). Score reliability and validity of the student risk screening scale: A psychometrically sound, feasible tool for use in urban middle schools. *Journal of Emotional and Behavioral Disorders, 18,* 211–224.

LeBuffe, P. A., & Naglieri, J. A. (1999). *The Devereux early childhood assessment.* Lewisville, NC: Kaplan Press Publishing.

Lewis, T. J., Jones, S. E. L., Horner, R. H., & Sugai, G. (2010). School-wide positive behavior support and students with emotional/behavioral disorders: Implications for prevention, identification and intervention. *Exceptionality, 18*(2), 82–93.

Maag, J. W., & Katsiyannis, A. (2008). The medical model to block eligibility for students with EBD: A response-to-intervention alternative. *Behavioral Disorders, 33*(3), 184–194.

McIntosh, K., Campbell, A. L., Russell-Carter, D., & Zumbo, B. D. (2009). Concurrent validity of office discipline referrals and cut points used in schoolwide positive behavior support. *Behavioral Disorders, 34,* 100–113.

Merrell, K. W. (2003). *Preschool and kindergarten behavior scales – Second edition.* Austin, TX: PRO-ED.

National Research Council and Institute of Medicine. (2009). *Preventing mental, emotional, and behavioral disorders among young people: Progress and possibilities.* Washington, DC: The National Academies Press.

Neisworth, J. T., Bagnato, S. J., Salvia, J., & Hunt, F. M. (1999). *TABS manual for the temperament and atypical behavior scale: Early childhood indicators of developmental dysfunction.* Baltimore, MD: Paul H. Brookes Publishing.

Peacock Hill Working Group. (1991). Problems and promises in special education and related services for children and youth with emotional or behavioral disorders. *Behavioral Disorders, 16,* 299–313.

Quay, H. C., & Peterson, D. R. (1996). *The revised behavior problem checklist.* Lutz, FL: Psychological Assessment Resources.

Scott, T. M., & Kamps, D. M. (2007). The future of functional behavioral assessment in school settings. *Behavioral Disorders, 32*(2), 146–157.

Scott, T. M., McIntyre, J., Liaupsin, C., Nelson, C. M., Conroy, M., & Payne, L. (2005). An examination of the relation between functional behavior assessment and selected intervention strategies with school-based teams. *Journal of Positive Behavior Interventions, 7*(4), 205–215.

Severson, H. H., & Walker, H. M. (1992). *Systematic screening for behavior disorders: Technical manua* (2nd edn.). Longmont, CO: Sopris West.

Severson, H. H., Walker, H. M., Hope-Doolittle, H., Kratochwill, T. R., & Gresham, F. M. (2007). Proactive, early screening to detect behaviorally at-risk students: Issues, approaches, emerging innovations, and professional practices. *Journal of School Psychology, 45,* 193–223.

Squires, J., & Bricker, D. (2009). *Ages and stages questionnaire: Third edition.* Baltimore, MD: Paul H. Brookes Publishing.

Stormont, M., Covington-Smith, S., & Lewis, T. J. (2007). Teacher implementation of precorrection and praise statements in Head Start classrooms as a component of a program-wide system of positive behavioral support. *Journal of Behavioral Education, 16,* 280–290.

Sugai, G., Horner, R. H., Dunlap, G., Hieneman, M., Lewis, T. J., Nelson, C. M., & Wilcox, B. (2000). Applying positive behavioral support and functional behavioral assessment in schools. *Journal of Positive Behavior Interventions, 2*, 131–143.

Tobin, T. J., & Sugai, G. M. (1999a). Discipline problems, placements, and outcomes for students with serious emotional disturbance. *Behavioral Disorders, 24*, 109–121.

Tobin, T. J., & Sugai, G. M. (1999b). Using sixth-grade school records to predict violence, chronic discipline problems, and high school outcomes. *Journal of Emotional and Behavioral Disorders, 7*, 40–53.

Tobin, T. J., Sugai, G., & Colvin, G. (1996). Patterns in middle school discipline records. *Journal of Emotional and Behavioral Disorders, 4*, 82–94.

Tolan, P., & Guerra, N. (1994). *What works in reducing adolescent violence: An empirical review of the field.* Center for the Study and Prevention of Violence, Boulder, CO.

U.S. Department of Education. (2004). *Twenty-fourth annual report to congress on the implementation of the Individuals with Disabilities Education Act.* Washington, DC: Author.

U.S. Department of Education. (2006). *Twenty-eighth annual report to congress on the implementation of the individuals with disabilities education act.* Washington, DC: Author.

VanAcker, R. (2004). Current status of public education and likely future directions for students with emotional and behavioral disorders. In L. M. Bullock & R. A. Gable (Eds.), *Quality personnel preparation in emotional/behavioral disorders: Current perspectives and future directions.* Denton, TX: Institute for Behavioral and Learning Differences.

Wagner, M., Kutash, K., Duchnowski, A. J., Epstein, M. H., & Sumi, W. C. (2005). The children and youth we serve: A national picture of the characteristics of students with emotional disturbances receiving special education. *Journal of Emotional and Behavioral Disorders, 13*(2), 79–96.

Walker, H., Stiller, B., Golly, A., Kavanagh, K., Severson, H., & Feil, E. (1997). *First step to success: Helping young children overcome antisocial behavior (an early intervention program for grades K-3).* Longmont, CO: Sopris West.

Webster-Stratton, C. (1984). A randomized trial of two parent-training programs for families with conduct-disordered children. *Journal of Consulting and Clinical Psychology, 52*(4), 666–678.

Webster-Stratton, C., & Hammond, M. (1998). Conduct problems and level of social competence in Head Start children: Prevalence, pervasiveness, and associated risk factors. *Clinical Child and Family Psychology Review, 1*(2), 101–123.

Webster-Stratton, C., Reid, M. J., & Hammond, M. (2004). Treating children with early-onset conduct problems: Intervention outcomes for parent, child, and teacher training. *Journal of Clinical Child and Adolescent Psychology, 33*, 105–124.

Ziglar, E., Taussig, C., & Black, K. (1992). Early childhood intervention: A promising preventative for juvenile delinquency. *American Psychologist, 47*, 997–1006.

APPENDIX

Sample Screening Instruments Targeting Emotional and Social Behavior Concerns

	School-Age Externalizing and Internalizing Screening Instruments			
Instrument	Description	Method(s)	Administration	Cost
Strengths & Difficulties Questionnaire (SDQ) Goodman (1997) Youthinmind.com	Grades K-12 Brief behavioral screening questionnaire that assesses conduct problems, hyperactivity, emotional symptoms, peer problems, and prosocial behavior Total difficulties score reported as low, medium or high risk	Teacher or parent report (ages 4–10) Teacher or parent report (ages 11–17) Student self-report (ages 11–17)	45 minutes to 1 hour/ class 25 items Online administration and scoring available Manual scoring = 10 minutes/student	No cost if administered and scored online One page per student if administered and scored by hand
Behavioral and Emotional Screening System (BASC-2 BESS) Kamphaus and Reynolds (2007)	Grades PreK-12 Assesses both behavioral problems and strengths, including internalizing problems, externalizing problems, school problems, and adaptive skills Scores reported as normal, elevated or extremely elevated	Teacher or parent report (ages 3–5) Teacher or parent report (K-12) Student self-report (grades 3–12)	5–10 minutes admin 25-30 items Computer scoring available using ASSIST software	Manual = $62 Teacher forms = ($100 for pkg of 100) Data Management System = $589

Name/Author	Description	Rating/Report	Time	Cost
Systematic Screening for Behavior Disorders (SSBD) H.M. Walker and Severson (1992)	Grades K-6 Uses three-stage, multi-gate process to screen and identify students who may be at risk of developing behavioral disorders	Rank orders 10 students with internalizing concerns and 10 students with externalizing concerns The top three students in each category are individually rated using The Critical Events Index (33 items) and the Combined Frequency Index that includes adaptive (12) and maladaptive (11) items	45 minutes to 1hour/ class (stages 1 and 2) Scoring = 15–30 minutes/class	Manual w/video = ($195)
Social Skills Improvement System (SSIS) Gresham and Elliot (2007)	Ages 3–19 Teacher compares student performance as measured against grade level expectations. A definition and performance-level descriptors are provided for each skill area. Teacher selects description that best fits the current level of functioning for each student	Teacher, parent and student self-rating options	Approximately 30 minutes per class 15–20 minutes per individual student	Performance screening guide ($41.25 for pack of 10) Manual = $101 Rating forms = Hand score ($42 for pack of 25) Scoring and reporting software = ($249)
The Revised Behavior Problem Checklist Quay and Peterson (1996)	Grades K-12 Six subscales measure conduct disorder, socialized aggression, attention problems, immaturity, anxiety-withdrawal, psychotic behavior, and motor tension-excess	Teacher or parent report on individual students (ages 5–18)	20 minutes per student Manual scoring 10 minutes/student	Manual = ($36) Test booklets = ($65 for pkg of 25) Profile sheets = ($30 for pkg of 25)

Preschool Externalizing and Internalizing Screening Instruments

Instrument	Description/purpose/use	Method(s)	Administration	Cost
Devereux Early Childhood Assessment Program (DECA) LeBuffe and Naglieri (1999)	2–5 years A Total Protective Factors (TPF) composite score is generated from results of scales assessing initiative, self-control, & attachment. A 10-item Behavioral Concerns scale assesses behavioral problems	Parent/caregiver Teacher	5–10 minutes/student 62 items Likert	Starter Kit = $200
Preschool and Kindergarten Behavior Scales – Second Edition (PKBS-2) Merrell (2003)	3–6 years Measures social skills and problem behaviors. Includes subtests for social cooperation, social interaction, social independence, self-centered/ explosive, attention problems/overactive, antisocial/aggressive, social withdrawal, anxiety/ somatic problems, externalizing problems, and internalizing problems	Parent/Caregiver Teacher	8–12 minutes/student 76 items Likert	Starter Kit = $120 No data management system
Temperament and Atypical Behavior Scale (TABS) Neisworth, Bagnato, Salvia, and Hunt (1999)	11–71 months (1–6 years) Brief screener identifies potential problems A separate assessment tool, is used when screening score indicates a concern. Results are provided for categories of detached, hypersensitive-active, underreactive, and dysregulated	Parent/Caregiver Teacher	15-item screener = 5 minutes/student 55-item checklist = 15 minutes/student	Introductory kit includes manual, screeners, and assessment tools = $95

Instrument	Age/Description	Informant	Administration	Cost/Materials
Ages and Stages Questionnaire: Third Edition (ASQ-3) Squires and Bricker (2009)	1–66 months Examines strengths and challenges in Self-regulation, compliance, communication, adaptive functioning, autonomy, affect, and interpersonal interactions	Parent/Caregiver	15–20 minutes/child 30 items 2–3 min to score	Starter kit = $250 Reproducible Data management system available
Early Screening Project (ESP) Feil, Walker, and Severson (1995)	3–5 years Process that allows for early intervention and identification of preschool adjustment problems Screens for emotional problems, speech and language difficulties, impaired cognitive ability, attention deficits, and hyperactivity Scores reported as at risk, high risk, or extreme risk	Teacher rating followed by direct observation completed by someone other than the classroom teacher	Stages 1 and 2 can be completed in approximately 1 hour Stage 3 requires two 10-minute observations in unstructured settings	

CHAPTER 7

ENGLISH LANGUAGE LEARNERS AND EMOTIONAL BEHAVIORAL DISORDERS

Diana L. Rogers-Adkinson, Theresa A. Ochoa and Stacy L. Weiss

ABSTRACT

This chapter provides the reader with a framework for understanding the needs of students that have concurrent needs as English Language Learners and Emotionally Behavioral Disturbed. Issues related to effective assessment practices, service delivery, and appropriate intervention are discussed.

Keywords: English Language Learners; Emotional Behavioral Disorders

INTRODUCTION

Currently, approximately 9% of all students in special education are English Language Learners (ELLs) (U.S. Department of Education, 2009). In addition, children who are ELLs are the fastest growing school population

Behavioral Disorders: Identification, Assessment, and Instruction of Students with EBD
Advances in Special Education, Volume 22, 151–171
Copyright © 2012 by Emerald Group Publishing Limited
All rights of reproduction in any form reserved
ISSN: 0270-4013/doi:10.1108/S0270-4013(2012)0000022010

(Serpa, 2011). Despite this fact, in the special education category of
Emotional Behavioral Disorders (EBD), research indicates ELLs are rarely
identified (Sullivan, 2011). Furthermore, dropout and retention rates are
also higher for this group suggesting a need for interventions within this
population (Duran, 2008). While these aspects are alarming, a more critical
concern is the core political, ideological, and educational "question of
whether or not to provide bilingual education services to learners for whom
English is not their dominant or native language" (Ehlers-Zalava, 2011,
p. 44). As a means of gaining understanding to part of this question, this
chapter provides comprehensive information on ELL with an emphasis on
determining appropriate assessment and educational interventions for
students with comorbid needs such as EBD that may assist in clarifying
the need for services for this population of students.

DEFINING ENGLISH LANGUAGE LEARNERS

A variety of terms have been utilized to describe students with varying
language exposures in the home. First, *Language Minority Students* refers to
students living in a home in which a language other than English is spoken.
These students may or may not use this language in their personal use. The
term *Limited English Proficient* applies to students who are experiencing
academic difficulty due to limited exposure to English. Finally, *ELLs* refers
to students whose first or native language is not English and who are in the
process of learning English to benefit from education (O'Malley, 1994). This
chapter utilizes the broad-based term ELL as it encompasses a majority of
the students experiencing the process of developing English language
proficiency in the schools.

Language proficiency varies across ELL in both home and school
language. Often, children who are ELLs live in a bilingual/bicultural
environment that includes multiple language exposures in the home
(Rogers-Adkinson, Ochoa, & Delgado 2003). Multiple language exposure
may be purposeful as many families wish to maintain speaking competence,
at minimum, in the family's native language. In the United States, educators
often have difficulty understanding this preference as they prefer that the
student be versed primarily in the language of school. This bias is often
confusing to families of recent immigrants, who come from countries that
promote multilingualism (Oliveira & Anca, 2009). Given this situation, it is
imperative that these educators be prepared to collaborate with families and
respect their wishes for multilingualism.

DEVELOPMENT OF ENGLISH LANGUAGE PROFICIENCY

Understanding the process of developing English language proficiency is important, particularly as it applies to students with disabilities generally and students with EBD more specifically. Key framework concepts embedded in this process are *Basic Interpersonal Communication Skills* (BICS) and *Cognitive Academic Language Proficiency* (CALP). According to Cummins (1999–2000), who is credited with first introducing these concepts about 30 years ago, BICS and CALP encompass the initial stage of second language acquisition commonly associated with immigrant children. Roessingh (2006), a former K-12 English as a second language (ESL) practitioner, delineates Cummins BICS original framework on English language development as having four quadrants. According to Roessingh, the first two quadrants are characterized broadly as being highly contextualized and cognitively undemanding. As such, these two BICS quadrants are characterized by simple grammar forms and include high-frequency vocabulary about family, clothes, food, money, and face-to-face interactions. Success at BICS quadrant one requires learners to master about 1,000–2,000 words. Mastery results from exposure to these words "hundreds and hundreds of times" (Roessingh, 2006, p. 93). In this BICS stage, initial reading skills are present and students' writing skills are for personal needs such as making lists or taking simple notes. Success at the BICS second quadrant necessitates that students acquire mastery of anywhere from 2,500 to 5,000 words and the integration of these words into grammar. The first two quadrants of the English language acquisition framework are commonly accepted as being the "here and now" and "my lived experiences" type of language and represent approximately 10% of the iceberg metaphors commonly used to illustrate the development of second language acquisition (Roessingh, 2006). For educators, it is important to note that in second language acquisition contexts, students often acquire peer-appropriate conversational fluency in English within two years.

CALP is represented by quadrants three and four of the English development framework and is characterized as academic language that is more cognitively demanding and decontextualized (Aukerman, 2007; Roessingh, 2006). According to Cummins (1999–2000) and Roessingh (2006), CALP takes approximately 5–10 years to develop and is the most important phase of language development to acquire and be fluent in so that students can experience academic success. At the third quadrant level, students have started to develop visual representations, their language is about the "there and then," there's a shift from learning to read to being able to learn from what they read and they have in their learning arsenal, access to reading strategies. The typical learner in this quadrant has approximately 3,000 high-frequency words and some academic words with an approximate combined vocabulary repertoire of 8,000 words. In the fourth and final quadrant of the English language acquisition framework, learners can access what is known as "educated imagination," which is the capacity to access language for abstract contexts. This access allows the language learner to understand metaphor, symbolism, and idioms. Learners attain a vocabulary that approximates 12,000 words between the seventh to ninth grades. By the end of grade 12, students have mastered a vocabulary between 40,000 and 100,000 words.

DISPROPORTIONAL REPRESENTATION OF ELLs FOR SPECIAL EDUCATION SERVICES

The disproportional referral, identification, and subsequent categorization of ELLs for special education services are perceived as problematic by many policy makers and educators in and outside of special education (see Black, 2010; Dyches & Prater, 2010; Green, 2010; Obiakor, 2010). One of the first notable allegations regarding this aspect was made in 1968 by Dunn, a special education researcher, who, citing statistics provided by the U.S. Office of Education, objected to the fact that special education classes were composed in large measure of students of color from low socioeconomic backgrounds and from homes where standard English was not the standard language of communication (Artiles, Harry, Reschly, & Chinn, 2002). His observations were subsequently echoed and supported by other scholars and concerns about the overrepresentation of ethnic minority students generally, and ELLs in particular continue to take front and center in discussions about the representation of students with English language limitations in categories of disability (see Ehlers-Zavala, 2011; Grossman, Utley, & Obiakor, 2003; Obiakor, 2011; Obiakor & Mukuria, 2007). Disproportionality is defined as an overrepresentation or underrepresentation of any given population of students in any given educational program based on the comparison of their makeup in the general population (Dyches & Prater, 2010). For example, if estimates of the number of Hispanic students in the

United States are 10% of the general population, the makeup of Hispanics in special education classes should also be 10%, no more or less.

Discussions on disproportional representation of culturally and linguistically diverse (CLD) students in special education are arguably synonymous with overrepresentation. However, the under referral, identification, and categorization of CLD for special education services is also an issue that has long been acknowledged as problematic (see Black, 2010; Dyches & Prater, 2010). To be sure, upon close scrutiny, Donovan and Cross (2002) reported that Hispanic students were only slightly overrepresented in the LD category and not at all in the EBD category. But less is known about the actual number of ELL in special education because state-level departments of education do not typically collect data about language proficiency (Klingner & Artiles, 2003). What is starting to become clear is that general education teachers of ELL, who typically are the first to notice academic struggles in the more mild categories disabilities of which the EBD category is considered to be part of, are hesitant to make a premature referral for special education evaluation. This hesitancy was noted by Ochoa et al. (2001), in a study of preservice educators who were presented with a young student exhibiting academic difficulties and who had English language limitations. According to Ochoa et al., these educators were reluctant to refer the student, who did not have full command of English, because the student's academic problems were believed to be a function of language deficits not disabilities. To be sure, the fear of misdiagnosis of ELL has caused confusion among educators charged with the education of students from diverse cultures and languages that they do not understand (Zetlin, Beltran, Salcido, Gonzalez, & Reyes, 2011).

LINGUISTICALLY APPROPRIATE ASSESSMENT RELATED TO EBD

Determination of disability status with ELL can be a challenge for educational teams. Before referring a student for evaluation, it is first recommended that the instructional program be evaluated to determine whether the current instructional practices are appropriate for ELL (Artiles & Ortiz, 2002). If the academic environment is appropriate for the student, progress in English is noted. Disability is suspected if English progress is not noted in spite of appropriate instruction.

Second, as a part of a pre-referral or response to intervention (RtI) and positive behavior support process (PBSP), an ELL need to be assessed in both the native and the English languages to determine both language dominance and language proficiency in each language (Artiles & Ortiz, 2002). Once language competence is determined, the team creates an intervention plan to support academic and behavioral competence. Both the RtI and the PBIS intervention processes serve to provide early intervention specific to disability; however, ELLs are excluded often from such a process initially due to perceptions that ELL services are being provided to the child (Rinaldi, 2010). In addition, Klingner and Harry (2006) determined child study teams often paid little attention to the effectiveness of pre-intervention strategies before referral for evaluation for eligibility. There has been limited work in this area, but early studies in the Boston Public Schools suggest that an RtI framework that supports the academic and behavioral concerns of ELL students can reduce the risk for referral and subsequent placement (Rinaldi, 2010). In addition, during the pre-referral process, if an ELL is a recent immigrant, it is important to note whether the child has previous school exposure, an interrupted attendance pattern, or an age appropriate educational experience (Rinaldi, 2010). Table 1 provides a set of helpful questions critical for discussion during the pre-intervention stage that assists

Table 1. Critical Questions during Pre-referral.

1. Have other adults working with the child in the school noticed similar difficulties?
2. Does the problem exist across contexts:
a. General education classes
b. During tutoring
c. At home?
3. Are the problem's evident in language?
4. Is the student's progress in acquiring English significantly different from that of peers who started at about the same level of English proficiency and have had comparable instruction?
5. Are the differences cross-cultural?
6. Are there other variables that could explain the difficulties or contribute to them?
7. Is there extreme test anxiety evidence?
8. Can problematic behaviors be caused or explained by procedural mistakes in the assessment process?
9. Can problematic behaviors be explained by bias during assessments?
10. Do data show that the student did not respond well to interventions?
11. Are the assessment results consistent with the concerns of the teachers and/or parents?

Source: Artiles and Ortiz (2002).

teams in exploring the impact of language proficiency in the educational environment (Artiles & Ortiz, 2002).

Once it is determined that a referral for special education is necessary, the assessment process can be challenging due to the lack of culturally appropriate assessment materials available for ELL. A majority of the research to date places an emphasis on identification of ELL in the area of learning disability (see Wagner, Francis, & Morris, 2005). Some of the principles applied in this area are germane to EBD as it is important to rule out a lack of socio-emotional and/or academic proficiency due to language acquisition when considering eligibility in EBD. It is also important to note that in states that require English immersion that the rate of ELLs that have been placed in special education has increased significantly (Artiles et al., 2002). This suggests a possible false positive due to the English only requirement of states such as Arizona and California. As a result, it is important to provide assessment materials that are in the native language of the student and English if available unless the student is English dominant (Artiles & Ortiz, 2002). Currently, tests of cognitive ability and achievement are widely available in Spanish, but few assessments are provided in other languages (see Salvia, Ysseldyke, & Bolt, 2010) In addition, in the area of behavioral assessment although translations are available in some measures, typically the normative sample is not reflective of the population identified in the translation.

Parental involvement may also bring additional challenges for assessment teams due to language and cultural barriers. Because parental interviews are needed to determine the student's sociological background and its impact on his/her school behavior, it is recommended that a "cultural broker" be included to not only assist with translation services but to also provide a culturally relevant context regarding the team's questions for the parents (Klotz & Canter, 2006). The cultural broker should also communicate to the team the family belief system regarding views of disability (Rogers-Adkinson et al., 2003) as these could impact the families' understanding of the need for intervention or placement and later in their involvement instructional intervention.

Determination of EBD eligibility should consider standardized assessments in both languages to document that an EBD is evident in both languages. In addition, descriptive data should confirm patterns of behavioral and academic performance noted in both standardized and performance-based measures (Artiles & Ortiz, 2002). It is imperative that all data suggest a systemic need for EBD supports and rule out that any behavioral concerns were due to communication frustration. Finally, once

EBD eligibility is determined, it is important that educational instruction and intervention address culturally responsive programming that develops skills both linguistically and behaviorally.

PROGRAMMING ISSUES FOR DUAL SERVICES ELL/EBD

Interventions for students with EBD have frequently focused on social and behavioral needs rather than academic needs (Wehby, Lane, & Falk, 2003). However, academic instruction is essential for students with EBD since these students often experience significant academic as well as behavioral difficulties (Epstein, Kinder, & Bursuck, 1989). ELL may also experience similar difficulties. For example, Kieffer (2008) reported that students, who began kindergarten with limited English proficiency, had lower initial reading skills than native English speakers through fifth grade. In contrast, Kieffer (2008) found that for students with a language minority background but demonstrated English proficiency in kindergarten, there was little difference in reading when compared to native English speakers.

For dual-identified ELL and EBD students, it is important to provide research-based instruction since students are likely to experience multiple academic and behavioral difficulties. In addition, the Individualized Education Program (IEP) team should view services in special education as specially designed instruction in the least restrictive language environment. Least restrictive ELL services would be provided through a two-way bilingual program. Ideally, these services would be implemented by an educator highly qualified in both ELL and special education licensure.

While there is a growing body of research regarding ELL with learning disabilities (e.g., Klingner & Vaughn, 1996; Saenz, Fuchs, & Fuchs, 2005), there is limited research on academic interventions serving ELLs with co-occurring EBD. As a result, it is necessary to identify those strategies that have support for either ELL or students with EBD as promising strategies for students who are identified as both EBD and ELL. In addition, it is necessary to highlight those practices that have been evaluated for dual-identified students. In the next section, potentially effective strategies for this population are reviewed. The strategies include direct, explicit instruction; cognitive strategy instruction; and peer-mediated instruction. First, we describe general instructional practices. Then, research specific to EBD and ELL is reviewed, including suggested modifications for the instructional practices.

DIRECT AND EXPLICIT INSTRUCTION

Direct, systematic, and explicit instruction includes clear, teacher-directed methods that can be implemented across content areas and grade levels. This type of instruction allows for teachers to present content in a logical sequence while providing students with multiple opportunities to respond to instruction and to receive corrective feedback and reinforcement. While there are important variations, the instructional model generally involves the teacher gaining students' attention and stating the goal or objective of the lesson followed by a short review of previously learned material. This brief opening is then followed by the main lesson of the teacher modeling the skills to be learned, providing extensive guided practice, and facilitating student independent practice. The conclusion of the lesson would involve a review of the days' learning. In their discussion of designing explicit lesson plans, Archer and Hughes (2011) highlight how to use physical, verbal, or visual prompts during guided practice. Verbal prompts can be broken down into "explicit directives (tell them what to do), questions (ask them what to do), or reminders (remind them what to do)" (Archer & Hughes, 2011, p. 33). Visual prompts include written or pictorial checklists. When a student is initially learning a skill, the prompts can be more intrusive (physical and verbal directives) and the prompts gradually lessen in intensity as students are able to complete the skills independently.

Vocabulary instruction can also be incorporated into a direct instruction lesson. In a variation of direct instruction called explicit instruction, Goeke (2009) recommends preteaching vocabulary words in the introduction to the lesson. For students with ELL, directly teaching new vocabulary and providing multiple interactions with novel vocabulary is beneficial. For example, fifth-grade students, including ELL, demonstrated increases in reading comprehension after receiving direct, explicit instruction in vocabulary (Carlo et al., 2004). During the 30- and 45-minutes of instruction 4 days a week for 15 weeks, students engaged in a variety of vocabulary activities, in both English and Spanish (Carlo et al., 2004). For example, students learned the Spanish cognate of English words or completed cloze passages in small groups with new vocabulary words.

The use of direct, explicit instructional practices are related to decreases in inappropriate behavior of students identified as EBD including those who are also identified as ELL. For example, in a comparison of three types of instructional practices with four students with EBD in a self-contained classroom, Nelson, Johnson, & Marchand-Martella (1996) found that the students consistently demonstrated greater levels of on-task behavior and less disruptive behavior during lessons utilizing direct, explicit instruction than when students engaged in cooperative group learning or independent work. Similarly, students in kindergarten through third grade who were identified as having reading difficulties and/or demonstrating aggressive classroom behaviors received either supplemental direct instruction or typical classroom instruction (Gunn, Smolkowski, Biglan, & Black, 2002). The supplemental reading instruction included either Reading Mastery (beginning readers) or Corrective Reading (older nonreaders). Both programs included principles of direct instruction, followed a strict scope and sequence of skill progression, and included scripted lessons in the structured code-based reading program. After participating in the supplemental instruction, these students had significantly higher scores on measures of word attack skills and oral reading fluency than those who did not receive the additional instruction (Gunn et al., 2002). Interestingly, there were no group differences on measures of comprehension or vocabulary (Gunn et al., 2002).

The Gunn et al. (2002) study included 158 Hispanic students, many who demonstrated inappropriate classroom behaviors. Hispanic students participating in the intervention program demonstrated improved performance in word attack, oral reading fluency, and passage comprehension, but not letter–word identification or vocabulary compared to those who did not participate (Gunn et al., 2002). Although they did not find a significant interaction between the level of English proficiency and student progress, the authors noted limited sample sizes to detect an effect.

In a study of four ELLs who demonstrated problematic classroom behaviors, Preciado, Horner, and Baker (2008) were able to effectively integrate academic and behavioral interventions. A functional behavioral assessment identified that the students engaged in inappropriate behaviors to escape from completing difficult work. The behaviors included disengagement from an activity, talking inappropriately, playing with objects, or refusing to work. The four-part intervention combined multiple practices including direct explicit instruction in decoding using the Reading Mastery program and a review of the next day's class reading lesson paired with vocabulary instruction. The student and his one-on-one tutor also addressed classroom behaviors including the review of directions for independent work and positive classroom social skills. Results of the single-subject across participants study demonstrated gains in oral reading fluency and task completion, with three of the four students also demonstrating improved behavior with the intervention (Preciado et al.).

For young ELL students, direct instructional practices can be effective in augmenting comprehension as well as word reading skills. Kindergarten students should receive daily direct, explicit instruction in phonemic awareness, letter knowledge, word reading, reading connected text, and comprehension (Vaughn et al., 2006). According to Vaughn et al. (2006), instruction should follow the principles of direct instructional practices and include a quick pace with multiple opportunities for responses, feedback, and scaffold instruction. Using these practices, Vaughn et al. reported significant gains in letter–word identification and phonemic awareness for ELL in the direct instruction supplemental intervention. Also, the researchers found that significant gains in comprehension were recorded for the ELL compared to those students who did not receive the instructional program. Vaughn et al. concluded that direct instructional practices are promising for ELL who also need behavioral supports.

COGNITIVE STRATEGY INSTRUCTION

Cognitive strategy instruction involves a systematic method requiring a series of steps to help a student complete a process or sequence when learning. Self-regulated strategy development (SRSD) can be used to help students process information to work through reading comprehension, mathematics, and written expression. SRSD involves six steps including some that are similar to direct explicit instruction. First, teachers activate student background knowledge (Nelson, Benner, & Mooney, 2008) by identifying necessary information and skills and then assessing student knowledge in that area (Reid & Leinemann, 2006). Next, teachers discuss the strategy to be taught to the student. At this point, it is very important to *sell* the strategy by explaining why it is important for the student to learn. The teacher then discusses the various steps in the strategy. The essential step involves the teacher modeling and thinking aloud through the strategy (Reid & Leinemann, 2006). This goes beyond just putting a math problem on the board and stating how to move the numbers around on the page. When modeling, the teacher explains why the steps are used and verbalizes the reasoning and thought process behind it. To help students master this strategy, Reid and Leinemann (2006) identified four questions the students can ask as they work. The questions are "Why am I doing this step in the task?; How did I know to do it?; What are the important actions, cues, or questions?; and What knowledge do I need?" (p. 39). The fourth step of SRSD involves memorizing the steps of the strategy.

After students are able to verbally recite the steps, they gradually begin to take over working problems, writing or answering questions independently. Reid and Leinemann (2006) suggest different three types of scaffolding during the guided practice, including, content, task, and material. Initially, the teacher can provide easier content for the student, or the student completes the easier steps and the teacher does the more difficult parts. Students also learn to evaluate their own performance. Students need to experience success when initially using the strategy. Eventually, students complete the last step of independent practice.

Academic instruction using the SRSD model can be used in conjunction with a Positive Behavioral Support model for students with behavioral difficulties. Lane, Graham, Harris, and Weisenbach (2006) describe the use of the mnemonics *POW* and *WWW, What = 2, How = 2* to teach narrative writing to two second graders. In addition to the SRSD steps described above, modifications were made that included providing additional verbal praise and using token reinforcement to promote positive behaviors. The *POW* strategy focuses on student planning of a story (*Pick* an idea, *Organize* notes, *Write*, and say more). The *WWW, What = 2, How = 2* strategy helps students ask questions to ascertain what to include when writing a story such as "who is the main character?" and "how does the story end?" Lane et al. (2008) noted that after instruction, students' stories included more story components and had greater clarity. In another study with the same strategy, six second-grade students included more story components in their writing and demonstrated improved writing quality after instruction (Lane et al., 2008). In the Lane et al. (2010) extension of the strategy with students who exhibited either internalizing or externalizing behavioral difficulties, similar gains in narrative story writing were found.

Strategy instruction has also been used to improve the persuasive writing for students with EBD. For example, Mason and Shriner (2007) taught six elementary school students with EBD, the *POW* and *TREE* strategies. After receiving instruction, students in both early elementary and later elementary placements demonstrated an increase in the number of essay parts written (topic sentence, three or more reasons for argument, ending), and writing quality ratings. Directly after instruction, these students wrote more words, but this effect was not as high after an elapsed period of time (Mason & Shriner, 2007).

SRSD can also be effective with reading comprehension. This was demonstrated in a study by Rogevich and Perin (2008) when they used a comprehension strategy with adolescent's students with EBD. The researchers combined the reading comprehension strategy of *Thinking before Reading, While Reading*, and *After Reading* with writing to facilitate the students reading of science texts. Rogevich and Perin reported that students with EBD who received the combined reading comprehension strategy instruction demonstrated greater gains on science posttests. In addition, students generalized the use of the strategy to other subject areas. and they expressed high levels of satisfaction with the strategy.

Olson and Land (2007) used cognitive strategy instruction with secondary ELL students. The use of the writing strategy resulted in a significant increase in writing proficiency by the students over a seven-year period. Olson and Land stressed that the utilization of cognitive modeling and extensive guided practice with strategies for both reading comprehension and written expression can produce significant gains. Although not as systematic and structured as the SRSD model, these researchers stressed that the Reader's and Writer's Tool Kit allowed teachers to model how to understand the strategies and know when, why, and how long to use them when reading and writing. According to Olson and Land (2007), this process lead to the students reflecting upon how they learn through journaling. Not only did students demonstrate gains in written expression skills in this program compared to their previous written expression skills, but they also demonstrated greater gains in writing than their peers in a different program (Olson & Land, 2007).

Cognitive strategy instruction is a valuable instructional practice because it provides students with a clear picture of what goes on in the process of reading and writing through teacher modeling and explanation. In addition, it provides the student with substantial practice while gradually decreasing levels of teacher support. For students with EBD and ELL, additional time in guided practice might be required, but it allows the students to feel successful as the strategy is employed. Cognitive strategy instruction for students with EBD and ELL works best when specific behavioral management supports are implemented to support appropriate student behavior (see Lane et al., 2010).

PEER-MEDIATED INSTRUCTION

Peer-mediated instruction involves students in homogeneous or mixed groupings working together toward academic outcomes. Students can work with partners or in small cooperative groups. Initially, a teacher provides instruction in how to work in the dyads and then peers provide each other with instruction and feedback. ELL and students identified as EBD have demonstrated gains when working in the roles of tutor and tutee in classwide peer tutoring programs (CWPT) or variations such as Peer-Assisted Learning Strategies (PALS).

There are several different variations of classwide peer tutoring that have been developed. CWPT was initially developed for students to receive additional practice on specific skills and multiple opportunities to respond to instruction to master specific content (Delaquadri, Greenwood, Stretton, & Hall, 1983). It involves a very specific set of guidelines in which a pair of students takes turns in the roles of tutor or tutee. The class is divided into two teams. Teachers provide the sight words, spelling lists, or math problems to be reviewed by each pair. The tutor is responsible for providing corrective feedback and recording the points earned by the tutor as he or she reads or spells words orally and in writing (J. Delaquadri, Greenwood, Whorton, Carta, & Hall, 1986). CWPT has also been found to be effective when used by teachers to address math computation (Arreaga-Mayer, 1989). For example, Aggeara-Mayer (1989) describes how teachers arranged the instructional situation such that if the tutee makes a math error, the tutor immediately corrects his partner, and the tutee has to practice the correct answer three times. Tutees are awarded points by the tutor: 2 points for a correct first response, 1 point for following through with the correct procedure, and 0 points for additional errors or not completing the corrective procedure. After one student completes the activities, the students switch roles. The teacher, who is monitoring the groups in the class, can also award both the tutor and the tutee for keeping an appropriate pace, following directions, providing encouraging remarks, and appropriately handling being informed that an answer was incorrect. The procedure is repeated four days per week and the pairs' points are totaled with the other members of their team. Additional points are awarded for accurate completion. At the beginning of the next week, students select a new partner.

One variation of CWPT is PALS. Instead of randomly pairing students through a weekly drawing, teachers purposefully pair one student performing in the top half of the class with a student performing in the bottom half of the class (Fuchs & Fuchs, 2005). In PALS, students still alternate roles, but the higher performing student is the tutor first. Additionally, the instructional material is geared toward the needs of the lower performing student and partner groupings change less frequently.

In their review of studies that included EBD students in peer-mediated instruction, Ryan, Reid, and Epstein (2004) found a large overall effect for peer-mediated interventions across subject areas regardless of age grouping (same age or cross-age groupings). Interestingly, they found that when students with EBD functioned only as tutees, the effect size was smaller than in the reviewed studies in which the students served in both roles or only participated in the role of the tutor. This finding was demonstrated in a study (Bell, Young, Blair, & Nelson, 1990) of adolescents with EBD while studying history. In this study, the students took on the role of a tutor and a tutee. Bell et al. (1990) reported that all students made substantial gains between the pretest and posttest on the history content. Another study (Falk & Wehby, 2001) with young children, who worked as both tutor and tutee in a phonemic awareness tutoring program, students with EBD demonstrated significant gains depending on the measure used. More specifically, pre- and post-interventions tests on blending and letter sound identification demonstrated significant gains, but segmentation skills were not changed (Falk & Wehby, 2001).

Peer tutoring has also been found to be effective with ELL (McMaster, Kung, Han, & Cho, 2008). For instance, McMaster et al. (2008) examined the performance of 60 kindergarten ELLs who participated in a peer tutoring through a K-PALS reading program that involved a variety of phonemic awareness activities and reading sight words. In this study, students (both ELL and non-ELL students) switched roles of tutor and tutee. McMaster et al. reported that the ELL participating in PALS scored higher on measures related to phonemic awareness but not on word reading or spelling than ELL who were exposed to their typical reading instruction program.

According to Greenwood, Arreaga-Mayer, Utley, Gavin, and Terry (2001) modifications may be necessary when using CWPT for ELL. For example, Greenwood et al. reported results on the use of CWPT for spelling with 117 ELLs. In this study, the students took turns in the role of tutor or tutee while one spelled a dictated word orally and in writing, while another checked the tutee's response and awarded points. Then, the students switched roles. ELL in first grade used flash cards to learn sight words, and a procedure was implemented to facilitate the pair asking for clarification if neither student knew the word. For ELL in second to fifth grades, words were presented at the beginning of the week in English and Spanish. Then, students who recently moved to the United States were paired with bilingual students. Greenwood et al. reported that overall the students had substantial gains on spelling and sight word knowledge tests between 52 and 67% over the pretest.

Intervention effectiveness for ELL may be influenced by reading ability. For instance, Wayman, McMaster, Saenz, and Watson (2010) reported on secondary ELL who participated in a PALS program that compared high reading and high language skills students with high reading and low language skills students. According to these researchers, both groups made progress in a PALS program. However, it appeared that secondary ELL with lower reading skills (regardless of language ability) benefitted more from supplemental reading programs that were more intensive than PALS such as partner retells with oral readings and paragraph shrinking that required summarization of the text.

Peer interventions can also be paired with direct instruction practices. This was the situation in a 12-week intervention that combined direct, explicit instruction program in reading, Open Court, with PALS in reading (Wehby, Falk, Barton-Arwood, Lane, & Cooley, 2003). In this study, eight students with EBD demonstrated significant growth in several measures of phonological awareness but not word reading (Wehby et al., 2003). Wehby et al. (2003) indicated that there were limited changes related to the improvement of student behavior.

Although CWPT have demonstrated substantial gains for students with EBD and students with ELL, there are cautions with using this program with dual-needs students. First, modifications will need to be made depending on student language proficiency. Students with limited English skills should be paired with students who are bilingual rather than random assignment (Arreaga-Mayer, 1989). Also, teachers will need to make sure students have ample practice with the directions. Furthermore, it is critical to present information to the students in advance of the actual tutoring. Lastly, contingencies need to be in place if neither pair knows that answer to the problem (Greenwood et al., 2001).

In recent years, there have been calls for additional research on academic strategies for students with ELLs (Vaughn & Klingner, 2004) and students with EBD (Wehby et al., 2003). While we echo this need for research on these populations, it is also important to consider students with both ELL and EBD. As the numbers of students with ELL increase across the country, those with ELL and EBD will continue to be an area of need. Students with multiple and intensive needs will continue to require evidence-based practices implemented with high rates of fidelity. Part of evidence-based practice is answering the question "For Whom?" As a result, additional research is needed on these strategies to ensure that they are effective for students from these populations and that necessary modifications based on student need for the strategies are considered and evaluated.

CONCLUSION

This chapter has addressed significant challenges related to the identification and intervention of children that are ELLs and EBD. The challenges include the limitations in pre-intervention strategies and a lack of culturally appropriate assessment devices. In addition, there are limited instructional interventions with evidence-based research specific to this population. As a result, practitioners must rely on promising or evidence-based practices specific to either children with EBD or ELL or an emphasis on integrating these practices to insure academic and behavioral success for this population.

REFERENCES

Archer, A. L., & Hughes, C. A. (2011). *Explicit instruction: Effective and efficient teaching.* New York, NY: Guilford Press.

Arreaga-Mayer, C. (1989). Increasing activity student responding and improving academic performance through classwide per tutoring. *Interventions in School and Clinic, 34*, 89–94.

Artiles, A. J., Harry, B., Reschly, D. J., & Chinn, P. C. (2002). Over-identification of students of color in special education: A critical overview. *Multicultural Perspectives, 4*(1), 3–10.

Artiles, A. J., & Ortiz, A. A. (2002). English Language Learners with special education needs. Center for Applied Linguistics. Retrieved from ERIC database (ED 482995).

Aukerman, M. (2007). A culpable CALP: Rethinking the conversations/academic language proficiency distinction in early literacy instruction. *The Reading Teacher, 60*(7), 626–635.

Bell, K., Young, K. R., Blair, M., & Nelson, R. (1990). Facilitating mainstreaming of students with behavioral disorders using class wide peer tutoring. *School Psychology Review, 19*(4), 564–573.

Black, R. S. (2010). Can underidentification affect exceptional learners?. In F. E. Obiakor, J. P. Bakken & A. F. Rotatori (Eds.), *Current issues and trends in special education: Identification, assessment, and instruction* (Vol. 19, pp. 37–51). Bingley, UK: Emerald Group Publishing Limited.

Carlo, M. S., August, D., McLaughlin, B., Snow, S., Dressler, C., Lippman, D., & White, C. E. (2004). Closing the gap: Addressing the vocabulary needs of English-language learners in bilingual and mainstream classrooms. *Reading Research Quarterly, 29*, 188–215.

Cummins, J. (1999–2000). BICS and CALP: Clarifying the distinction. Retrieved from ERIC database (ED 438551).

Delaquadri, J., Greenwood, C. R., Whorton, D., Carta, J. J., & Hall, R. V. (1986). Classwide peer tutoring. *Exceptional Children, 52*, 535–542.

Delaquadri, J. C., Greenwood, C. R., Stretton, K., & Hall, R. V. (1983). The peer tutoring spelling game: A classroom procedure for increasing opportunity to respond and spelling performance. *Education & Treatment of Children, 6*, 225–239.

Donovan, M. S., & Cross, C. T. (2002). *Minority students in special and gifted education.* Washington, DC: National Research Council.

Duran, R. P. (2008). Assessing English-language learners' achievement. *Review of Research in Education, 32*(1), 292–327. doi:10.3102/0091732x07309372

Dyches, T. T., & Prater, M. A. (2010). Disproportionate representation in special education: Overrepresentation of selected subgroups. In F. E. Obiakor, J. P. Bakken & A. F. Rotatori (Eds.), *Current issues and trends in special education: Identification, assessment, and instruction* (Vol. 19, pp. 53–71). Bingley, UK: Emerald Group Publishing Limited.

Ehlers-Zavala, F. P. (2011). History of bilingual special education. In A. F. Rotatori, F. E. Obiakor & J. P. Bakken (Eds.), *History of special education* (Vol. 21, pp. 343–361). Bingley, UK: Emerald Group Publishing Limited.

Epstein, M. H., Kinder, D., & Bursuck, B. (1989). The academic status of adolescents with behavioral disorders. *Behavioral Disorders, 14*, 157–165.

Falk, K. B., & Wehby, J. H. (2001). The effects of peer-assisted learning strategies on beginning reading skills of young children with emotional or behavioral disorders. *Behavioral Disorders, 26*, 344–359.

Fuchs, S., & Fuchs, L. S. (2005). Peer-assisted learning strategies: Prompting word recognition, fluency, and reading comprehension in young children. *The Journal of Special Education, 39*, 34–44.

Goeke, J. L. (2009). *Explicit instruction: A framework for meaningful direct teaching.* Upper Saddle River, NJ: Pearson.

Green, L. S. (2010). Multicultural education: A necessary tool for general and special education. In F. E. Obiakor, J. P. Bakken & A. F. Rotatori (Eds.), *Current issues and trends in special education: Research, technology, and teacher preparation* (Vol. 20, pp. 1207–1232). Bingley, UK: Emerald Group Publishing Limited.

Greenwood, C. R., Arreaga-Mayer, C., Utley, C. A., Gavin, K. M., & Terry, B. J. (2001). Classwide peer tutoring learning management system: Applications with elementary-level English Language Learners. *Remedial and Special Education, 22*, 34–47.

Grossman, H., Utley, C. A., & Obiakor, F. E. (2003). Multicultural learners with exceptionalities in general and special education settings. In F. E. Obiakor, C. A. Utley & A. F. Rotatori (Eds.), *Effective education for learners with exceptionalities* (Vol. 15, pp. 445–463). Oxford, UK: Elsevier Science Ltd.

Gunn, B., Smolkowski, K., Biglan, A., & Black, C. (2002). Supplemental instruction in decoding skills for Hispanic and non-Hispanic students in early elementary school: A follow-up. *The Journal of Special Education, 36*, 69–79.

Kieffer, M. J. (2008). Catching up or falling behind? Initial English language proficiency, concentrated poverty, and the reading growth of language minority learners in the United States. *Journal of Educational Psychology, 100*, 851–868.

Klingner, J. K., & Artiles, A. J. (2003). When should bilingual students be in special education? *Educational Leadership, 44*(October), 66–71.

Klingner, J. K., & Harry, B. (2006). The special education referral and decision-making process for English Language Learners: Child study team meetings and placement conferences. *Teachers College Record, 108*(11), 2247–2281.

Klingner, J. K., & Vaughn, S. (1996). Reciprocal teaching of reading comprehension strategies for students with learning disabilities who use English as a second language. *The Elementary School Journal, 96,* 275–293.

Klotz, M. B., & Canter, A. (2006). Culturally competent assessment and consultation. Retrieved from http://www.nasponline.org/resources/principals/culturally%20competent%20assessment%20and%20consultation%20nassp.pdf. Accessed on July 11, 2011.

Lane, K. L., Graham, S., Harris, K. R., Little, A., Sandmel, K., & Brindle, M. (2010). The effects of self-regulated strategy development for second-grade students with writing and behavioral difficulties. *The Journal of Special Education, 44,* 107–128.

Lane, K. L., Graham, S., Harris, K. R., & Weisenbach, J. L. (2006). Teaching writing strategies to young students struggling with writing and at risk for behavioral disorders: Self-regulated strategy development. *Teaching Exceptional Children, 39*(1), 60–64.

Lane, K. L., Harris, K. R., Graham, S., Weisenbach, J. L., Brindle, M., & Morphy, P. (2008). The effects of self-regulated strategy development on the writing performance of second-grade students with behavioral and writing difficulties. *The Journal of Special Education, 41,* 234–253.

Mason, L. H., & Shriner, J. G. (2007). Self-regulated strategy development instruction for writing an opinion essay: Effects for six students with emotional/behavioral disorders. *Reading and Writing: A Multidisciplinary Journal, 21,* 71–93.

McMaster, K. L., Kung, S., Han, I., & Cho, M. (2008). Peer-assisted learning strategies: A "Tier 1" approach to promoting English learners' response to intervention. *Exceptional Children, 74,* 194–214.

Nelson, J. R., Benner, G. J., & Mooney, P. (2008). *Instructional practices for students with behavioral disorders: Strategies for reading, writing, and math.* New York, NY: Guilford Press.

Nelson, J. R., Johnson, A., & Marchand-Martella, N. (1996). Effects of direct instruction, cooperative learning, and independent learning practices on the classroom behavior of students with behavioral disorders: A comparative analysis. *Journal of Emotional and Behavioral Disorders, 4,* 53–62.

Obiakor, F. E. (2010). Multicultural education: Not a general and special education panacea. In F. E. Obiakor, J. P. Bakken & A. F. Rotatori (Eds.), *Current issues and trends in special education: Research, technology, and teacher preparation* (Vol. 20, pp. 123–141). Bingley, UK: Emerald Group Publishing Limited.

Obiakor, F. E. (2011). Historical and cotemporary contexts, challenges, and prospects in the education of students with exceptionalities. In A. F. Rotatori, F. E. Obiakor & J. P. Bakken (Eds.), *History of special education* (Vol. 21, pp. 363–378). Bingley, UK: Emerald Group Publishing Limited.

Obiakor, F. E., & Mukuria, G. M. (2007). Special education leadership in urban schools. In F. E. Obiakor, A. F. Rotatori & S. Burkhardt (Eds.), *Current perspectives in special education administration* (Vol. 17, pp. 55–70). Oxford, UK: Elsevier.

Ochoa, T. A., Gerber, M. M., Leafstedt, J. M., Hough, S., Kyle, S., Rogers-Adkinson, D., & Koomar, P. (2001). Web technology as a teaching tool: A multicultural special education case. *Journal of International Forum of Educational Technology & Society, 4*(1), 50–60.

Oliveira, A. L., & Anca, M. H. (2009). "I speak five languages": Fostering plurilingual competence through language awareness. *Language Awareness, 18*(3/4), 403–421.

Olson, C. B., & Land, R. (2007). A cognitive strategies approach to reading and writing instruction for English Language Learners in secondary school. *Research in the Teaching of English, 41,* 269–303.

O'Malley, J. M. (1994). State assessment policies, practices, and language minority students. *Educational Assessment, 2*(3), 213–255.

Preciado, J. A., Horner, R. H., & Baker, S. K. (2008). Using a function-based approach to decrease problem behavior and increase academic engagement for Latino English Language Learners. *The Journal of Special Education, 42*, 227–240.

Reid, R., & Leinemann, T. O. (2006). *Strategy instruction for students with learning disabilities.* New York, NY: Guilford Press.

Rinaldi, C. (2010). Ask the experts: Can you provide examples or research on implementing RtI in dual language immersion schools? A response from Claudia Rinaldi. In RTI Network. Retrieved from http://www.rtinetworkorg/connect/askexperts.

Roessingh, H. (2006). BICS-CALP: An introduction for some, a review for others. *TESL Canada Journal, 23*(2), 91–96.

Rogers-Adkinson, D. L., Ochoa, T., & Delgado, B. (2003). Developing cross-cultural competence in serving families with significant developmental needs. *Focus on Autism and Other Developmental Disabilities, 18*(1), 4–8.

Rogevich, M. E., & Perin, D. (2008). Effects on science summarization of a reading comprehension intervention for adolescents with behavior and attention disorders. *Exceptional Children, 74*, 135–154.

Ryan, J. B., Reid, R., & Epstein, M. H. (2004). Peer-mediated intervention studies on academic achievement for students with EBD: A review. *Remedial and Special Education, 25*(6), 330–341.

Saenz, L. M., Fuchs, L. S., & Fuchs, D. (2005). Peer-assisted learning strategies for English language learners with learning disabilities. *Exceptional Children, 71*, 231–247.

Salvia, J., Ysseldyke, J., & Bolt, S. (2010). *Assessment in special and inclusive education.* New York, NY: Houghton Mifflin.

Serpa, M. (2011). *An imperative for change: Bridging special and English language education to ensure a free and appropriate education in the least restrictive environment for ELLS with disabilities in Massachusetts.* Cambridge, MA: The Mauricio Gaston Institute for Latino Community Development and Public Policy.

Sullivan, A. (2011). Disproportionality in special education identification and placement of English Language Learners. *Exceptional Children, 77*(3), 317–334.

U.S. Department of Education. (2009). *28th annual report to Congress on the implementation of the Individuals with Disabilities Education Act.* Washington, DC: Office of Special Education Programs.

Vaughn, S., & Klingner, J. K. (2004). Strategies for struggling second-language readers. In T. L. Jetton & J. A. Dole (Eds.), *Adolescent literacy research and practice* (pp. 183–209). New York, NY: Guildford Press.

Vaughn, S., Mathes, P., Linan-Thompson, S., Cirino, P., Carlson, C., Pollard-Durodoloa, S., & Francis, D. (2006). Effectiveness of an English intervention for first-grade English Language Learners at risk for reading problems. *The Elementary School Journal, 107*, 153–180.

Wagner, R. K., Francis, D. J., & Morris, R. D. (2005). Identifying English language learns with learning disabilities: Key challenges and possible approaches. *Learning Disabilities Research, 20*(1), 30–38.

Wayman, M. M., McMaster, K. L., Saenz, L. M., & Watson, J. A. (2010). Using curriculum-based measurement to monitor secondary English Language Learners' responsiveness to peer-mediated reading instruction. *Reading & Writing Quarterly, 26*, 308–332.

Wehby, J. H., Falk, K. F., Barton-Arwood, S., Lane, K. L., & Cooley, C. (2003). The impact of comprehensive reading instruction on the academic and social behavior of students with emotional and behavioral disorders. *Journal of Emotional and Behavioral Disorders, 11,* 225–238.

Wehby, J. H., Lane, K. L., & Falk, K. B. (2003). Academic instruction for students with emotional and behavioral disorders. *Journal of Emotional and Behavioral Disorders, 11,* 194–197.

Zetlin, A., Beltran, D., Salcido, P., Gonzalez, T., & Reyes, T. (2011). Building a pathway of optimal support for English Language Learners in special education. *Teacher Education and Special Education, 34*(1), 59–70.

CHAPTER 8

BEHAVIOR MODIFICATION/ TRADITIONAL TECHNIQUES FOR STUDENTS WITH EMOTIONAL AND BEHAVIORAL DISORDERS

Paul Mooney, Joseph B. Ryan, Philip L. Gunter and R. Kenton Denny

ABSTRACT

In addressing positive general education teaching practices for use with students with or at risk for emotional and behavioral disorders (EBD), the chapter emphasizes teacher behavior change research that has been informed by applied behavior analytic (ABA) principles. Its central theme is that general education teachers can access research informed by ABA in developing prosocial instructional and management practices. Highlighted teaching practices include fostering correct academic responses from students, increasing active student response, and using contingent praise with regularity. The chapter also discusses functional behavioral assessment, positive behavioral interventions and supports, and controversial behavior change issues surrounding seclusion and restraints and medication, topics related to teaching students with or at risk for EBD in general education settings.

Behavioral Disorders: Identification, Assessment, and Instruction of Students with EBD
Advances in Special Education, Volume 22, 173–202
Copyright © 2012 by Emerald Group Publishing Limited
All rights of reproduction in any form reserved
ISSN: 0270-4013/doi:10.1108/S0270-4013(2012)0000022011

Keywords: Applied behavior analysis; teacher behavior change; functional behavioral assessment; positive behavioral interventions and supports; restraint; medication

Behavior modification has been described as a scientific approach to analyzing and modifying human behavior in meaningful ways (Kazdin, 2001; Miltenberger, 2001). In the field of emotional and behavioral disorders (EBD), meaningful behavior change research has largely taken place by employing principles of applied behavior analysis (ABA). Cooper, Heron, and Heward (2007) define ABA as "the science in which tactics derived from the principles of behavior are applied systematically to improve socially significant behavior and experimentation is used to identify the variables responsible for behavior change" (p. 20). Accurate application of behavior change principles assumes that we specify, understand, and systematically manipulate temporal and functional relationships between a socially relevant behavior and what occurs before, during, and after that behavior in a given context. In this way, we can increase the likelihood of meaningful change by teaching replacement behaviors, altering the environment, and/or reducing problem behavior (Lewis, Lewis-Palmer, Newcomer, & Stichter, 2004).

In this chapter, we examine research targeting teacher behavior change that is informed by ABA. We highlight teacher behavior change as the unit of analysis because changes in teacher behavior impact both teacher and student behavior. The chapter focuses on several major themes including (a) research addressing specific actions (e.g., promoting correct student responding, increasing student opportunities to respond, and increasing rates of praise) that teachers can take to promote prosocial student–teacher interactions and classroom environments; (b) the potential for research to continue to identify factors that increase active student engagement, promote student achievement, and reduce the likelihood for coercive interactions between students and teachers; and (c) commonly used yet controversial methods of behavior management for students with EBD. We begin by providing a rationale for attending to teacher behavior in schools. Following the rationale, we discuss the utility of functional behavioral assessment (FBA), provide both a historical and a current perspective on research into teacher–student interactions in classrooms for students with or at risk for EBD, and discuss both schoolwide and controversial behavior modification practices and issues. We conclude the chapter by addressing avenues for future research across the areas introduced. Throughout the chapter, we make an empirical case that teachers can be positive change agents in classrooms and schools for students with or at risk for EBD by effectively specifying, understanding, and systematically manipulating their instructional interactions with students in their environment.

RATIONALE FOR FOCUS ON TEACHER BEHAVIOR CHANGE

Our rationale for targeting teacher behavior change using principles of ABA is multidimensional and informed by factors impacting students, teachers, classrooms, and schools. Over the past decade, research has demonstrated that teachers who provide frequent negative reactions to their students' problem behaviors while ignoring positive behaviors may unintentionally increase the likelihood of future maladaptive behavior continuing (Sutherland & Oswald, 2005); in this case, the hypothesis indicates that maladaptive behaviors are positively reinforced by teacher attention. Similarly, when teachers focus on positively reinforcing prosocial behaviors, these behaviors increase through positive reinforcement while the number of maladaptive behaviors decrease if those behaviors are not positively reinforced (Leflot, van Lier, Onghena, & Colpin, 2010). Focusing on teacher behaviors is critical given that students with EBD are increasingly likely to be educated in less restrictive environments. Fig. 1 displays data from the Office of Special Education Programs' last eight annual reports to Congress and shows the percent of the school day that students with emotional disturbance – the legal term introduced in federal disabilities legislation – are being educated in the general education classroom. Review of the graph demonstrates that there has been steady growth in the percentage of students verified with emotional disturbance who receive the majority of their instruction from the general education teacher. Moreover, Fig. 1 also shows an accompanying decrease in the percentage of students with emotional disturbance who spend the majority of their instructional time in more restrictive settings. When we consider these related trends alongside the widely held belief that the population of students with emotional disturbance receiving special education services is underidentified (Kauffman, 2005), we can assume that a significant number of students with emotional disturbance (hereafter referred to as EBD) are taught in general classroom settings. Hence, it is a

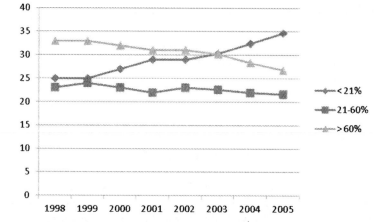

Figure 1. Percent of the School Day Students with Emotional Disturbance are Educated Outside of the General Education Classroom.

reasonable assertion to suggest that targeting meaningful teacher behavior change across all educational environments is worthy of attention. Couple that with recent research findings (Maggin, Wehby, Moore Partin, Robertson, & Oliver, 2011) indicating that students identified as at risk for EBD who were being taught in a general classroom tended to perform better academically and behaviorally than their counterparts in self-contained settings, and there is even more reason to believe that the general classroom setting is an arena in which positive behavior change should be promoted.

The second group of factors contributing to a focus on teacher behaviors encompasses recent trends toward the implementation of prevention-oriented systems such as Positive Behavioral Interventions and Supports (PBIS) and Response to Intervention (RTI) along with the move to greater collaboration practices in schools. In terms of prevention, both PBIS and RTI are based on problem-solving models and grounded in differentiated instruction that offer multiple levels of support that are systematically applied to students based on demonstrated need (Office of Special Education Programs Technical Assistance Center on PBIS, n.d.). These systems aim to avert school failure through the systematic application of evidence-based behavioral (PBIS) and academic (RTI) practices. In terms of collaboration, there has been increasing attention paid to collaborative teaching practices, inclusive education, and collaboration in general that likely has been spurred through legislation (Friend, Cook, Hurley-Chamberlain, & Shamberger,

2010). For example, passage of the No Child Left Behind Act of 2001 requires that all students, including those with EBD, access the general curriculum, be included in accountability systems, and be taught by highly qualified teachers. Furthermore, reauthorization of the Individuals with Disabilities Education Act (IDEA) in 2004 continued special education's emphasis on student access to and progress in the general curriculum. As a whole, successful implementation of prevention systems and collaborative practices is likely to continue the trend of students with EBD being served in less-restrictive settings.

The final group of factors contributing to our focus on classroom settings relates to teachers themselves. These factors are multi-faceted and directly related to the previous combinations of factors. On the one hand, and precisely because larger numbers of practicing and preservice general classroom teachers will be interacting with greater numbers of students with EBD than they may have previously, there is a greater likelihood of a mismatch between teacher capabilities and student behaviors. This mismatch could contribute to the continuation of the coercive teaching practices that have been frequently documented in the literature (Shores, Gunter, & Jack, 1993). Related to that is the body of literature that continues to document the lack of differentiation and individualization of teaching for students with special needs in public school classrooms (Scruggs, Mastropieri, & McDuffie, 2007; Vaughn, Moody, & Schumm, 1998). For example, in spite of the intuitive appeal of co-teaching as an instructional approach that facilitates access of students with disabilities to the general curriculum, there remains little variability in terms of the co-teaching models implemented in general education classrooms (Scruggs et al., 2007). That is, while varied co-teaching models that encourage equal status in teaching and managing content are described in the literature, the predominant model in practice remains the one teach, one assist model in which the special education teacher serves in a support role to the general classroom teacher (Harbort et al., 2007). And furthermore, Scruggs et al. (2007) noted that specialized instructional practices such as strategy instruction, use of mnemonics, and self-monitoring were rarely observed in practice. General education classroom observations conducted by Maggin et al. (2011) yielded teacher practices that included low rates of teacher praise and opportunities for students to respond to academic questions in settings that included students at risk for EBD.

On the other hand, research continues to point to the potential for positive behavior change that teachers can have. The "teacher effects" research (Rosenshine & Stevens, 1986) is seminal scholarship and points teachers in the direction of effective teacher behavior for all students, including those with disabilities. Ryan, Pierce, and Mooney (2008) highlighted academic interventions that demonstrated meaningful academic outcomes with students with EBD. And recently, a number of researchers have used ABA principles in attempting to promote meaningful teacher behavior change in the classroom. Stichter, Hudson, and Sasso (2005) used structural analysis to determine setting events that affect disruptive behavior in classroom settings. Haydon, Mancil, and Van Loan (2009) demonstrated that teacher increases in the rates of student opportunities to respond to academic content (OTR) in the general classroom resulted in increases in on-task behavior and correct responding and a decrease in disruptive behavior for a student at-risk for EBD. And Lane, Barton-Arwood, Spencer, and Kalberg (2007) demonstrated how intensive teacher training in the design, implementation, and evaluation of function-based interventions could be successfully carried out by general education teachers. As we turn our attention to FBA, the chapter's underlying message is that teachers can be agents of positive, meaningful, and adaptive change for students with or at risk for EBD.

FUNCTIONAL BEHAVIORAL ASSESSMENT

Initially, as part of IDEA 1997 and later IDEA 2004, FBA was required as an integral part of building behavior intervention plans for students with disabilities. FBA has been a part of the practice of applied behavior analysts for many years. Determining the antecedents, consequences, and contextual/ environmental variables associated with maladaptive behavior has long been promoted as the basis for developing effective behavioral interventions (Horner, 1994; Sasso et al., 1992). By gaining a better understanding of particular conditions that are reliably associated with the occurrence of challenging behavior, interventionists are in a position to attempt to prevent the problem behavior or respond to it in a fashion that will build appropriate replacement behavior(s).

Some authors (Heckaman, Conroy, Fox, & Chait, 2000; Sasso, Conroy, Stichter, & Fox, 2001) have questioned the validity of FBA procedures applied to students with a broader range of emotional and behavioral challenges than early research had examined. Students with EBD most frequently impact classroom environments where considerations regarding the instructional as well as the social-behavioral are critical in the appropriate analysis of classroom-based behavior problems. Many of the procedures designed for students with significant intellectual disabilities could be considered narrow for assessing environmental influences for students with EBD.

There is a growing research base that has extended the application of FBA procedures to students with EBD with consistently favorable results (Briere & Simonsen, 2011; Kamps, Wedland, & Culpepper, 2006; Kern, Delaney, Clarke, Dunlap, & Childs, 2001; Lane, Weisenbach, Little, Phillips, & Wehby, 2006; Lewis & Sugai, 1996; Umbreit, 1995; Umbreit, Lane, & Dejud, 2004). FBA has been used to successfully address a range of behaviors exhibited by students with EBD in a range of environments. Interventions, based on functional assessment, have increased academic engagement (Ingram, Lewis-Palmer, & Sugai, 2005; Stahr, Cushing, Lane, & Fox, 2006; Umbreit & Blair, 1997; Umbreit et al., 2004), improved levels of social engagement (Lane, Thompson, Reske, Gable, & Barton-Arwood, 2006), decreased off-task and disruptive behavior (Kern, Childs, Dunlap, Clarke, & Falk, 1994; Umbreit & Blair, 1997), and decreased aggressive behaviors (Dufrene, Doggett, Henington, & Watson, 2007). Interventions based in functional assessment have proven effective in self-contained schools (Stahr et al., 2006), self-contained classrooms (Dunlap, Kern-Dunlap, Clarke, & Robbins, 1991; Lane, Thompson et al., 2006), preschools (Umbreit, 1995), and general education classrooms (Ingram et al., 2005; Kamps et al., 2006; Kern et al., 2001; Umbreit et al., 2004).

While the range of methods for conducting FBA varies widely (Dunlap & Kincaid, 2001; O'Neil et al., 1997), the process traditionally follows a systematic approach to clearly identify the challenging behavior; observe the frequency/duration of the behavior under specified conditions and times; identify the most common antecedents and consequences through direct and indirect methods; and form testable hypothesis of the function or purpose that the problem behavior serves for the individual (Anderson & Scott, 2006; O'Neil et al., 1997). The data from the various sources of information (direct observations, interviews, record reviews, social behavior checklists, etc.) are reviewed to identify the tentative function or functions of the problem behaviors (Umbreit, Ferro, Liaupsin, & Lane, 2007). Consistent with a focus on student behavior, functions are generally simply identified as positively reinforcing (gaining objects/attention) or negatively reinforcing (escape/avoidance) or in some instances self-stimulation functions.

Once the function of behavior is tentatively identified, interventionists may propose procedures to make the inappropriate behavior less effective and less efficient in meeting the function/purpose and appropriate replacement behavior(s) more effective and more efficient in obtaining positive consequences (Sugai, Lewis-Palmer, & Hagan-Burke, 2001). Through the manipulation of antecedent or consequent conditions, the focus becomes one of identifying more appropriate behavior to teach systematically and reinforce consistently and/or to rearrange antecedent conditions to prevent problem behavior (Umbreit et al., 2007).

Umbreit et al. (2007) provide an extension of the process to examine contextual variables (e.g., physical space, instruction, and management procedures) to provide a decision matrix for intervention based on the identification of replacement behavior. A determination is made as a result of the FBA whether a student has the appropriate behavior in their repertoire. Students lacking the behavior are taught the skill systematically (O'Neil et al., 1997; J. Witt & Beck, 1999). Students possessing the behavior but failing to demonstrate with appropriate frequency are provided contingency-based interventions (Umbreit et al., 2007; J. Witt & Beck, 1999). An analysis of the environment in terms of teacher and teaching behavior identifies possible improvements and so the environment responds more effectively and efficiently to problem behavior (Sugai et al., 2001). Ideally, this process identifies interventions that may be more acceptable to significant others in the environment (Martens, Witt, Elliott, & Darveaux, 1985; J.C. Witt & Elliott, 1985), have a higher likelihood of being consistently applied (Gunter & Denny, 2004; Kamps et al., 2006; Lane, Weisenbach et al., 2006), and lead to the provision of more positive consequences to students with EBD (Shores, Gunter et al., 1993).

FBA provides a process for addressing problem behavior of students with EBD within the contexts of schools. It has the potential to provide information on the environmental conditions that predict or maintain behavior, provide information on the selection and targeting of interventions (student focus or teacher focus), and is a process that can be implemented by trained teachers in the classroom (Grey, Honan, McClean, & Daly, 2005; Maag & Larsen, 2004) especially with support of consultants or coaches (Kamps et al., 2006; Lane et al., 2006). Ellingson, Miltenberger, Sticker, Galensky, and Garlinghouse (2000) evaluated the reliability of teacher-collected data on the antecedents and consequences of problem behavior. The teachers used a checklist format to note the occurrence of behavior, along with the relevant antecedents and consequences. Inter-observer agreement was collected between experimenters and classroom teachers. For the three teachers, mean percentages of agreement on the antecedents and consequences recorded for each behavior were 92%, 86%, and 73%, with a range of 57–100% across observations. Ellingson et al. (2000) indicated that the level of agreement between the teachers and the experimenters was adequate to produce the same conclusions about the consequence maintaining problem behavior and suggested that relatively inexperienced observers can collect descriptive data with a high degree of precision especially when given limited measurement options. Lane et al. (2007) have also demonstrated that with training, elementary school teams, which included both general and special educators, successfully designed, implemented, and evaluated function-based assessment and intervention procedures that resulted in decreases in problem behavior and increases in the use of functionally equivalent replacement behaviors.

HISTORY OF RESEARCH ON THE BEHAVIORS OF TEACHERS FOR STUDENTS WITH EBD

Given the poor academic outcomes for students with EBD (M.M. Wagner, 1995; M. Wagner et al., 2006), perhaps an important application of the constructs of ABA is toward academic instruction. Shores, Jack, and colleagues (1993) provided one of the first studies using a computerized sequential analysis of behaviors of participants in instructional settings in which a student with EBD was present. Individual events of any target participant (teacher or paraprofessional, student with EBD, and other students) were compared to events that preceded and followed the given event of interest using probability statements. Additionally, unconditional probabilities of events in the classroom interactions were reported. The findings from the study provided tremendous insight into the behavioral interactions of the classroom participants. For example, the unconditional probability data indicated that teacher directives to students were the most likely behaviors to occur in the classrooms. Interestingly, student compliance responses to teacher directives were the most likely behaviors to occur subsequent to teacher directives. One interpretation of this finding was that students with EBD most often attempt to respond to teacher directives.

Gunter, Shores, Jack, Denny, and DePaepe (1994) used the same lag sequential methodology employed by Shores, Jack, and colleagues (1993) in an attempt to understand the impact of modifying interactions between a teacher and student with EBD in an instructional setting. In the study, they demonstrated that altering behavior sequences from the teacher requesting a response from the student to requiring the teacher to provide information related to the question immediately before the teacher asking the question was associated with a decreased unconditional probability of disruptive behaviors from the student. Gunter and colleagues speculated that providing the information needed to successfully answer a teacher question reduced the aversive nature of the instructional behavior of teachers asking questions in isolation; the hypothesis that the disruptive behaviors were maintained to escape questions for which the student could not respond correctly was supported. In short, they hypothesized that many disruptive behaviors of students with EBD in instructional settings could be explained as being supported through a negative reinforcement paradigm (cf., Gunter & Coutinho, 1997). That is, disruptive behaviors were maintained by avoidance or removal of a stimulus (e.g., academic instruction) that has aversive characteristics for the students.

Obviously, since academic instruction is imperative if students with EBD are to gain the skills needed for further education and adult life, simply removing instruction is not an option, even though this may be an inadvertent outcome. For example, Wehby, Symons, Canale, and Go (1998) and Van Acker, Grant, and Henry (1996) provided compelling data suggesting a reciprocal relationship between ratings of aggression and academic instruction; that is, as students were identified as more aggressive, the level of academic engagement with the teacher was lower than for students identified with less aggression. To address the need for academic instruction for students with EBD, Gunter and Reed (1997) evaluated the impact of teachers' use of lesson scripts as a mechanism to insure that students had information necessary to respond to teachers' mands. They found significant reductions in disruptive behaviors when teachers used scripted narratives that ensured that information to successfully answer teachers' questions was provided before the actual question. This reduction in disruptive behavior was inversely related to the frequency of correct responses, which was positively correlated with information provided before assessment and praise for correct academic responses. Gunter and Reed suggested that the need for the students in the study to escape instructional interactions (through disruptive behaviors) that were perceived as aversive was removed by removing the aversive aspect of the instruction interaction; that is, the students were provided the information they needed to respond correctly in the instructional exchange.

The series of studies just reviewed and others (e.g., Gunter, Jack, Shores, Carrell, & Flowers, 1993; Jack et al., 1996; Sutherland, Alder, & Gunter, 2003) have contributed to a body of literature that supports the study of classroom instructional and social interactions of students with EBD from an ABA perspective. The theoretical framework provided from this perspective has allowed discussion to understand and modify classroom interactions to increase learning and decrease undesirable social behaviors through more effective instructional procedures (cf., Gunter & Coutinho, 1997; Gunter, Denny et al., 1994; Gunter & Denny, 1998; Gunter, Hummell, & Conroy, 1998; Harrison, Gunter, Lee, & Reed, 1996; Sutherland et al., 2003). For this to happen though, the literature supports the need for teachers' responsibilities to modify the interactions. "The teacher who laments, 'I'd like to reinforce that student but s/he just doesn't do the right thing,' is ignoring the teacher's role in instruction. It is the teacher's job to design instruction so that students are likely to be successful" (Scott, Nelson, & Liaupsin, 2001, p. 318). Pianta (1996) indicates that these instructional exchanges place "a disproportionate amount of responsibility on the adult for the quality of the relationship" (p. 73).

Pfeffner, Rosen, and O'Leary (1985) found that classrooms in which teacher praise toward students was approximately three times greater than teacher attention to undesirable behavior were classrooms that were much better managed with fewer instances of undesirable behavior. Stage (1997) suggested that punishment strategies based on withholding instructional opportunities (e.g., in-school suspension) will likely not be effective unless the classroom instructional interaction is that described by Pfeffner and colleagues. Again, the construct presented is one that is easily described through the tools of ABA. If the desired behavior for students in instructional settings is increased academic achievement, which, at that micro-analytic stage, might be described as correct responses, then the teacher has an obligation to provide a stimulus to elicit a student response. Van Acker et al. (1996) provided data demonstrating that the most likely behavior that preceded teacher praise was correct academic responding. Gunter and Coutinho (1997) indicated that this sequence of behaviors (teacher provides information, teacher assesses by asking a question about the information, student responds correctly, and teacher praises) represents a positive reciprocal instructional interaction that can be described by the A-B-C (antecedent, behavior, consequence) (Bijou, Peterson, & Ault, 1968) tool of ABA.

Gunter, Denny et al. (1994) went a step further in an attempt to describe outcomes for teachers of students with EBD using the A-B-C analysis. They provided explanations for observed limitations of academic engagement by teachers of students with EBD (cf., Vaughn, Levy, Coleman, & Bos, 2002) and for the high attrition rates of these teachers (Gunter, Denny et al., 1994). Just as for students with EBD, Gunter, Denny et al. (1994) suggested that there are likely aversive stimuli in classroom interactions for the teachers. Obviously, disruptive and aggressive behaviors are undesired and likely aversive stimuli for teachers, but Gunter, Denny et al. suggested that even inadequate academic responding by students (i.e., incorrect responses) could serve as aversive stimuli. Hence, they suggested that escape and avoidance for teachers of students with EBD could account for much of the high attrition rate of these teachers. That is, to escape or avoid undesirable social behaviors (e.g., cursing, shouting, hitting, and disrespect), many teachers may simply leave the teaching profession. Attrition is higher for teachers of students with EBD than for any other group of teachers.

The A-B-C analysis for interactions that lead to escape, avoidance, or even counter-control behaviors of teachers seems just as applicable to them as to their students. For example, if the teacher asked a question and the student provided the wrong answer, the wrong answer might be an aversive stimulus for the teacher, who may then not ask the student questions as frequently (cf., Good & Brophy, 2000). The hypothetical social interaction sequence that might follow is that the student then engages in disruptive behaviors in an attempt to solicit teacher attention. Van Acker et al. (1996) purports this is a more predictable way for students with EBD to engage teachers' attention that serves as a positive reinforcer for more disruptive behavior. As the cycle escalates, it is possible that both the teacher and the student are engaging in behaviors that the other participant finds aversive with both attempting to exit the interaction. In short, the ABA model provides a framework in which teachers can analyze variables that maintain both their own behavior and the behavior of their students.

RECENT ABA RESEARCH TARGETING TEACHER BEHAVIOR CHANGE

As we have noted, the research of Shores, Gunter et al. (1993) and others has indicated that targeting teacher efforts to elicit correct student responses is a pivotal teacher behavior contributing to positive outcomes. Studies indicated that students' correct academic responses were the only behaviors to be reliably followed by teacher praise in classrooms for students with EBD (e.g., Van Acker et al., 1996). Additionally, correct academic responses were found to be positively correlated with teachers' use of effective instruction procedures (cf., Gunter & Reed, 1997). Finally, correct academic responses have consistently been found to be inversely related to disruptive behaviors of student with EBD (Gunter & Reed, 1997). Recent research by Haydon et al. (2010) has focused on teacher efforts to increase students' rates of positive and meaningful response to instruction.

Greenwood, Delquadri, and Hall (1984) defined opportunity to respond (OTR) as "the interaction between (a) teacher formulated instruction … (the materials presented, prompts, questions asked, signals to respond, etc.) and (b) its success in establishing the academic responding desired or implied by materials, the subject matter goals of instruction" (p. 64). From an ABA perspective, teacher actions to increase opportunities to respond sets the stage (i.e., acts as an antecedent) for a student response (the middle component of the three-term contingency or learning trial), which then can be consequenced through praise or corrective feedback. Teachers who provide increased academic requests through questioning and/or cueing strategies produce greater student learning, among other positive outcomes (Haydon, Borders, Embury, & Clarke, 2009).

A number of strategies have been employed to increase active student response to the curriculum, including individual student responding, choral – or group – responding, or a mixture of individual and choral responding. Sutherland et al. (2003), for example, demonstrated that when a teacher used choral responding to increase the rate of student OTR in a self-contained classroom with nine students with EBD that there were more correct responses, fewer disruptions, and increased on-task behavior during math lessons. These positive findings were replicated by Haydon, Mancil et al. (2009) in a study using science content and targeting a general education student at risk of EBD. That is, the teachers' increased rate of delivering questions, providing more opportunities for student response, resulted in increases in the students' correct responding and on-task behavior.

Haydon et al. (2010) extended OTR research involving students with EBD by comparing choral responding with individual and mixed (i.e., 70% choral/30% individual) responding conditions for a group of elementary-aged students who, through systematic screening procedures, were deemed to be at risk for EBD. Following a two-phase training protocol that involved an explanation of the procedures and practice until mastery regimen, teachers were instructed to implement a randomly selected OTR strategy, eliciting student responses at a rate of approximately five per minute during sight word and syllable review activities. Results from the alternating treatments design generally favored implementation of the mixed responding treatment. That is, the mean rate of disruptive behavior per minute was lowest in the mixed responding condition for five of the six students. In terms of off-task behavior, the lowest mean percentage of off-task behavior for five of the six students was demonstrated in the mixed conditioning. For active responding, three of the six students demonstrated a higher mean percentage of active student responding in the mixed condition, whereas the remaining three were shown to be most active in the choral conditioning. All six students were least active during the individual responding condition.

OTR is a critical antecedent teacher behavior to a correct student response in the three-term contingency. Teachers can implement contingent praise as an effective consequence of correct student responding as well. A rich literature demonstrates that effective teacher praise statements – those that explicitly indicate the desired behavior and offer adequate feedback about the correctness of the students' behavior – can act as reinforcers of appropriate student behavior (Moore Partin, Robertson, Maggin, Oliver, & Wehby, 2010). For teachers of students with EBD, use of goal setting, ongoing feedback, and self-evaluation have collectively been shown to increase rates of teacher-initiated praise (Moore Partin et al., 2010). Sutherland and Wehby (2001) trained teachers to audiotape selected instructional activities and then listen to portions of the tapes to collect data on their rates of praise statements directed at students. Following the calculation of praise rates, teachers then graphed their daily praise rates and then praised themselves for evaluating their teaching behavior. Sutherland and Wehby found that teachers who self-monitored their use of praise during the treatment condition reported higher rates of praise than did teachers who were not taught to self-monitor. Researchers at the Vanderbilt Behavior Research Center (cf., Moore Partin et al., 2010) extended the Sutherland and Wehby treatment condition to provide for teacher training designed to increase both contingent praise statements and student OTR. Moore Partin et al. (2010) highlighted the positive findings from one teacher who nearly tripled both her rate of praise statements (to 25–30 in 15 minutes of instruction from fewer than 10) and student OTR (to more than 100 OTR per 15 minutes of instruction from 40 to 60) from baseline to treatment. Overall, ongoing research continues to demonstrate that principles of ABA directed toward teachers of students with EBD can have prosocial and meaningful outcomes for students, teachers, classrooms, and school buildings and systems.

POSITIVE BEHAVIORAL INTERVENTIONS AND SUPPORTS

In the past 20 years, researchers and practitioners have shifted toward looking at the school as the basis for change (Horner & Sugai, 2000; Walker, Ramsey, & Gresham, 2004). Schools have been encouraged and supported to replace reactive discipline plans that rely heavily on negative consequences for rule infractions (Shores, Jack et al., 1993). Instead, they are supported in moving to proactive, instructional approaches to preventing problem behavior through teaching, prompting, and reinforcing desired behavior patterns within the context of three-tiered models of support (Horner & Sugai, 2000; Lane, 2007). PBIS is a process for addressing the context of problem behavior through progressively more intensive evidenced-based interventions (Horner & Sugai, 2000).

The PBIS process focuses on the design, implementation, and maintenance of primary, secondary, and tertiary interventions to reduce problem behaviors and support desired behavior for all students within a school. At the primary level, schools are supported in the process of identifying the expectations for student behavior across multiple within school environments, systematically teaching and prompting the desired behavior at a schoolwide level and reinforcing students who meet the expectations. The focus is to support all students in more appropriate school behavior and to establish a process for screening students who may need additional levels of support (Lane, Gresham, & Shaughnessy, 2002). Schools identify students at risk or in need of more intensive interventions through the systematic screening of all students using a variety of social behavior assessments and the histories of problem behaviors through office discipline referrals.

The secondary level reflects students who require additional levels of support through targeted group interventions within the schools. Students who have multiple office discipline referrals or exhibit more extreme forms of behavior are provided an additional level of intervention. In addition, the process includes more frequent monitoring of student behavior to determine the impact of interventions on student behavior. While the range of possibilities for interventions is very broad and based on the particular forms of problem behavior, the most frequent components include reteaching expectations, targeted social skills training, academic assistance, and teaching self-management procedures.

The tertiary level reflects the development of a more intensive individualized system of support for students who exhibit chronic or intensive behavior challenges. Using a team-based process, individualized interventions are developed based on the results of a systematic FBA (described previously). The team monitors and supports the intervention through the established school system based on office discipline referrals as well as the implementation and response to the intervention using more common behavioral measures (e.g., frequency and duration measures of problem behaviors in school environments). The process is intended to address issues not only related to developing an intervention plan but for providing the needed support for teachers, families, and support personnel to implement the interventions with fidelity. In addition, services and environments may be expanded for individuals beyond the school setting as part of individual support systems as part of "wraparound" services (Duchnowski & Kutash, 2006; Eber & Keenan, 2004; Eber, Sugai, Smith, & Scott, 2002).

Research is beginning to address not only the impact of the schoolwide implementation of PBIS but also the response of students with EBD to the varying levels of support. For example, Lane et al. (2007) studied the impact of movement through increasing levels of support for two students considered at-risk of being identified as EBD. One student exhibited internalizing behavior (e.g., physical ailments before social engagement; purposeful social isolation; avoiding participation in activities with peers) and the other more externalizing behaviors (e.g., noncompliance). Through the systematic assessment and intervention process, the researchers documented the history of interventions through the primary and secondary levels that led to the development of individualized interventions. Results indicated that the application of interventions based on FBA were effective in increasing the levels of participation for one student and increasing compliance for the other student. The study is notable for illustrating how the process of behavioral interventions and support could be used to progressively build interventions for students at risk of being identified as EBD for both internalizing and externalizing behavior.

A major contribution of PBIS to the intervention process is the structure and support of the interventionists in monitoring student behavior. Researchers and teacher educators have long identified the failure to use data to guide interventions, especially for students with EBD. Teachers often question the extensive time and effort involved in the FBA/PBIS process given the demands they face to change behavior quickly in the classroom/school setting (Miller, Gunter Venn, Hummel, & Wiley, 2003). Gunter and Denny (2004) reviewed the literature on the use of data to guide interventions (academic and social behavior) and suggested that teachers needed systematic support in the collection and interpretation of student-level data. The use of team-based intervention support and the progressive and systematic increase in data collection contained within the levels of the PBIS process are features that can ultimately reduce the response cost of data collection for teachers and administrators leading to more effective and efficient behavioral intervention.

CONTROVERSIAL INTERVENTIONS

Researchers have long posited that preventive approaches can reduce challenging behavior of students (George, 2000; Miller, Hunt, & George, 2006). As previously discussed, ineffective educational programming (e.g., failure to provide appropriate curricular, instructional, and/or behavioral interventions) often exacerbates the behavioral difficulties of some students, leading to a vicious cycle of antecedents that set the stage for problem behaviors (Long, 1996). When students become escalated to a level where they begin displaying verbal and physical aggression, schools sometimes elect to implement questionable behavior management practices to cope with these disruptive behaviors.

Several highly controversial procedures used with this population of students include seclusion, restraint, and medication therapy. The contentiousness of these interventions is highlighted because many parents, advocacy groups, and researchers believe these procedures are used far too frequently, each intervention poses potential safety concerns, and there are currently insufficient policies and/or guidelines established governing their use. For instance, a recent review of existing state policies for restraint and seclusion found only 31 states had established guidance concerning the use of these crisis intervention procedures, with several additional states considering developing a policy in the near future. Where state laws do exist, they typically vary drastically regarding scope and content (Ryan, Robbins, Peterson, & Rozalski, 2009; U.S. Government Accountability Office (GAO), 2009).

Restraint

Physical restraint occurs when one or more staff members use their bodies to restrict an individual's body movement as a means for reestablishing behavioral control and establishing and maintaining safety for the individual, his/her peers, and staff (Ryan et al., 2009). While there are currently no standardized reporting procedures to accurately monitor the use of restraint procedures nationwide, several states have begun to monitor their use within educational settings. Two states (California and Texas) that have recently begun monitoring the use of these procedures reported using restraints over 33,000 times during the 2007/2008 academic school year (U.S. GAO, 2009). Even more disconcerting is that researchers have shown that these procedures are frequently used when less restrictive procedures would have been a more appropriate response. One study investigating the use of restraint in a special day school found that nearly all of these procedures (96.8%) were performed for reasons other than safety, with the vast majority performed due to student noncompliance, or leaving an assigned area (Ryan, Peterson, Tetreault, & van der Hagen, 2007).

While poor state and federal reporting procedures limit the ability to accurately track the number of deaths and injuries that occur each year due to improperly performed restraint procedures, advocacy agencies estimate that as many as 8–10 individuals die each year due to restraint (Child Welfare League of America, 2011). The vast majority of these fatalities are caused by either (a) positional asphyxia (suffocation) during a prone (face down) floor restraint caused by staff members placing their body weight on an individual's back or chest, or (b) aspiration (choking) during a supine (face up) floor restraint (Mohr, Petti, & Mohr, 2003). Other risk factors included individuals prescribed specific psychotropic medications (e.g., antipsychotics) that can make them more susceptible to heart conditions that can lead to sudden death. In addition to the hazards of death and injury, there are also serious concerns that restraints may cause psychological trauma to students, particularly among those who have a history of either physical and/or sexual abuse.

Seclusion Time-out

Seclusion is a highly restrictive form of time-out in which a student is removed from the classroom environment and isolated in a room in which they are prevented from leaving (Busch & Shore, 2000). The theoretical framework within the psychiatric literature justifying seclusion is based on this time-out serving two primary functions, including (a) as a therapeutic modality to establish appropriate limit setting and/or decreased stimulation from sensory overload; and (b) as a means of containing violent behavior to protect either the student or others (Busch & Shore, 2000). The efficacy of seclusion has also been sparsely studied in educational settings and with mixed results. A review by Ryan, Peterson, and Rozalski (2007) showed there have been a limited number of studies conducted investigating the efficacy of seclusion and those that were performed had mixed results.

Medication Therapy

Over the past several decades, the rapid growth of child psychopharmacology has been nothing short of phenomenal, with drug therapy becoming the most common medical intervention for treating children and adolescents with EBD (Epstein, Singh, Luebke, & Stout, 1991; Ryan, Reid, & Ellis, 2008). While the National Institute of Mental Health (2003) estimates that only 2–3% of all children and adolescents are currently being prescribed some type of psychotropic medication, medication rates among students with EBD have been reported to be as high as 65–94%, with an overall medication rate of 76% among students placed in residential care (Ryan et al., 2008). The increased use of psychotropic medications is in part due to the availability and efficacy of new medications that demonstrated have been to be effective at altering moods and behavior, coupled with an increased awareness of mental health problems among children (Thomas, Conrad, Casler, & Goodman, 2006). Their demonstrated efficacy has helped medication therapy become a common form of treatment for students with EBD (Connor, Boone, Steingard, Lopez, & Melloni, 2003; Sweeney, Forness, & Levitt, 1998). Studies such as those conducted by the MTA Cooperative Group (1999) have demonstrated medication therapy can be a quick and effective alternative for managing student behavior. As a result, the number and types of psychotropic medications developed and currently prescribed for the treatment of emotional and behavioral problems have continued to increase.

According to Stahl and Mignon (2009), it is hypothesized that medication therapy can positively affect several regions of the brain related to executive functioning (e.g., response inhibition, ability to identify cause and effect) as well as motor control (e.g., ability to sit still). It is important to caution though that all psychotropic medications can have an adverse side effect, ranging from physical symptoms (i.e., skin rash and difficulty breathing) to behavioral changes (i.e., irritability and aggression) to severe reactions with the potential of death (Dulcan, 2007; Ryan, Katsiyannis, & Hughes, 2011). Children and adolescents are often placed at increased risk, because some medications are prescribed off label (without Food and Drug Administration (FDA) approval). This is especially true when the children are not close to the age, size, and weight of the adult population for which the medication was tested and approved for use. Individuals may respond in dramatically different ways to psychotropic medications based on their individual genetic variation, which affects the body's ability to metabolize a drug. For instance, individuals whose bodies have difficulty metabolizing a drug may be more likely to experience adverse side effects when taking a medication (Bray, Clarke, Brennen, & Muncey, 2008).

FUTURE RESEARCH

As evidenced in our narrative to this point, behavior change research using principles of ABA has stamped a clear, rich footprint on the field of EBD. It has provided teachers, students, parents, administrators, interventionists, and researchers with a theoretical and empirical road map that guides all of us toward "socially significant" end points such as improved student outcomes and efficacious teacher practices. Stakeholders have taken and likely will continue to take different "roads" to their end goals, including continued empiricism directed at FBA, teacher behaviors such as OTR and praise, schoolwide efforts involving PBIS and RTI, and more controversial methodologies including restraint and medication therapy. Future research in ABA should follow its historical direction, the application of the somewhat tentative principles of behavior to the understanding and treatment of socially valued behavior in applied settings (Baer, Wolf, & Risley, 1968). Before concluding, we offer a few thoughts as to where some of those roads might take the field of EBD.

FBA

While much progress has been made on the procedural processes of FBA, there remain additional research areas to be examined. There continues to be a need for a more streamlined and standardized approach for behavioral assessments. Given that the research appears to support at least acceptable levels of agreement between the various sources of assessment data (student interview, parent interviews, checklists, analog probes, and direct observation), there is a need to examine the level of assessment necessary to guide intervention selection in an accurate and efficient measure. As with other forms of formative assessment, there continues to be a need to provide relatively quick forms of initial assessments to guide efforts with the depth, frequency, and complexity of assessment procedures increasing if students fail to respond to indicated interventions.

Another promising area for research is the validation of procedures for prescribing interventions based on the outcomes of the assessment processes. The work by Umbreit et al. (2007) provides an initial framework for tentative links between assessment and intervention. Being able to discriminate quickly and efficiently between classroom-level interventions that address the general classroom environment (instruction, routines, expectations, and broad reinforcement systems) and more intensive and individualized interventions remains a positive area for future research efforts.

Teacher Behavior Change

Bushell and Baer (1994) proposed that "close, continual contact with relevant outcome data" [ought to be] "a fundamental, distinguishing feature" (p. 7) of both ABA and classroom teaching, arguing that educators had largely been unsuccessful in developing relevant outcome measures for directly measuring student performance "of what is taught as it is taught" (p. 7). Teacher behavior change research described herein may provide researchers with clues as to what may be relevant teaching outcome measures. With correct student responses to teacher directives associated with greater student engagement and outcomes, fewer student disruptive behaviors, and greater rates of teacher praise, it makes sense to intensify the systematic study of eliciting correct student responses (Gunter & Denny, 1998, 2004). For example, what is an empirically derived rate of student correct responses to teacher requests for academic tasks? Does that level of performance differ in different settings (i.e., general vs. special classroom) or with different subject matter (e.g., English Language Arts vs. math vs. science), grade levels of students (e.g., preschool vs. elementary school vs. middle school), or teaching methodology (e.g., co-teaching model). Given that correct student response as a metric of effective teaching practice has nowhere near the acceptance or stature that curriculum-based measurement (Deno, 1985) procedures do as indicators of student academic growth, then we need to apply principles of ABA to questions surrounding why teachers do not use this measure to inform their practice. ABA research should seek to systematically address the complexities of teacher behavior in applied contexts. In gaining a greater understanding of the existing contingencies for more effective teacher behavior and the multiple, competing, and concurrent schedules of reinforcement in existence for teachers, we may better design programs of intervention that support and maintain not only more effective teaching behavior but also produce desired changes in student academic and social behavior.

PBIS

Given the current trend toward the adoption of PBIS on a wide scale, we are cautiously optimistic that the application of evidence and empirically based behavioral interventions will increase. However, for students with the most challenging behaviors such as students with EBD, the demonstration of initial and long-term impact of such an approach is still in an early stage. As discussed previously, there are demonstrations of the initial impact of tiered interventions on the challenging behavior of students with EBD. We believe strongly that the effort to show the history of intervention efforts as part of student descriptions in research will help in the development of more effective interventions. The impact of tiered behavioral interventions on the identification rates of students with EBD and the impact of these procedures specifically addressing outcomes for students with EBD (lower office discipline referrals, suspensions, academic performance, etc.) is a first area of research that remains to be studied in sufficient detail.

A second area of research in PBIS is related to the overall orientation of this chapter. Specifically, the challenges associated with implementation with fidelity and the sustainability of interventions remain critical areas for future research. A better understanding of the seemingly complex contingencies that govern adult/teacher behavior appear critical to developing interventions that will actually be applied, be applied correctly and consistently, and be maintained over time as needed. The structures for shaping and reinforcing more effective and efficient teacher behavior (coaching, co-teaching, standard treatment protocols, etc.) are a critical need for future research. Reid and Nelson (2002) suggest that standard treatment protocols could serve to not only assist teachers in developing skill in the intervention delivery but also aid in the fidelity and maintenance of skill over time. For example, Carter and Horner (2007) examined the combination of a "manualized" intervention and FBA with a 6-year-old with challenging behavior. They found that the standard treatment protocol, First Steps (Walker et al., 1997), could be enhanced by addressing the specific functions of behavior. The enhanced treatment protocols produced consistently lower levels of disruptive behavior and higher levels of academic engagement. The advantage of the standardized treatment approach plus FBA is the efficiency by which well-described validated interventions can be implemented and reflect the possibly unique individual and environmental features.

To the extent that the above structures support strategies such as providing frequent opportunities to respond, clear and taught expectations, high rates of correct academic responding, and other critical instructional behaviors, they may well serve to make some instructional behavior more reinforcing for teachers or at least less aversive (Gunter & Denny, 2004; Gunter, Denny et al., 1994; Shores, Gunter et al., 1993). The opportunities provided by the support structures being placed within schools through RTI and PBIS are very promising in supporting a broader research agenda for students with EBD.

Controversial Procedures

To date, there has been little research investigating the efficacy of either seclusion or restraint procedures in reducing maladaptive behaviors of students with EBD. Researchers believe the key to reducing and/or eliminating these controversial procedures is dependent on staff training, specifically in the areas of prevention (PBIS) and conflict de-escalation (Couvillian, Peterson, Ryan, Scheuermann, & Stegall, 2011; Ryan, Peterson, Tetreault et al., 2007). As for medication therapy, the combination of significant advances within the field of pharmacology, cost-effectiveness, and an increased willingness of many parents to treat their child's mental health disorders with drug therapy is likely to make this form of treatment even more popular. Medications have become heavily relied on given their ability to help modify student behavior by (a) decreasing symptoms; (b) improving functioning within school, home, and other environments; and (c) helping increase the effectiveness of behavioral and academic interventions (Ryan et al., 2011). Unfortunately, many medications given to students with EBD are prescribed off label (without FDA approval). This is potentially dangerous, especially for young children who are not close to the age, size, and weight of the adult population the medication was tested and approved for by the FDA (Ryan et al., 2008). Specifically, the central nervous system of a child is still developing, and the range of responses to medications may vary considerably. Complicating matters is that many students with EBD are prescribed multiple medications (polypharmacy), which can increase the risk of adverse side effects and drug interactions (Pappadopulos et al., 2003). Additional research is necessary to determine both the efficacy and safety of medication therapy.

SUMMARY

Almost three decades ago, Michael Nelson and Lewis Polsgrove (1984) raised the question of whether behavioral principles in special education were a "White Elephant or a White Rabbit". They concluded that even though the impact of behavioral principles applied to special education had been considerable, its potential had yet to be realized. Even though this chapter has highlighted many of the substantial contributions made to date and the challenges we continue to face, we believe their conclusions are as applicable today.

REFERENCES

Anderson, C., & Scott, T. (2006). Implementing function based support within school-wide positive behavioral support. In W. Sailor, G. Dunlap, G. Sugai & R. Horner (Eds.), *Handbook of positive behavior support* (pp. 705–728). New York, NY: Springer Publishing.

Baer, D. M., Wolf, M. M., & Risley, T. R. (1968). Some current dimensions of applied behavior analysis. *Journal of Applied Behavior Analysis, 1*, 91–97.

Bijou, S. W., Peterson, R. F., & Ault, M. H. (1968). A method to integrate descriptive and experimental field studies at the level of data and empirical concepts. *Journal of Applied Behavior Analysis, 1*, 175–191.

Bray, J., Clarke, C., Brennen, G., & Muncey, T. (2008). Should we be pushing meds? The implications of pharmacogenomics. *Journal of Psychiatric and Mental Health Nursing, 15*, 357–364.

Briere, D. E., & Simonsen, B. (2011). Self-monitoring interventions for at-risk middle school students: The importance of considering function. *Behavioral Disorders, 36*, 129–140.

Busch, A. B., & Shore, M. F. (2000). Seclusion and restraint: A review of recent literature. *Harvard Review of Psychiatry, 8*, 261–270.

Bushell, D., Jr., & Baer, D. M. (1994). Measurably superior instruction means close continual contact with the relevant outcome data revolutionary! In R. Gardener, III, D. M. Sainato, JO. Cooper, T. E. Heron, W. Heward, J. W. Eshleman & T. A. Grossi (Eds.), *Behavior analysis in education: Focus on measurably superior instruction* (pp. 3–11). Pacific Grove, CA: Brooks/Cole.

Carter, D. R., & Horner, R. H. (2007). Adding functional behavioral assessment to first steps to success: A case study. *Journal of Positive Behavioral Interventions, 9*(4), 229–238.

Child Welfare League of America. (2011). Behavior management in residential care fact sheet, 1-2. Retrieved from www.cwla.org/advocacy/secresfactsheet.htm. Accessed on May 23, 2011.

Connor, D. F., Boone, R. T., Steingard, R. J., Lopez, I. D., & Melloni, R. H. (2003). Psychopharmacology and aggression: II. A meta-analysis of nonstimulant medication effects on overt aggression-related behaviors in youth with SED. *Journal of Emotional and Behavioral Disorders, 11*, 157–168.

Cooper, J. O., Heron, T. E., & Heward, W. L. (2007). *Applied behavior analysis* (2nd ed.). Upper Saddle River, NJ: Pearson.

Couvillian, M., Peterson, R. L., Ryan, J. B., Scheuermann, B. K., & Stegall, J. (2011). A review of crisis intervention training programs for schools. *Teaching Exceptional Children, 42*(5), 6–17.

Deno, S. L. (1985). Curriculum-based measurement: The emerging alternative. *Exceptional Children, 52*, 219–232.

Duchnowski, A. J., & Kutash, K. (2006). Integrating PBS, mental health services, and family-driven care. In W. Sailor, G. Dunlap, G. Sugai & R. Horner (Eds.), *Handbook of positive behavior support* (pp. 705–728). New York, NY: Springer Publishing.

Dufrene, B. A., Doggett, R. A., Henington, C., & Watson, T. S. (2007). Functional assessment and intervention for disruptive classroom behavior in preschool and Head Start classrooms. *Journal of Behavioral Education, 16*, 368–388.

Dulcan, M. K. (2007). *Helping parents, youth, and teachers understand medications for behavioral and emotional problems* (3rd ed.). Arlington, VA: American Psychiatric Press.

Dunlap, G., Kern-Dunlap, L., Clarke, S., & Robbins, F. R. (1991). Functional assessment, curricular revision, and severe behavior problems. *Journal of Applied Behavior Analysis, 24*, 387–397.

Dunlap, G., & Kincaid, D. (2001). The widening world of functional assessment: Comments on four manuals and beyond. *Journal of Applied Behavior Analysis, 34*, 365–377.

Eber, L., & Keenan, S. (2004). Collaboration with other agencies: Wraparound and systems of care for children and youths with emotional and behavioral disorders. In R. B. Rutherford, M. M. Quinn & S. R. Mathur (Eds.), *Handbook of research in emotional and behavioral disorders* (pp. 502–516). New York, NY: Guilford Press.

Eber, L., Sugai, G., Smith, C. R., & Scott, T. M. (2002). Wraparound and positive behavioral interventions and supports in schools. *Journal of Emotional and Behavioral Disorders, 10*(3), 171–180.

Ellingson, S. A., Miltenberger, R. G., Sticker, J., Galensky, T. L., & Garlinghouse, M. (2000). Functional assessment and intervention for challenging behaviors in the classroom by general classroom teachers. *Journal of Positive Behavior Interventions, 2*, 85–97.

Epstein, M. H., Singh, N. N., Luebke, J., & Stout, C. E. (1991). Psychopharmacological intervention. II: Teacher perceptions of psychotropic medication for students with learning disabilities. *Journal of Learning Disabilities, 24*, 477–483.

Friend, M., Cook, L., Hurley-Chamberlain, D., & Shamberger, C. (2010). Co-teaching: An illustration of the complexity of collaboration in special education. *Journal of Educational and Psychological Consultation, 20*, 9–27.

George, M. P. (2000). Establishing and promoting disciplinary practices at the building level that ensure safe, effective and nurturing school environments. In L. M. Bullock & R. A. Gable (Eds.), *Positive academic and behavioral supports: Creating safe, effective, nurturing schools for all students* (pp. 11–15). Reston, VA: Council for Children with Behavioral Disorders.

Good, T. L., & Brophy, J. E. (2000). *Looking in classrooms* (8th ed.). New York, NY: Longman.

Greenwood, C. R., Delquadri, J. C., & Hall, R. V. (1984). Opportunity to respond and student academic performance. In W. L. Heward, T. E. Heron, D. S. Hill & J. Trap-Porter (Eds.), *Focus on behavior analysis in education* (pp. 58–88). Columbus, OH: Merrill.

Grey, I. M., Honan, R., McClean, B., & Daly, M. (2005). Evaluating the effectiveness of teacher training in applied behavioural analysis. *Journal of Intellectual Disabilities, 9*, 209–227.

Gunter, P. L., & Coutinho, M. J. (1997). The growing need to understand negative reinforcement in teacher training programs. *Teacher Education and Special Education, 20*, 249–264.

Gunter, P. L., & Denny, R. K. (1998). Trends, issues, and research needs regarding academic instruction of students with emotional and behavioral disorders. *Behavioral Disorders, 24*, 44–50.

Gunter, P., & Denny, R. K. (2004). Data collection issues in behavioral disorders research. In R. Rutherford, M. Quinn & S. Mathur (Eds.), *Handbook of research in emotional and behavior disorders* (pp. 582–595). New York, NY: Guilford Publishing.

Gunter, P. L., Denny, R. K., Jack, S. L., Shores, R. E., Reed, T., & Nelson, C. M. (1994). Teacher escape, avoidance, and countercontrol behaviors: Potential responses to disruptive and aggressive behaviors of children with severe behavior disorders. *Journal of Child and Family Studies, 3,* 211–223.

Gunter, P. L., Hummell, J. H., & Conroy, M. A. (1998). Increasing correct academic responding: An effective intervention strategy to decrease behavior problems. *Effective School Practices, 17,* 55–61.

Gunter, P. L., Jack, S. L., Shores, R. E., Carrell, D., & Flowers, J. (1993). Lag sequential analysis as a tool for functional analysis of student disruptive behavior in classrooms. *Journal of Emotional and Behavioral Disorders, 1,* 138–148.

Gunter, P. L., & Reed, T. M. (1997). Academic instruction of children with emotional and behavioral disorders using scripted lessons. *Preventing School Failure, 42,* 33–37.

Gunter, P. L., Shores, R. E., Jack, S. L., Denny, R. K., & DePaepe, P. A. (1994). A case study of the effects of altering instructional interactions on the disruptive behavior of a child identified with severe behavior disorders. *Education & Treatment of Children, 17,* 435–444.

Harbort, G., Gunter, P. L., Hull, K., Venn, M. L., Brown, Q., Wiley, L. P., & Wiley, E. (2007). Behaviors of co-teachers in inclusive high-school classrooms. *Teacher Education and Special Education, 30,* 13–23.

Harrison, J., Gunter, P. L., Lee, J., & Reed, T. M. (1996). Teacher instructional language and negative reinforcement: A conceptual framework for working with students with emotional and behavioral disorders. *Education & Treatment of Children, 19,* 183–196.

Haydon, T., Borders, C., Embury, D., & Clarke, L. (2009). Using effective instructional delivery as a classwide management tool. *Beyond Behavior, 18*(2), 12–17.

Haydon, T., Conroy, M. A., Scott, T. M., Sindelar, P. T., Barber, B. R., & Orlando, A. (2010). A comparison of three types of opportunities to respond on student academic and social behaviors. *Journal of Emotional and Behavioral Disorders, 18,* 27–40.

Haydon, T., Mancil, G. R., & Van Loan, C. (2009). Using opportunities to respond in a general education classroom: A case study. *Education & Treatment of Children, 32,* 267–278.

Heckaman, K., Conroy, M., Fox, J., & Chait, A. (2000). Functional assessment-based intervention research for students with or at risk for emotional and behavioral disorders in school settings. *Behavioral Disorders, 25,* 196–210.

Horner, R. H. (1994). Functional assessment: Contributions and future directions. *Journal of Applied Behavior Analysis, 27,* 401–404.

Horner, R. H., & Sugai, G. (2000). School-wide behavior support: An emerging initiative. *Journal of Positive Behavior Interventions, 2,* 231–232.

Ingram, K., Lewis-Palmer, T., & Sugai, G. (2005). Function-based intervention planning: Comparing the effectiveness of FBA functionbased and nonfunction-based intervention plans. *Journal of Positive Behavior Interventions, 7,* 224–236.

Jack, S. L., Shores, R. E., Denny, R. K., Gunter, P. L., DeBriere, T., & DePaepe, P. (1996). An analysis of the relationship of teachers' reported use of classroom management strategies on types of interactions. *Journal of Behavioral Education, 6,* 67–87.

Kamps, D. M., Wedland, M., & Culpepper, M. (2006). Active teacher participation in functional behavior assessment for students with emotional and behavioral disorders in the general education classroom. *Behavioral Disorders, 31,* 128–146.

Kauffman, J. M. (2005). *Characteristics of emotional and behavioral disorders of children and youth* (8th ed.). Upper Saddle River, NJ: Pearson.

Kazdin, A. E. (2001). *Behavior modification in applied settings* (6th ed.). Belmont, CA: Wadsworth/Thomson Learning.

Kern, L., Childs, K. E., Dunlap, G., Clarke, S., & Falk, G. D. (1994). Using assessment-based curricular intervention to improve the classroom behavior of a student with emotional and behavioral challenges. *Journal of Applied Behavior Analysis, 27,* 7–19.

Kern, L., Delaney, B., Clarke, S., Dunlap, G., & Childs, K. (2001). Improving the classroom behavior of students with emotional and behavioral disorders using individualized curricular modifications. *Journal of Emotional and Behavioral Disorders, 9*(4), 239–247.

Lane, K. L. (2007). Identifying and supporting students at risk for emotional and behavioral disorders within multi-level models: Data driven approaches to conducting secondary interventions with an academic emphasis. *Education & Treatment of Children, 30,* 135–164.

Lane, K. L., Barton-Arwood, S. M., Spencer, J. L., & Kalberg, J. R. (2007). Teaching elementary school educators to design, implement, and evaluate functional assessment-based interventions: Successes and challenges. *Preventing School Failure, 51,* 36–46.

Lane, K. L., Gresham, F., & Shaughnessy, Y. (2002). Serving students with or at-risk for emotional and behavioral disorders: Future challenges. *Education & Treatment of Children, 25*(4), 507–521.

Lane, K. L., Thompson, A., Reske, C., Gable, L., & Barton-Arwood, S. (2006). Reducing skin picking via competing activities. *Journal of Applied Behavior Analysis, 39,* 459–462.

Lane, K. L., Weisenbach, J. L., Little, M. A., Phillips, A., & Wehby, J. (2006). Illustrations of function-based interventions implemented by general education teachers: Building capacity at the school site. *Education & Treatment of Children, 29,* 549–571.

Leflot, G., van Lier, P., Onghena, P., & Colpin, H. (2010). The role of teacher behavior management in the development of disruptive behaviors: An intervention study with the good behavior game. *Journal of Abnormal Child Psychology, 38,* 860–882.

Lewis, T. J., Lewis-Palmer, T., Newcomer, L., & Stichter, J. (2004). Applied behavior analysis and the education and treatment of students with emotional and behavior disorders. In R. B. Rutherford, Jr., M. M. Quinn & S. R. Mathur (Eds.), *Handbook of research in emotional and behavioral disorders* (pp. 523–545). New York, NY: Guilford.

Lewis, T. J., & Sugai, G. (1996). Functional assessment of problem behavior: A pilot investigation of the comparative and interactive effects of teacher and peer social attention on students in general education settings. *School Psychology Quarterly, 11,* 1–19.

Long, N. (1996). The conflict cycle paradigm on how troubled students get teachers out of control. In N. Long, W. Morse & R. Newman (Eds.), *Conflict in the classroom* (5th ed., pp. 90–108). Austin, TX: PRO-ED.

Maag, J. W., & Larsen, P. J. (2004). Training a general education teacher to apply functional assessment. *Education & Treatment of Children, 27,* 26–36.

Maggin, D. M., Wehby, J. H., Moore Partin, T. C., Robertson, R., & Oliver, R. M. (2011). A comparison of the instructional context for students with behavioral issues enrolled in self-contained and general education classrooms. *Behavioral Disorders, 36,* 84–99.

Martens, B. K., Witt, J. C., Elliott, S. N., & Darveaux, D. (1985). Teacher judgments concerning the acceptability of school based interventions. *Professional Psychology: Research and Practice, 16,* 191–198.

Miller, K. A., Gunter, P. L., Venn, M. L., Hummel, J., & Wiley, L. P. (2003). Effects of curricular/materials modifications on the academic performance and task engagement of three students with emotional/behavioral disorders. *Behavioral Disorders, 28,* 130–149.

Miller, J., Hunt, D., & George, M. (2006). Reduction of physical restraints in residential treatment facilities. *Journal of Disability Policy Studies, 16,* 202–208.

Miltenberger, R. G. (2001). *Behavior modification: Principles and procedures* (2nd ed.). Belmont, CA: Wadsworth/Thomson Learning.

Mohr, W. K., Petti, T. A., & Mohr, B. D. (2003). Adverse effects associated with physical restraint. *Canadian Journal of Psychiatry, 48*(5), 330–337.

Moore Partin, T. C., Robertson, R. E., Maggin, D. M., Oliver, R. M., & Wehby, J. H. (2010). Using teacher praise and opportunities to respond to promote appropriate student behavior. *Preventing School Failure, 54,* 172–178.

MTA Cooperative Group. (1999). A 14-month randomized clinical trial of treatment strategies for attention-deficit/hyperactivity disorder. *Archives of General Psychiatry, 56,* 1073–1086.

National Institute of Mental Health. (2003). Attention deficit disorder with hyperactivity. Retrieved from http://www.nimh.nih.gov. Accessed on July 10, 2008.

Nelson, C. M., & Polsgrove, L. (1984). Behavior analysis in special education: White elephant or white rabbit?. *Remedial and Special Education, 5*(4), 6–15.

Office of Special Education Programs Technical Assistance Center on PBIS. (n.d.). Retrieved from www.pbis.org/. Accessed on May 20, 2011.

O'Neil, R. E., Horner, R. H., Albin, R. W., Storey, K., Sprague, J. R., & Newton, J. S. (1997). *Functional assessment of problem behavior: A practical assessment guide.* Pacific Grove, CA: Brooks/Cole.

Pappadopulos, E., MacIntyre, J. C., Crimson, M. L., Findling, R. L., Malone, R. P., Derivan, A., & Jensen, P. S. (2003). Treatment recommendations for the use of antipsychotics for aggressive youth (TRAAY). Part II. *Journal of the American Academy of Child and Adolescent Psychiatry, 42*(2), 145–161.

Pfeffner, L. J., Rosen, L. A., & O'Leary, S. G. (1985). The efficacy of an all-positive approach to classroom management. *Journal of Applied Behavior Analysis, 18,* 257–261.

Pianta, R. C. (1996). *High-risk children in schools: Constructing sustaining relationships.* New York, NY: Routledge.

Reid, R., & Nelson, J. R. (2002). The utility, acceptability, and practicality of functional behavioral assessment for students with high-incidence problem behaviors. *Remedial and Special Education, 23,* 15–23.

Rosenshine, B., & Stevens, R. (1986). Teaching functions. In M. C. Wittrock (Ed.), *Handbook of research on teaching* (3rd ed., pp. 376–391). New York, NY: Macmillan.

Ryan, J. B., Katsiyannis, A., & Hughes, E. M. (2011). Medication treatment for attention deficit hyperactivity disorder. *Theory Into Practice, 50*(1), 1–9.

Ryan, J. B., Peterson, R. L., & Rozalski, M. (2007). Review of state policies concerning the use of timeout in schools. *Education & Treatment of Children, 30,* 215–239.

Ryan, J. B., Peterson, R. L., Tetreault, G., & van der Hagen, E. (2007). *Examining the safety of high-risk interventions for children and young people.* Ithaca, NY: Cornell University Press.

Ryan, J. B., Pierce, C. D., & Mooney, P. (2008). Evidenced-based teaching strategies for students with EBD. *Beyond Behavior, 17*(3), 22–29.

Ryan, J. B., Reid, R., & Ellis, C. (2008). A survey of special educator knowledge regarding psychotropic interventions for students with emotional and behavioral disorders. *Remedial and Special Education, 29,* 269–279.

Ryan, J. B., Robbins, K., Peterson, R. L., & Rozalski, M. (2009). Review of state policies concerning the use of physical restraint procedures in schools. *Education & Treatment of Children, 32,* 487–504.

Sasso, G. M., Conroy, M., Stichter, J., & Fox, J. (2001). Slowing down the bandwagon: The misapplication of functional assessment for students with emotional or behavioral disorders. *Behavioral Disorders, 26,* 282–296.

Sasso, G. M., Reimers, T. M., Cooper, L. J., Wacker, D., Berg, W., & Steege, M. (1992). Use of descriptive and experimental analyses to identify the functional properties of aberrant behavior in school settings. *Journal of Applied Behavior Analysis, 25,* 809–821.

Scott, T. M., Nelson, C. M., & Liaupsin, C. J. (2001). Effective instruction: The forgotten component in preventing school violence. *Education & Treatment of Children, 24,* 309–322.

Scruggs, T. E., Mastropieri, M. A., & McDuffie, K. A. (2007). Co-teaching in inclusive classrooms: A metasynthesis of qualitative research. *Exceptional Children, 73,* 392–416.

Shores, R. E., Gunter, P. L., & Jack, S. L. (1993). Classroom management strategies: Are they setting events for coercion? *Behavioral Disorders, 18,* 92–102.

Shores, R. E., Jack, S. L., Gunter, P. L., Ellis, D. N., DeBriere, T., & Wehby, J. (1993). Classroom interactions of children with severe behavior disorders. *Journal of Emotional and Behavioral Disorders, 1,* 27–39.

Stage, S. (1997). A preliminary investigation of the relationship between in-school suspension a the disruptive classroom behavior of students with behavior disorders. *Behavioral Disorders, 23,* 57–76.

Stahl, S. M., & Mignon, L. (2009). *Stahl's illustrated: Attention deficit hyperactivity disorder.* New York, NY: Cambridge University Press.

Stahr, B., Cushing, D., Lane, K. L., & Fox, J. (2006). Efficacy of a function-based intervention in decreasing off-task behavior exhibited by a student with ADHD. *Journal of Positive Behavior Interventions, 8,* 201–211.

Stichter, J. P., Hudson, S., & Sasso, G. M. (2005). The use of structural analysis to identify setting events in applied settings for students with emotional/behavioral disorders. *Behavioral Disorders, 30,* 403–420.

Sugai, G., Lewis-Palmer, T., & Hagan-Burke, S. (2001). Overview of the functional behavioral assessment process. *Exceptionality, 8,* 149–160.

Sutherland, K. S., Alder, N., & Gunter, P. L. (2003). The effect of varying rates of opportunities to respond to academic requests on the classroom behavior of students with EBD. *Journal of Emotional and Behavioral Disorders, 11,* 239–248.

Sutherland, K. S., & Oswald, D. P. (2005). The relationship between teacher and student behavior in classrooms for students with emotional and behavioral disorders: Transactional processes. *Journal of Child and Family Studies, 4,* 1–14.

Sutherland, K. S., & Wehby, J. H. (2001). The effect of self-evaluation on teaching behavior in classrooms for students with emotional or behavioral disorders. *Journal of Special Education, 35,* 161–171.

Sweeney, D. P., Forness, S. R., & Levitt, J. G. (1998). An overview of medications commonly used to treat behavioral disorders associated with autism, Tourette syndrome, and pervasive developmental disorders. *Focus on Autism and Other Developmental Disabilities, 13*, 144–150.

Thomas, C. P., Conrad, P., Casler, R., & Goodman, E. (2006). Trends in the use of psychotropic medications among adolescents, 1994 to 2001. *Psychiatric Services, 57*(1), 63–69.

Umbreit, J. (1995). Functional assessment and intervention in a regular classroom setting for the disruptive behavior of a student with attention deficit hyperactivity disorder. *Behavioral Disorders, 20*, 267–278.

Umbreit, J., & Blair, K. C. (1997). Using structural analysis to facilitate the treatment of noncompliance and aggression in a young child at risk for behavioral disorders. *Behavioral Disorders, 22*, 75–86.

Umbreit, J., Ferro, J., Liaupsin, C., & Lane, K. (2007). *Functional behavioral assessment and function-based intervention: An effective, practical approach.* Upper Saddle River, NJ: Prentice-Hall.

Umbreit, J., Lane, K. L., & Dejud, C. (2004). Improving classroom behavior by modifying task difficulty: Effects of increasing the difficulty of too-easy tasks. *Journal of Positive Behavior Interventions, 1*, 13–20.

U.S. Government Accountability Office. (2009, May 19). *Seclusions and restraints: Selected cases of death and abuse at public and private schools and treatment centers.* Washington, DC: Author.

Van Acker, R., Grant, S. H., & Henry, D. (1996). Teacher and student behavior as a function of risk for aggression. *Education & Treatment of Children, 19*, 316–334.

Vaughn, S., Levy, S., Coleman, M., & Bos, C. S. (2002). Reading instruction for students with LD and EBD. *Journal of Special Education, 36*, 2–13.

Vaughn, S., Moody, S. W., & Schumm, J. S. (1998). Broken promises: Reading instruction in the resource classroom. *Exceptional Children, 64*, 211–225.

Wagner, M., Friend, M., Bursuck, W. D., Kutash, K., Duchnowski, A. J., & Sumi, W. C. (2006). Educating students with disturbances: A national perspective on school programs and services. *Journal of Emotional and Behavioral Disorders, 14*, 12–30.

Wagner, M. M. (1995). Outcomes for youth with serious emotional disturbance in secondary school and early adulthood. *Future of Children, 5*, 9–113.

Walker, H. M., Ramsey, E., & Gresham, F. M. (2004). *Antisocial behavior in school: Evidence-based practices* (2nd ed.). Belmont, CA: Wadsworth/Thomson Learning.

Walker, H. M., Stiller, B., Golly, A., Kavanagh, K., Severson, H. H., & Feil, E. G. (1997). *First step to success: Helping children overcome antisocial behavior: Implementation guide.* Longmont, CO: Sopris West.

Wehby, J. H., Symons, F. J., Canale, J. A., & Go, F. J. (1998). Teaching practices in classrooms for students with emotional and behavioral disorders: Discrepancies between recommendations and observations. *Behavioral Disorders, 24*, 51–56.

Witt, J., & Beck, R. (1999). *One minute academic functional assessment and interventions: "Can't" do it ... or "won't" do it?.* Longmont, CO: Sopris West.

Witt, J. C., & Elliott, S. N. (1985). Acceptability of classroom intervention strategies. In T. R. Kratochwill (Ed.), *Advances in school psychology* (Vol. 4, pp. 251–288). Mahwah, NJ: Erlbaum.

CHAPTER 9

DIFFERENTIATED INSTRUCTION FOR STUDENTS WITH EMOTIONAL AND BEHAVIORAL DISORDERS

Christy Borders, Stacey Jones Bock
and Nichelle Michalak

ABSTRACT

Today's classroom differs greatly from the classroom a decade ago. This is due, in part, to the changing demographics of students across the United States where diversity is now the norm. As children enter the educational system with diverse backgrounds, they are exposed to new experiences that facilitate changes in interests, behaviors, and learning styles. One way to address diversity in the classrooms is to focus on the model of differentiated instruction (DI). The purpose of this chapter is to discuss DI and its relationship to Universal Design for Learning (UDL), provide information why DI is a valuable model for students with EBD, and review DI modifications and adaptations that serve as academic and behavior change elements in the classroom. At the core of both of these models lies the need for flexibility and adaptations to the learning environment and materials to meet the needs of all students. Furthermore, there is a heavy emphasis from both of these constructs to allow all students access to the general education environment – not just physical

Behavioral Disorders: Identification, Assessment, and Instruction of Students with EBD
Advances in Special Education, Volume 22, 203–219
Copyright © 2012 by Emerald Group Publishing Limited
All rights of reproduction in any form reserved
ISSN: 0270-4013/doi:10.1108/S0270-4013(2012)0000022012

but the educational benefits. To best address the social, emotional, behavioral, and academic needs of students with EBD, educators must differentiate their instruction.

Keywords: Direct instruction; universal design for learning; differing content; differing process; differing product; differing learning environment

Educators and researchers agree that today's classrooms are increasingly composed of students who are diverse in a variety of ways (Lawrence-Brown, 2004). Students bring diversity in the areas of language, socioeconomic backgrounds, religion, race, experiences, interests, behaviors, and learning styles. Children come into the education system at a very early age with diversity, and as they age, many students become more diverse particularly in the areas of experiences, interests, behaviors, and learning styles. It is not surprising that the traditional education system, in its current form, can no longer accommodate this group of diverse learners. According to Broderick, Mehta-Parekh, and Reid (2005), "offering the same lesson to all makes no sense when every indication is that U. S. classrooms are inherently diverse" (p. 196). Unfortunately, offering the same lesson to all may come out of the necessity that teachers have too little time to cover too much information to too large classrooms. This results in lessons that are delivered at a single pace and through a single instructional approach. "We do one thing in one way and hope for the best, but for many of our students, it will not be good enough" (Tomlinson & Kalbfleisch, 1998, p. 53). One way to address diversity in the classrooms is to focus on the model of differentiated instruction (DI). This is particularly important for students with emotional and behavior disorders (EBD) because they consistently perform below their typically developing peers in all academic areas and have disappointing post-school outcomes (Lane, Carter, Pierson, & Glaeser, 2006). The purpose of this chapter is to discuss DI and its relationship to Universal Design for Learning (UDL), provide information why DI is a valuable model for students with EBD, and review DI modifications and adaptations that serve as academic and behavior change elements in the classroom.

DIFFERENTIATED INSTRUCTION

According to Hall, Strangman, and Meyer (2003), the package of DI lacks an empirical research base; however, it stems from principles that are rooted in years of educational research. Tomlinson (2000), best known for her work in defining the philosophical principles associated with DI, authored several articles and books that have promoted the advancement of effective classrooms for all. DI, according to Tomlinson, is an effort for teachers to respond to diverse learners in their classrooms by teaching in a variety of ways to address differing readiness levels, interests, and preferred modes of learning. Tomlinson identified the areas of content, process, products, and the learning environment as the four classroom elements that can be differentiated.

Differentiating Content

Differentiating content is identifying what the student needs to learn and how they will learn it. Content selection should be informed by state learning standards (Hall et al., 2003) and delivered by emphasizing varying levels of readiness, interests, and learning profiles (Tomlinson & Kalbfleisch, 1998). Access to the content should be supported by the use of various materials and instructional supports. All students should have access to the same content, but the content complexity should be adapted to meet each student's level of readiness.

Differentiating Process

Differentiating the process identifies the levels of student interaction and the activities they will engage in to learn the identified content. According to Hall et al. (2003), students must work together to learn. With that in mind, a large part of differentiating the process is practicing dynamic grouping and regrouping; grouping that changes with the content, activities, and projects. In addition to dynamic grouping, varying the length of time for content mastery and providing opportunities for content enrichment allows the learner to master the information being presented at their own pace.

Differentiating Products

Differentiating products refers to how the student will demonstrate the content they have learned and how they will show generalization of this new information. Providing students with a choice of activities and providing guidelines and rubrics for those activities allows students to select the product or output that is most conducive to their learning style (Tomlinson,

2000). The choice of product encourages the student to actively participate in their learning and apply and extend what they have learned.

Differentiating the Learning Environment

Differentiating the learning environment denotes the classroom procedures and the "climate" that the teacher sets for learning. The learning environment should include areas designated for independent learning and small group collaboration. The student should feel comfortable and valued as a member of the learning environment (Tomlinson, 2000). This can be accomplished by teaching about tolerance and diversity and the value of each learner in the learning community.

UNIVERSAL DESIGN FOR LEARNING

The universal design movement began in architecture and focused on designing physical and learning structures to meet the needs of individuals with disabilities (Hall et al., 2003). The original focus of the movement was a purposeful or intentional plan to minimize barriers, specifically physical barriers, and create equal access for all learners. The educational principles of UDL were developed following the reauthorization of the Individuals with Disabilities Education Act in 1997, which stemmed from the push for inclusion for all students. According to Edyburn (2010), "While students with disabilities had gained physical access to the general education classroom, concerns were being raised about how these students would gain access to the "general education curriculum" (p. 33). Comparable to DI, the education community recognized that the needs of a diverse population of students could not be met by the one-size-fits-all approach to curriculum and teaching.

Similar to DI, UDL has little scientific evidence to support the theoretical principles. The term was defined in the Assistive Technology Act of 1998 (Edyburn, 2010). In this act, UDL refers to a framework that provides flexibility in the way information is presented and in the way students can respond. It also addresses different ways students can be engaged in their learning and it emphasizes including all students through appropriate accommodations and supports.

There are many commonalities between the DI and the UDL theoretical perspectives. Table 1 outlines a comparison between DI and UDL. At the core of both of these models lies the need for flexibility and adaptations to

Table 1. A Comparison between Differentiated Instruction and Universal Design for Learning.

Differentiated Instruction	Universal Design for Learning
Content • The manner in which students gain access to important content learning • Aligning tasks and objectives to learning goals drives the instructional "next-steps." • Concept-focused instruction with adjusted degrees of complexity	*Recognition learning* • Focuses on pattern recognition and multiple, flexible, and teaching methods • Methods include providing multiple examples, multiple media formats that highlight critical features and highlight critical features to support background knowledge
Process • Flexible grouping that includes small group or paired work that allows for dynamic regrouping • Classroom management benefits students and teachers and includes organization and instructional delivery strategies	*Strategic learning* • Students receive instruction through their desired method of learning strategies • These models include flexible models of skilled performance, supported practice, and flexible opportunities for skill demonstration
Product • Pre- and ongoing assessment informs teachers so that they can better provide a menu of approaches and choices and address varying needs through interests and abilities • Students become active and responsible learners when tasks are interesting, engaging, and accessible • Varying expectations and requirements allows varying levels of task difficulty, evaluation, and scoring	*Affective learning* • Supporting affective learning by engaging them in instructional tasks • Methods of engagement include offering choice of content and tools, providing adjustable levels of challenge, and offering a choice of learning context
Environment • Locations for students to work without distraction as well as to work collaboratively • Materials that reflect a variety of cultures and home environments • Clear guidelines for independent work • Classroom procedures and routines • Teaching learning diversity to classmates	

Source: Compiled from Hall et al. (2003) and Tomlinson (2000).

the learning environment and materials to meet the needs of all students. Furthermore, there is a heavy emphasis from both of these constructs to allow all students access to the general education environment – not just physical but the educational benefits.

DI FOR STUDENTS WITH EBD

All children should have access to the general education curriculum. All students refer not only to typically developing general education students but also to students receiving special education services, even children who receive services for EBD. Regular and special education teachers are accountable for ensuring this access. The Individuals with Education Improvement Act of 2004 requires schools to focus on positive intervention in the areas of academic instruction and behavior supports. It also mandates that general and special educators have the knowledge of both curricular accommodations and behavior interventions and supports (Gable, Hendrickson, Tonelson, & Van Acker, 2000).

Students with EBD typically receive intervention to reduce problem behavior that may interfere with learning. This occurs even though research shows us that students with EBD have significant learning needs (Lane, 2007; Yell, Busch, & Rogers, 2008). With that in mind, it is hard to determine the directionality of the relationship between behavioral issues and academic needs (Gunter & Coutinho, 1997; Wehby, Symons, Canale, & Go, 1998) or which is causal. Furthermore, even though educators supporting students with EBD have worked for years to improve the quality of the education that is provided, the outcomes for students with EBD remain dismal (Lane et al., 2006).

According to Sutherland, Lewis-Palmer, Stichter, and Morgan (2008), ignoring poor academic achievement and primarily focusing on aberrant behavior limits the teacher's ability to comprehensively meet the needs of students with EBD. Sutherland and colleagues point to the research that focuses on targeting the classroom learning demands and specific academic skill instruction as a way to best support students with EBD. Once students understand the academic content and the classroom expectations, they will naturally be more engaged. "Although reducing disruptive behavior might have positive effects on the classroom environment and associated variables, increasing task engagement might increase the efficacy of instructional procedures in the classroom, resulting in increases in achievement and concomitant positive developmental outcomes, including providing incidental opportunities for prosocial instruction in the context of instructional demands" (p. 230). Increasing task engagement can be accomplished by differentiating content, process, product, and the learning environment – all components of DI.

Teachers who use DI expect students to bring a variety of experiences, abilities, interests, and learning styles. They acknowledge this natural diversity and design and deliver responsive, yet relevant curriculum (Broderick et al., 2005). This approach to instruction addresses both the academic and behavioral needs of students with EBD. This holistic approach targets the whole child and does not rely on the outdated theoretical perspective that behavior must be under control before a student can learn.

MODIFICATIONS AND ADAPTATIONS TO ANTECEDENTS IN THE CLASSROOM

To best address the social, emotional, behavioral, and academic needs of students with EBD, educators must differentiate their instruction. As stated above, there are several avenues in which differentiation can occur during the learning process. These include differentiation of content, process, product, and the environment.

When supporting students with EBD, behavioral and academic interventions have occurred in a reactive nature (Bock, Bakken, & Kempel-Michalak, 2009). Behavioral interventions with EBD students have been rooted in the use of consequences, more specifically, punitive or aversive in nature (Burke, Ayers, & Hagan-Burke, 2004; Wheeler & Richey, 2010). These viewpoints exist even though, for years, educators and researchers have linked social and behavioral deficits with academic difficulties (Lane, 2007; Yell et al., 2008). Unfortunately, these methods have proven ineffective for this population of learners (Burke et al., 2004; Gable et al., 2000). Furthermore, there is a bidirectional correlation between significant behavioral challenges and academic deficits (Sutherland et al., 2008).

With that said, addressing the diverse needs of students with EBD through both academic and behavioral interventions using the underlying principles of DI allows students to become more successful. The principles of DI specifically focus on the design of instruction, placing the idea of meeting student needs at the forefront of lesson planning. It is a collection of best practices, strategically employed to maximize student learning by providing them with the tools to handle anything that comes their way.

It also provides them with appropriate challenges allowing them to thrive in the learning environment.

There are several different adaptations and modifications to instruction that teachers can incorporate for students with EBD. Deschenes, Ebeling, and Sprague (1994) described nine different types of adaptations for instruction. While this source may seem outdated, the authors of this chapter agree that the adaptations listed encompass current best practice and include a comprehensive look at ways to alter the learning process so that all learners can actively participate with success. The nine instructional adaptations also address the areas of modifying content, process, product, and environment, all components of DI. The adaptations include size, time, level of support, input, difficulty, output, participation, alternative curricular goals, and substitute curriculum (Deschenes et al., 1994).

Size

The initial adaptation to consider is the modification of size. Size modification refers to a reduction in the amount of work that is expected. Possible adaptations include decreasing the number of problems in an assignment (e.g., complete the even numbered problems, complete 50% of problems, and complete the first five problems per page), altering the presentation of a full assignment (e.g., to cover problems on a paper, to give multiple strips of problems rather than an entire page, give papers with only a small number of problems at a time) or breaking up an assignment into smaller tasks. Modification of size is an example of differentiating instruction at the level of process. While this is a common teacher practice and assumed to be an effective strategy for differentiation, it is noted there is limited empirical research to reinforce the efficacy of this strategy for students.

Dunlap, Kern-Dunlap, Clarke, and Robbins (1991) illustrated that the use of shortened tasks versus long resulted in an increase of on-task behavior. Furthermore, they observed a decrease in disruptive behavior for students with EBD. This finding was replicated by Dunlap et al. (1993) who found that short tasks resulted in better on-task behavior and fewer disruptive behaviors for students with EBD.

Time

Another way instruction or an assignment could be differentiated is through time. The time element refers to the time allowed (3 days versus 5 days) or the time allotted for a student to complete a learning task. Providing a student extended time to complete tasks and assignments is the most frequently used time modification. While teachers often use this strategy, it may not be the best way to differentiate for students with EBD. More often than not, students with EBD view assignments as aversive. Granting extended or additional time may allow the student more time to avoid the assignment or to engage in disruptive behavior. One way to address this is by adapting the time of lessons through pacing (Vannest, Harrison, Temple-Harvey, Ramsey, & Parker, 2010). For instance, a teacher can provide students with extra processing time by extending the time between the initial request and the anticipation of a response. Providing a wait time of 3–5 seconds between question and response (Rowe, 1987) has shown to be effective with multiple populations of students (Dyer, Christian, & Luce, 1982; Fagan, Hassler, & Szabo, 1981; Koegel, Dunlap, & Dyer, 1980; Tincani & Crozier, 2008; Tobin, 1987; Tobin & Capie, 1982). Additionally, Cybriwsky and Schuster (1990) and McCurdy, Cundari, and Lentz (1990) found teacher provided wait times of 4–8 seconds, respectively, were effective at increasing performance in reading and math for students with EBD. Differentiating instruction through altering the time allowed for completion of assignments, the pace of teaching, and providing wait time addresses differentiation in the area of process.

Levels of Support

Providing assistance to the learner by differing levels of support includes matching their diverse needs to their skill level. Levels of support may include differentiating at the environmental level by modifying the classroom setting or by adding visual and structural supports (e.g., study carrels and room dividers). A teacher could also differentiate the level of support for students with EBD at the product level by modifying materials in the classroom/assignment (e.g., graphic organizers and guided notes). Tomlinson (2000) notes the importance of environmental and material modifications in her model of DI. There is a dearth of research available in this area for supporting students with EBD. The backing for several of these strategies, including environmental and material modification, comes from a theoretical background based in Vygotsky's (1978) work on the zone of proximal development (ZPD). The underlying beliefs of ZPD implies there is an optimal range for learning to occur that falls between what a learner can do independently and what a learner can do with support.

Research has been conducted on the differentiation of instruction through the use of social or personal levels of support such as differentiating the process of learning through the use of peers (see Fuchs et al., 2001; Hall et al., 2003; Ryan, Reid, & Epstein, 2004). As noted in Hall et al. (2003), there is a lack of specific empirical evidence for the strategies practiced and accepted as effective. Peer strategies such as Peer-Assisted Learning Strategies (PALS) have been successful interventions to increase on-task behavior, decrease disruptive behavior, as well as increase content knowledge for students with EBD (Fuchs et al., 2001). Ryan et al. (2004) reviewed 14 studies that utilized peer-mediated strategies for academic content areas and found them to be successful in the reduction of disruptive behaviors and escalation of academic skills with students with EBD. Differentiating the level of support addresses the DI principles of content, process, and the learning environment.

Input

Another highly effective way teachers differentiate instruction for students with EBD is to adapt the way in which content is delivered. While this may include strategies such as computer-assisted instruction, it also includes other pedagogical practices used in the classroom such as direct and strategy instruction. Students with EBD are more successful when information is presented through clear, systematic instruction at an appropriate pace (Coleman & Vaughn, 2000). Kern, Childs, Dunlap, Clarke, and Falk (1994) found that students with EBD responded with higher rates of attending and on-task behavior when they were not required to engage in drill and practice activities as part of instruction.

The teacher may also differentiate at the student level by utilizing information from his or her background and identifying reinforcers specific to each diverse learner (Vannest et al., 2010). The use of purposeful activities (Dunlap et al., 1993) and student interests (Clarke et al., 1995; Vannest et al., 2010) can be used to increase student motivation and engagement.

Additionally, providing choice is a strategy that has proven effective for students with EBD. Dunlap et al. (1994) demonstrated that the opportunity for choice in an activity dramatically increased on-task behavior and decreased off-task behavior for two students with EBD. Romaniuk et al. (2002) also described the power of providing choice and related it back to the functions underlying students' behavior. In this study, choice was effective for students when the function of the student's behavior was escape and not when the function was to gain attention. Using the input strategy of adapting content and providing choice are ways to differentiate at the content and process levels of DI.

Difficulty

Adapting the difficulty of a task is another strategy used to differentiate instruction for students with EBD. This may include using state board of education standards to identify tasks that meet the content at varying levels. For example, a typically developing fourth grader needs to be able to identify the states and their capitals. A student receiving a modified task might be required to identify regions of the country rather than individual states. Modification of difficulty of tasks would include differentiating at the content level.

DePaepe, Shores, Jack, and Denny (1996) demonstrated that when presented with difficult tasks opposed to easy tasks, two students with EBD engaged in an increased level of inappropriate behavior. Lee, Sugai, and Horner (1999) similarly hypothesized that the presentation of difficult tasks would be viewed as aversive and result in disruptive behavior. They modified instruction by delivering content of difficult tasks through individually designed instruction. Breaking down the content and altering the level of difficulty resulted in a decrease of disruptive and off-task behaviors. Adapting the difficulty of the task differentiates at the process and content levels.

Output

Changing the output requirement is another way teachers can modify the way in which learners can demonstrate they have a clear understanding of the content. There are an unlimited number of ways that a student may respond to instruction. To name a few, learner output includes hand raising, typing a response, or turning in an alternate product.

Educators can modify many areas in an effort to shape a learner's response. Too often, teachers expect students to listen intently to teacher-led instruction, raise hands to answer questions, and then work independently on paperwork intended to show mastery of the content. Teacher expectations of how students will respond can result in behavioral changes. Offering more opportunities to respond during a lesson is an effective strategy to increase engagement of students and to decrease negative behaviors (Haydon, Mancil, & VanLoan, 2009; Heward, 1994; Sutherland, Alder, & Gunther, 2003). Other means for student responding that are empirically validated include the use of response cards or choral responding (Heward, 1994; Heward et al., 1996). Output may also be modified through the use of alternate forms of expression (Tomlinson, 2000). This may include having a student demonstrate understanding through making a movie or drawing a picture rather than using handwriting as the means of expression.

Differentiating student output is an example of differentiation at the product level. Differentiation of output is critical for students with EBD as it allows for students to have an increased sense of autonomy within the classroom.

Participation

Another differentiation strategy tied to opportunities to respond and active participation is to modify the extent and type of student participation. Using strategies mentioned above, such as the use of peers during instruction, can allow students with EBD to engage in instruction that will offer group corrective feedback versus individual feedback, which can sometimes viewed as aversive. Additionally, through active engagement strategies, the students can alter how they participate in the classroom. Sutherland et al. (2003) investigated changing the rate of opportunities for response with a classroom of students with EBD. Increasing the number of opportunities resulted in students displaying a higher level of accuracy of responses and increased on-task behavior. Altering the level of participation addresses differentiating instruction at the process and product level.

Alternative Curricular Goals and Substitute Curriculum

Adding additional alternative curricular goals for students with EBD is another option for differentiating instruction. Adapting content to meet specific social and behavioral deficits is one method of differentiation with this population of students. Embedding additional goals, often targeted through an individualized education plan, allows educators to individualize a student's learning within a common curriculum. If a student with EBD requires additional support to the embedding of alternative curricular goals, he may also benefit from a substitute curriculum. An example of substitute curricula is one that can be used to teach functional life skills.

Students with EBD often struggle with social situations in the classroom (Sutherland et al., 2008). For instance, how to ask for assistance, how to appropriately accept correction or feedback, or how to manage frustration are areas students with EBD repeatedly show great difficulty. Incorporating specific social and behavioral goals and content to the curriculum allows teachers to address multiple deficit skills within instruction. The schoolwide positive behavioral support (SWPBS) model is a good example of embedding social skills training within the general education curriculum for all students (Lewis, Jones, Horner, & Sugai, 2010). Schools that implement the three-tiered SWPBS model provide educators with the tools to identify and intervene with behaviors before the behavior becomes chronic (Lewis et al., 2010). Thus, positively changing the outcomes of students entering the system at different levels.

Differentiating expectations for content mastery through the use of "Big Ideas" (Kameenui & Carnine, 1998) allows for educators to select the most important, functional concepts for each student and prioritize content. Teaching through "Big Ideas" involves teachers selecting the most relevant and applicable concepts that a student should gain from a unit of study rather than focusing on all points presented. Teachers frequently practice the addition of alternative curricular goals or substitute curriculum; however, there is a lack of empirical evidence backing up this strategy in the literature. Use of these strategies differentiates at the content, process, and learning environment levels.

CONCLUSION

Today's classroom differs greatly from the classroom a decade ago. This is due, in part, to the changing demographics of students across the United States where diversity is now the norm. As children enter the educational system with diverse backgrounds, they are exposed to new experiences that facilitate changes in interests, behaviors, and learning styles. The traditional education system, in its current form, can no longer accommodate this group of diverse learners. This is particularly relevant for students with EBD because they have both behavioral and academic needs that require flexibility and creativity of curriculum delivery. To meet the needs of diverse learners, preservice and practicing teachers should be prepared to address errors in learning and behavior through a variety of interventions including appropriate curricular accommodations and a strong knowledge base of positive behavioral interventions and supports (Gable et al., 2000).

The underlying philosophy of DI is based on the premise that learners differ in important ways. It is a collection of best practices strategically employed to maximize students' learning outcomes. DI addresses diversity in learners by specifically differing readiness levels, interests, and preferred modes of learning. In addition, DI addresses a child's behavioral needs by accommodating their specific classroom learning style. According to Sutherland et al. (2008), targeting classroom learning demands and specific academic instruction leads to naturally engaged students.

Engaging learners can be accomplished by addressing the four classroom elements originally described by Tomlinson (2000). Differentiating the content that the student needs to learn, the interaction and the activities that are used for content delivery, the way in which the students display content knowledge, and setting the climate of the classroom build the foundation for engaging all learners. Without DI, all students including those with EBD will continue to perform below their typically developing peers in all academic areas and continue to have disappointing post-school outcomes.

REFERENCES

Bock, S. J., Bakken, J. P., & Kempel-Michalak, N. (2009). Behavioral interventions for children and youth with autism spectrum disorders. In V. G. Spencer & C. G. Simpson (Eds.), *A handbook for teachers: Teaching students with autism in the general education classroom* (pp. 109–141). Waco, TX: Prufrock Press, Inc.

Broderick, A., Mehta-Parekh, H., & Reid, D. K. (2005). Differentiating instruction for disabled students in inclusive class- rooms. *Theory Into Practice, 44*(3), 194–202. doi:10.1207/s15430421tip4403_3

Burke, M. D., Ayers, K., & Hagan-Burke, S. (2004). Preventing school-based antisocial behaviors with school-wide positive behavior support. *Journal of Early and Intensive Behavior Intervention, 1*, 65–73.

Clarke, S., Dunlap, G., Foster-Johnson, L., Childs, K., Wilson, D., White, R., & Vera, A. (1995). Improving the conduct of students with behavioral disorders by incorporating student interests into curricular activities. *Behavioral Disorders, 20*, 221–237.

Coleman, M., & Vaughn, S. (2000). Reading interventions for students with emotional/behavioral disorders. *Behavioral Disorders, 25*, 93–104.

Cybriwsky, C. A., & Schuster, J. W. (1990). Using constant time delay procedures to teach multiplication facts. *Remedial and Special Education, 11*, 54–59. doi:10.1177/074193259001100108

DePaepe, P. A., Shores, R. E., Jack, S. L., & Denny, R. K. (1996). Effects of task difficulty on the disruptive and on-task behavior of students with severe behavior disorders. *Behavioral Disorders, 21*, 216–225.

Deschenes, C., Ebeling, D. G., & Sprague, J. (1994). *Adapting curriculum and instruction in inclusive classrooms: A teacher's desk reference.* Bloomington, IN: Institute for the Study of Developmental Disabilities.

Dunlap, G., dePerczel, M., Clarke, S., Wilson, D., Wright, S., White, R., & Gomez, A. (1994). Choice making to promote adaptive behavior for students with emotional and behavioral challenges. *Journal of Applied Behavior Analysis*, *27*, 505–518. doi:10.1901/jaba.1994.27-505

Dunlap, G., Kern-Dunlap, L., Clarke, S., & Robbins, F. R. (1991). Functional assessment, curricular revision, and severe behavior problems. *Journal of Applied Behavior Analysis*, *24*, 287–397. doi:10.1901/jaba.1991.24-387

Dunlap, G., Kern, L., dePerczel, M., Clarke, S., Wilson, D., Childs, K. E., & Falk, G. D. (1993). Functional analysis of classroom variables for students with emotional and behavioral disorders. *Behavioral Disorders*, *18*, 275–291.

Dyer, K., Christian, W., & Luce, S. (1982). The role of response delay in improving the discriminative performance of autistic children. *American Journal of Mental Deficiency*, *88*, 194–202.

Edyburn, D. L. (2010). Would you recognize universal design for learning if you saw it? Ten propositions for new direction for the second decade. *Learning Disability Quarterly*, *33*, 33–41.

Fagan, E., Hassler, D., & Szabo, M. (1981). Evaluation of questioning strategies in language arts instruction. *Research in the Teaching of English*, *15*, 267–273.

Fuchs, D., Fuchs, L. S., Thompson, A., Svenson, E., Yen, L., Al-Otaiba, S., & Saenz, L. (2001). Peer-assisted learning strategies in reading: Extensions for kindergarten, first grade and high school. *Remedial and Special Education*, *22*, 15–21. doi:10.1177/074193250102200103

Gable, R. A., Hendrickson, J. M., Tonelson, S. W., & Van Acker, R. (2000). Changing disciplinary and instructional practices in the middle school to address IDEA. *The Clearing House*, *73*, 205–208. doi:10.1080/00098650009600951

Gunter, P. L., & Coutinho, M. J. (1997). Negative reinforcement in classrooms: What we're beginning to learn. *Teacher Education and Special Education*, *35*(2), 30–34.

Hall, T., Strangman, N., & Meyer, A. (2003). Differentiated instruction and implications for UDL implementation. Wakefield, MA: National Center on Accessing the General Curriculum. Retrieved from http://aim.cast.org/learn/historyarchive/backgroundpapers/differentiated_instruction_udl. Accessed on May 2011.

Haydon, T., Mancil, G. R., & VanLoan, C. (2009). The effects of opportunities to respond on the on-task behavior for a student emitting disruptive behaviors in a general education classroom: A case study. *Education & Treatment of Children*, *32*, 267–278.

Heward, W. L. (1994). Three "low-tech" strategies for increasing the frequency of active student responding during group instruction. In R. Gardner, III, D. M. Sainato, J. O. Cooper, T. E. Heron, W. L. Heward, J. Eshleman & T. A. Grossi (Eds.), *Behavior analysis in education: Focus on measurably superior instruction* (pp. 283–320). Pacific Grove, CA: Brooks/Cole.

Heward, W. L., Gardner, R. I., Cavanaugh, T. A., Courson, F. H., Grossi, T. A., & Barbetta, P. M. (1996). Everyone participates in this class: Using response cards to increase active student responses. *Teaching Exceptional Children*, *28*, 4–10.

Kameenui, E. J., & Carnine, D. W. (1998). *Effective teaching strategies that accommodate diverse learners*. Columbus, OH: Merrill.

Kern, L., Childs, K. E., Dunlap, G., Clarke, S., & Falk, G. D. (1994). Using assessment-based curricular intervention to improve the classroom behavior of a student with emotional and behavioral challenges. *Journal of Applied Behavior Analysis*, *27*, 7–19. doi:10.1901/jaba.1994.27-7

Koegel, R., Dunlap, G., & Dyer, K. (1980). Intertrial interval duration and learning in autistic children. *Journal of Applied Behavior Analysis, 13*, 91–99. doi:10.1901/jaba.1980.13-91

Lane, K. L. (2007). Identifying and supporting students at risk for emotional and behavioral disorders within multi-level models: Data driven approaches to conducting secondary interventions with an academic emphasis. *Education & Treatment of Children, 30*, 135–164. doi:10.1353/etc.2007.0026

Lane, K. L., Carter, E. W., Pierson, M. R., & Glaeser, B. C. (2006). Academic, social, and behavioral characteristics of high school students with emotional disturbances or learning disabilities. *Journal of Emotional and Behavioral Disorders, 14*, 108–117. doi:10.1177/10634266060140020101

Lawrence-Brown, D. (2004). Differentiated instruction: Inclusive strategies for standards-based learning that benefit the whole class. *American Secondary Education, 32*(3), 34–62.

Lee, Y., Sugai, G., & Horner, R. H. (1999). Using an instructional intervention to reduce problem and off-task behaviors. *Journal of Positive Behavior Intervention, 1*, 195–204. doi:10.1177/109830079900100402

Lewis, T. J., Jones, S. E. L., Horner, R. H., & Sugai, G. (2010). School-wide positive behavior support and students with emotional/behavioral disorders: Implications for prevention, identification and intervention. *Exceptionality, 18*, 82–93. doi:10.1080/09362831003673168

McCurdy, B. L., Cundari, L., & Lentz, F. E. (1990). Enhancing instructional efficiency: An examination of time delay and the opportunity to observe instruction. *Education & Treatment of Children, 13*(3), 227–238.

Romaniuk, C., Miltenberger, R., Conyers, C., Jenner, N., Jurgens, M., & Ringenberg, C. (2002). The influence of activity choice on problem behaviors maintained by escape versus attention. *Journal of Applied Behavior Analysis, 35*(4), 349–362. doi:10.1901/jaba.2002.35-349

Rowe, M. (1987). Wait time: Slowing down may be a way of speeding up. *American Educator, 11*, 38–43.

Ryan, J. B., Reid, R., & Epstein, M. H. (2004). Peer-mediated intervention studies on academic achievement for students with EBD. *Remedial and Special Education, 25*(6), 330–341. doi:10.1177/07419325040250060101

Sutherland, K. S., Alder, N., & Gunther, P. L. (2003). The effect of increased rates of opportunities to respond on the classroom behavior of students with emotional/behavioral disorders. *Journal of Emotional and Behavioral Disorders, 11*, 239–248. doi:10.1177/10634266030110040501

Sutherland, K. S., Lewis-Palmer, T., Stichter, J., & Morgan, P. L. (2008). Examining the influence of teacher behavior and academic outcomes for students with emotional or behavioral disorders. *Journal of Special Education, 41*, 223–233. doi:10.1177/0022466907310372

Tincani, M., & Crozier, S. (2008). Comparing brief and extended wait time during small group instruction for children with challenging behavior. *Journal of Behavioral Education, 17*, 79–92. doi:10.1007/s10864-008-9063-4

Tobin, K. (1987). The effect of an extended teacher wait-time on science achievement. *Journal of Research in Science Teaching, 17*, 469–475.

Tobin, K., & Capie, W. (1982). Relationship between classroom process variables and middle school science achievement. *Journal of Educational Psychology, 14*, 441–454. doi:10.1037/0022-0663.74.3.441

Tomlinson, C. A. (2000). Differentiation of instruction in the elementary grades. *ERIC Digest*, August. Champaign, IL: ERIC Clearinghouse on Elementary and Early Childhood Education. (ERIC Document No. ED443572). Retrieved from http://eric.ed.gov/ERICWebPortal/detail?accno=ED443572. Accessed on May 2011.

Tomlinson, C. A., & Kalbfleisch, M. L. (1998). Teach me, teach my brain: A call for differentiated classrooms. *Educational Leadership, 56*, 52–55.

Vannest, K. J., Harrison, J. R., Temple-Harvey, K., Ramsey, L., & Parker, R. I. (2010). Improvement rate differences of academic interventions for students with emotional and behavioral disorders. *Remedial and Special Education*. Advance online publication. doi:10.1177/0741932510362509.

Vygotsky, L. (1978). *Mind in society: The development of higher psychological processes*. Cambridge, MA: Harvard University Press.

Wehby, J. H., Symons, F. J., Canale, J. A., & Go, F. J. (1998). Teaching practices in classrooms for students with emotional and behavioral disorders: Discrepancies between recommendations and observations. *Behavioral Disorders, 24*, 51–56.

Wheeler, J. J., & Richey, D. R. (2010). *Behavior management: Principles and practices of positive behavior supports* (2nd ed.). Upper Saddle River, NJ: Pearson.

Yell, M. L., Busch, T. W., & Rogers, D. C. (2008). Planning instruction and monitoring student performance. *Beyond Behavior, 17*, 31–38.

CHAPTER 10

HOBSON'S CHOICE: ILLUSORY INTERVENTION CHOICE FOR CULTURALLY AND LINGUISTICALLY DIVERSE LEARNERS WITH PROBLEM BEHAVIORS

Festus E. Obiakor

ABSTRACT

Hobson's choice is a "no-choice" choice that gives general and special educators the traditional impetus to do what they want in classrooms. While there is some "goodness" in having this power and audacity to control whatever happens in classrooms, it does not allow for creativity, flexibility, adaptability, modification, especially in behavior management, assessment practices, instructional delivery. In addition, it presents many practical problems in this era of response-to-intervention (Rtl) and actually devalues the integrity of any form of remedial or special education. For many culturally and linguistically diverse (CLD) learners who are already operating at different cultural, linguistic, and racial levels with their teachers and service providers, the Hobson's choice can have

Behavioral Disorders: Identification, Assessment, and Instruction of Students with EBD
Advances in Special Education, Volume 22, 221–231
Copyright © 2012 by Emerald Group Publishing Limited
All rights of reproduction in any form reserved
ISSN: 0270-4013/doi:10.1108/S0270-4013(2012)0000022013

some unintended devastating educational effects. For example, by not allowing any alternatively creative options, CLD learners can be misidentified, misassessed, miscategorized, misplaced, and misinstructed. More so, it can lead to school drop out and increase in school and societal problems. Clearly, rather than impose the "no-choice" choice on CLD students who are sometimes disenfranchised because of the differences that they bring to school programs, it is important for general and special educators to be innovative in managing inappropriate behaviors in today's multicultural classrooms. This is the premise of this chapter.

Keywords: Hobson's choice; inflexibility; disenfranchisement; cultural and linguistic diversities; response-to-intervention; innovative behavior management

Thomas Hobson was a livery stable owner who lived in the 17th century at Cambridge, England. He routinely told his customers that they had the option to take the next horse available or to leave because he was going to rotate his horses equally (Martin, 2010; Webster's New World College Dictionary, 2010). Mr. Hobson's rule was implemented with such fidelity that many would coin the term "Hobson's choice" after him. Hobson's choice is a choice with no real alternative and essentially presents the "take-it-or-leave-it" scenario. Though we are centuries removed from Mr. Hobson's era, far too many general and special education practitioners still present many culturally and linguistically diverse (CLD) learners with a Hobson's choice, especially in their behavior intervention/management philosophy. While this philosophy highlights the sole power of teachers and service providers, its genesis is in antipathy with the wisdom of special education. According to Blackhurst and Berdine (1993), special education is the provision of services different from, additional to, and supplementary with those provided in the regular classroom with a systematic modification and adaptation of instruction, materials, and equipment. In other words, central to special education or behavior management is the valuing of (a) human differences, (b) personal realities and experiences, (c) multidimensional pedagogical and intervention strategies, (d) collaborative consultations between professionals and families, and (e) the unique "specialness" in special education (Obiakor, 2001; Obiakor, Harris-Obiakor, Garza-Nelson, & Randall, 2005).

Hobson's choice assumes that general or special education practitioners or service providers have all the answers to questions on students' behaviors and learning styles. It exposes the unidimensionality in traditional educational programming which basically is in consonance with the "one-size-fits-all" philosophy. This choice further fails to recognize that problem behaviors do not occur in isolation, that is, that behaviors occur in multidimensional ways. In addition, it encourages the blindness in valuing interindividual and intraindividual differences in students (James, 1958) and to a large extent fails to recognize the positive or negative energies of students, teachers, families, communities, and government agencies, especially as they affect behavioral patterns and manifestations (Obiakor, Utley, Smith, & Harris-Obiakor, 2002). As it appears, the focus today is on how best to increase appropriate behaviors and decrease inappropriate behaviors that impinge upon learning. General and special educators are encouraged to use innovative assessment and intervention strategies to manage problem behaviors. One such innovation is the Response-to-Intervention (RTI) strategy. Hobson's choice fails to realize the multi-dimensionalities associated with behaviors, assessments, and interventions (Obiakor, 1999a, 1999b, 2007, 2008; Stoiber & Good, 1998). Without this realization, how can reasonable success-oriented behavior intervention options be explored, revisited, and implemented, especially as they involve the student, school, home, community, and government?

In most traditional classrooms, the teacher's rules are exposed in some classroom corner. One of those rules is "obey my rule," which is an embodiment of Hobson's choice. While the "obey my rule" philosophy respects the supreme power of the teacher or service provider, it ignores the real problems of students and teachers. For example, when does a behavior become a disordered behavior? Does it not depend on the teacher or the student? Before a behavior is a disordered behavior, should it not depart from acceptable standards, based on culture, norms, and gender? Should a behavior disorder not consider the circumstance and situation? And should it not have frequency and duration? In addition to these traditional problems, there is a preponderance of evidence that savage inequalities exist within today's school systems (Epps, 2001; Kozol, 1991; West, 1993). These inequalities are evident in the higher rates at which CLD learners are disciplined, detained, suspended, and placed in negatively stigmatizing special education programs. As a result, these learners fall into a circle of failure and get entangled in criminal arrests and subsequent incarceration (Lovitt, 2000; Obiakor & Algozzine, 1995). Central to these problems is the lack of preparation or ill-preparation of teachers and service providers who work with these students. Clearly, there appears to be a cultural disconnect between these professionals and their students (Gay, 2002). Even when these professionals care and want to help, they do not have the cultural skills, knowledge, and capital to tackle the endemic problems confronting their students in and out of school. Consequently, they resort to (a) solving problems that do not exist, (b) avoiding problems that they should solve, and (c) engaging in fraudulent multiculturalism that leaves students and parents confused about professional intentions and integrity. In this chapter, I analyze problems associated with the Hobson's choice and discuss innovative strategies for managing problem behaviors of CLD learners.

STRUGGLING WITH CHANGE IN AN ERA OF CHANGE

Haberman (1995) stated that the majority of teaching programs are inadequate for all learning environments. Since the browning of America is not a recent phenomenon, it is alarming that institutions of higher learning have repeatedly failed to change the core curriculum at the same pace (Gay, 2002; Obiakor & Algozzine, 1995). It should be noted that although today's classrooms are more culturally diverse, the teaching population remains predominantly filled with white women (Chang & Shimizu, 1999; Smith & Sapp, 2005). This does not imply that a white person cannot effectively teach a diverse classroom or that CLD educators will rectify the problem. I argue that misinformed, ill-prepared, or unprepared teachers and service providers tend to miseducate their students and sometimes jeopardize their future by their deliberate or unintended actions.

It is common knowledge that the government has tried to intervene through court cases (e.g., *Brown vs. Board of Education*, Topeka, Kansas) and well-intended legislation (e.g., the 1975 Education for All Handicapped Children Act, the 1990 Individuals with Disabilities Act, the 2001 No Child Left Behind Act, and the 2004 Individuals with Disabilities Education Improvement Act). However, plans to implement changes legislatively have appeared to be a great hassle to program planners and educational leaders (Obiakor, 1999b, 2001, 2008). These efforts have not been successful because they have not fully impacted the changes they are supposed to support. For example, many CLD learners are still misidentified, misassessed, miscategorized, misplaced, and misinstructed. Specifically, they are sometimes (a) misidentified because of their different behavioral patterns; (b) misassessed because of instruments that lack validity and reliability; (c) miscategorized because of errors in identification and assessment; (d) misplaced because of errors in miscategorization; and (e) misinstructed because of ill-preparation and poor preparation of teachers and service providers (Obiakor, 2001, 2007).

Apparently, cultural differences that separate CLD students and educators create barriers between parents and educators. At the heart of such barriers are race, culture, language, and socioeconomics (Obiakor, Grant, & Dooley, 2002). For example, there is a problem when teachers do not view the home as an asset, but as the source of the problem. This is communicated implicitly or explicitly in many cases. The rising number of single family homes, blended families, the same-sex partners, children living with nonparental relatives, and those in foster care creates further problems in relationship building (Gordon, 1993; Harry, 1992; Obiakor & Algozzine, 1995). The home–school collaboration is grounded in the fact that all voices are important and must be heard (Obiakor, Grant et al., 2002).

Recent demographic changes in the American society suggest changes in the sociocultural and educational frameworks of schools. Unfortunately, the more things change, the more they remain the same. Even educators and service providers who are well intentioned continue to struggle with how best to manage problem behaviors. Their cultures, personal idiosyncrasies, and embedded educational traditions continue to intrude in how they do their jobs. For example, while new ideas (e.g., RTI) are thrown around in educational circles, educators and service providers continue to be tied to the apron string of old thinking that seems to have no relevance for today's changing world (e.g., the archaic theory of biological determinism that stipulates that intelligence or behavior is genetically handed down). In addition, while people and their behaviors are known to be different and multidimensional, many general and special education professionals seem to be unidimensional in their behavioral assessment/intervention approaches (Obiakor & Beachum, 2005).

FROM HOBSON'S CHOICE TO CULTURALLY RESPONSIVE INTERVENTION

We have seen wonderful isolated examples of star teachers and educators dedicated to making a change in classrooms all across America (Collins & Tamarkin, 1990; Haberman, 1995; Ladson-Billings, 1994; Obiakor, 2001, 2007, 2008). Though schools as a whole have shown little success in the area of cultural competence, it is important to study and duplicate the quiet heroes and risk-takers in the classroom that have made outstanding contributions to the lives of their students. To respond to change, there must be innovation on how teachers and service providers work with CLD learners, especially those with problem behaviors. One of those new ways is culturally responsive intervention, a technique that uses effective and appropriate cultural knowledge, experiences, and styles of intervention (Gay, 2002; Obiakor, 2007, 2008). Effective educators and practitioners utilize culturally responsive teaching and intervention techniques instinctively and routinely. They are frequently honest with themselves on a myriad of issues. In addition, they (a) know who they are, (b) learn the facts when in doubt, (c) change their thinking, (d) use resource persons, (e) build self-concepts, (f) teach with divergent techniques, (g) make the right choices, and (h) continue to learn (see Obiakor, 2008). Culturally responsive teachers/ practitioners recognize that all the answers are not available with them, a rule that is central to Hobson's choice. Rather than using the "teacher's rule," these professionals incorporate the voices of students, families, and community members in behavior management. In a society where differences are considered deficits, effective educators and service providers are willing to learn about others and go beyond ceremonial displays of one size that fits all (Obiakor, 1999a; Obiakor & Beachum, 2005).

Culturally responsive teachers and practitioners are change agents who use innovative techniques to manage problem behaviors. They understand the importance of the home and school (Gay, 2002) and attempt to make contact with each parent. They understand that they may have to extend the proverbial olive branch to help mend current pains and even pains they did not create. They allow parents to become active equal participants in the educational growth of their child (Harry, 1992; Mehring, 1996) and understand that the environment is important in the creation of an atmosphere conducive to academic and social success (Bluestein, 2008; Kapalka, 2009; Obiakor & Algozzine, 1995; Obiakor & Beachum, 2005). Clearly, they understand that the parent is the true bridge to help connect to the student, borrow from other successful teachers and programs, and implement new strategies based on the student as client (Obiakor, Grant et al., 2002). They are willing to go beyond the duties of the job description, seek advice, and seek help from those who are more knowledgeable, and they are not afraid to think outside the box. To a large measure, effective educators and service providers are willing to implement culturally responsive behavior intervention/management techniques without prescribed scripts (e.g., "obey my rule") or state mandates. Though these educators and service providers are overworked, underpaid, and underappreciated (Haberman, 1995), they feel obligated to be professionals who value their job and clients (Kozol, 1991; Obiakor, 1999a, 2001, 2007, 2008; Obiakor et al., 2005).

MANAGING PROBLEM BEHAVIORS: LOOKING FORWARD

Without human valuing as a central focus, it is impossible to create a culturally responsive classroom intervention and process. If the goal is to reduce inappropriate behaviors and increase appropriate behaviors, the human being must be a valued entity. As a consequence, cultures and their embodiments must be valued. Since culturally different behaviors increase the wonders of individuality (Gay, 2002), there should be greater emphasis on having smaller class sizes to allow teachers to be in proximity with their students. A small teacher to student ratio is ideal, but in areas where this is not acceptable, ample space and supplies are compulsory. Even more, a situation where children are not confined within the walls of school is a definite benefit (Obiakor & Beachum, 2005; Obiakor et al., 2005).

The curriculum and instruction are important tools for managing problem behaviors in the classroom. What we teach and how we teach it are important (Bluestein, 2008; Kapalka, 2009). The curriculum should include the core areas needed to survive in this world (e.g., reading, writing, and arithmetic); however, it should be inclusive of other topics that relate to students or that will benefit them immediately and in the future. It should be noted that a curriculum that is culturally responsive is not an enemy to the current curriculum; in fact, it is a great equalizer and supplement. Even if culturally responsive methods are forced upon teachers, they would look different in every class because of the personal idiosyncrasies that exist within each educator or service provider (Gay, 2002; Obiakor, 2001). The instruction or intervention style must be within the natural style of the individual teacher or interventionist. Instruction flows well when one feels comfortable; thus, it is critical that teachers and service providers understand why culturally responsive pedagogy and intervention are effective (Obiakor, 2007, 2008).

Frankly, to reduce problem behaviors and allow educators to reclaim their classes or reverse the staggering epidemic of failure in behavior intervention, school leaders must create environments for success (Bluestein, 2008; Kapalka, 2009; Mendler, Curwin, & Mendler, 2008). The majority of CLD students want to learn, even when they state something different.

Many have had difficult experiences in the past and will be less likely to trust significant adults. The culturally responsive educator or service provider can recognize these students and place them in situations where success will be within their grasp. It is true that every student cannot be saved, and it is also true that culturally responsive teaching or intervention is not a panacea that will cure all of the evils of the world. Every child can be reached, but even the most versed culturally competent teacher cannot reach everyone. Sometimes removal from the institution is not only practical but necessary. In other words, culturally responsive professionals are creative and caring as they deal with problem behaviors. To get students interested in learning and increasing their positive behaviors, educational leaders and professionals must be creative and caring (Obiakor & Beachum, 2005). For example, culturally responsive teaching manifests itself in a plethora of ways (e.g., audio, visual, and kinesthetic) and in a myriad of settings (Mehring, 1996; Newby, 2006; Obiakor, 2007, 2008). Hands-on projects that make assignments come to life are necessary. It is a different experience to read about art history than it is to explore a museum with an art history display. In addition to out-of-school field trips, it is necessary to bring in community personalities (e.g., from churches, mosques, or synagogues) who will inspire and expose students to different worlds outside their own worlds. This is also an opportunity to expose students to adventures and places they have not only experienced but also never knew about. These experiences will surely encourage a good mental and psychological health of students, parents, and professionals (Smith & Sapp, 2005).

With the recent emphasis on RTI, Hobson's choice will restrict all the necessary choices to manage problem behaviors. Shores (2009) noted that RTI "involves an instructional framework of increasingly intensive assessment and interventions designed to address a continuum of academic and behavioral problems" (p. 2). By definition and practice, there are myriad assessment and intervention processes associated with the RTI. This is contrary to what Hobson's choice is all about. The "take-it-or-leave-it" philosophy generally restricts fundamental choices in education and creates "victims" out of CLD learners who are already leery about the system. Specifically, when there are no choices, how can target and intensive interventions in behavior management be provided? If there are no choices, how will problem behaviors be defined? How can behavior plans be implemented? And how can the student's progress be evaluated? Since special education focuses on how the potential of individual students can be maximized, it is reasonable to conclude that Hobson's choice is an anti-special education psychological philosophy. In reality, this philosophy assumes an inherent pathology that can only be eliminated by the teacher's sole power. When human differences are devalued, CLD learners fail to maximize their fullest potential. In the words of James (1958),

> We are practical beings, each of us with limited functions and duties to perform. Each is bound to feel intensely the importance of his[her] own duties and the significance of the situations that call these forth. But this feeling is in each of us a vital secret for sympathy which we vainly look to others ... Hence the falsity of our judgments, so far as they presume to decide in an absolute way on the value of other persons' conditions of ideals. (p. 149)

CONCLUSION

This chapter has focused on how problem behaviors can be reduced or eliminated using multidimensional choices, instead of the Hobson's choice, a choice that was never a choice in the first place. Hobson's choice makes dictators out of teachers and service providers and prevents them from responding to demographic changes. Since the goal is to reduce problem behaviors, we must care for students' physical, mental, and spiritual well-being. This requires support from the student, family, school, community, and government. Clearly, problems that exist within our school systems cannot be fixed overnight with one initiative; however, we must start somewhere. It is imperative that we reduce problem behaviors in classrooms to create a positive culture of learning. That is the more reason why we need well-prepared educators and service providers to help rebuild relationships with parents and hold students accountable in culturally responsive ways. We truly need professional leaders to avoid the use of Hobson's choice in managing problem behaviors and to help CLD learners to maximize their fullest potential. Finally, our overall mission must be to value personal realities and experiences, multidimensional pedagogical and intervention strategies, collaborative consultations between professionals and families, and the unique "specialness" in special education.

REFERENCES

Blackhurst, A. E., & Berdine, W. H. (1993). *An introduction to special education* (3rd ed.). New York, NY: Harper Collins.

Bluestein, J. (2008). *The win-win classroom: A fresh and positive look at classroom management.* Thousand Oaks, CA: Corwin Press.

Chang, J. L., & Shimizu, W. (1999). Educating the Asian-Pacific American exceptional English-language learners. In F. E. Obiakor, J. O. Schwenn & A. F. Rotatori (Eds.), *Advances in special education: Multicultural education for learners with exceptionalities* (pp. 33–51). Stanford, CT: JAI Press.

Collins, M., & Tamarkin, C. (1990). *Marva Collins' way: Returning to excellence in education.* Los Angeles, CA: Tarcher.

Epps, E. (2001). Race, class, social inequality, and special education: Summary comments. In C. A. Utley & F. E. Obiakor (Eds.), *Special education, multicultural education, and school reform: Components of quality education for learners with mild disabilities* (pp. 228–236). Springfield, IL: Charles C. Thomas.

Gay, G. (2002). Preparing for culturally responsive teaching. *Journal of Teacher Education, 53,* 106–116.

Gordon, B. M. (1993). African American cultural knowledge and liberatory education: Dilemmas, problems, and potentials in a postmodern America society. *Urban Education, 27*(4), 448–470.

Haberman, M. (1995). *Star teachers of children in poverty.* West Lafayette, IN: Kappa Delta Pi.

Harry, B. (1992). *Cultural diversity, families, and the special education system: Communication and empowerment.* New York, NY: Teachers College Press.

James, W. (1958). *Talks to teachers on psychology, and to students on some of life's ideals.* New York, NY: W. W. Norton.

Kapalka, G. (2009). *Eight steps to classroom management success: A guide for teachers of challenging students.* Thousand Oaks, CA: Corwin Press.

Kozol, J. (1991). *Savage inequalities: Children in American schools.* New York, NY: Crown Publishers.

Ladson-Billings, G. (1994). *The dreamkeepers: Successful teachers of African American children.* San Francisco, CA: Jossey-Bass.

Lovitt, T. (2000). *Preventing school failure: Tactics for teaching adolescents* (2nd ed.). Austin, TX: PRO-ED.

Martin, G. (2010). The phrase finder. Retrieved from http://www.phrases.org.uk/meanings/hosons-choice.html

Mehring, T. A. (1996). Authentic assessment: The link to special education. In A. F. Rotatori, J. O. Schwenn & S. Burkhardt (Eds.), *Advances in special education: Assessment and psychological issues in special education* (pp. 158–176). Greenwich, CT: JAI Press.

Mendler, B. D., Curwin, R. L., & Mendler, A. N. (2008). *Strategies for successful classroom management: Helping students succeed without losing your dignity or sanity.* Thousand Oaks, CA: Corwin Press.

Newby, R. F. (2006). *Your struggling child: A guide to diagnosing, understanding, advocating for your child with learning, behavioral, or emotional problems.* New York, NY: Harper Collins.

Obiakor, F. E. (1999a). Multicultural education: Powerful tool for educating learners with exceptionalities. In F. E. Obiakor, J. O. Schwenn & A. F. Rotatori (Eds.), *Advances in special education: Multicultural education for learners with exceptionalities* (pp. 1–14). Stanford, CT: JAI Press.

Obiakor, F. E. (1999b). Teacher expectations of minority exceptional learners: Impact on "accuracy" of self-concepts. *Exceptional Children, 66*(1), 39–53.

Obiakor, F. E. (2001). *It even happens in good schools: Responding to cultural diversity in today's classrooms.* Thousand Oaks, CA: Corwin Press.

Obiakor, F. E. (2007). *Multicultural special education: Culturally responsive teaching.* Upper Saddle River, NJ: Pearson Merrill/Prentice Hall.

Obiakor, F. E. (2008). *The eight-step approach to multicultural learning and teaching* (3rd ed.). Dubuque, IA: Kendall Hunt.

Obiakor, F. E., & Algozzine, B. (1995). *Managing problem behaviors: Perspectives for general and special educators.* Dubuque, IA: Kendall Hunt.

Obiakor, F. E., & Beachum, F. D. (2005). *Urban education for the 21st century: Research, issues, and perspectives.* Springfield, IL: Charles C. Thomas.

Obiakor, F. E., Grant, P. A., & Dooley, E. A. (2002). *Educating all learners: Refocusing the comprehensive support model.* Springfield, IL: Charles C. Thomas.

Obiakor, F. E., Harris-Obiakor, P., Garza-Nelson, C., & Randall, P. (2005). Educating urban learners with and without special needs: Life after the Brown case. In F. E. Obiakor & F. D. Beachum (Eds.), *Urban education for the 21st century: Research, issues, and perspectives* (pp. 20–33). Springfield, IL: Charles C. Thomas.

Obiakor, F. E., Utley, C. A., Smith, R., & Harris-Obiakor, P. (2002). The comprehensive support model for culturally diverse exceptional learners: Interventions in an age of change. *Intervention in School and Clinic, 38*(1), 14–27.

Shores, C. (2009). *A comprehensive RTI model: Integrating behavioral and academic interventions.* Thousand Oaks, CA: Corwin Press.

Smith, R., & Sapp, M. (2005). Insights into educational psychology: What urban school practitioners must know. In F. E. Obiakor & F. D. Beachum (Eds.), *Urban education for the 21st century: Research, issues, and perspectives* (pp. 100–113). Springfield, IL: Charles C. Thomas.

Stoiber, K. C., & Good, B. (1998). Risk and resilience factors linked to problem behavior among culturally diverse adolescents. *School Psychology Quarterly, 9*(4), 1–22.

Webster's New World College Dictionary. (2010). *Hobson's choice.* Cleveland, OH: Wiley.

West, C. (1993). *Race matters.* New York, NY: Vintage Books.